Dungeon

Twilight
Volume 4:

The End of Dungeon

Joann SFAR, Lewis TRONDHEIM, story
Art for High Septentrion: ALFRED
Art for The End of Dungeon: MAZAN
color: WALTER

NANTIER · BEALL · MINOUSTCHINE
Publishing inc.
new york

Also available
Dungeon, Zenith, vols. 1, 2: $14.95 each, 3: $14.99
Dungeon Early Years, vols. 1: $14.99, 2: $12.95
Dungeon, Twilight, vols. 1, $12.95, 2: $14.99, 3: $12.99
Dungeon, Parade, vol. 2: $9.95
Dungeon, Monstres, vols. 2: $12.95, 3: $12.99, 4: $14.99
Also by Trondheim:
Little Nothings, vols. 2, 3: $14.95 each
Mr. I, $13.95
with Thierry Robin:
Happy Halloween, $14.95

See previews, get exclusives and order from:
NBMPUB.COM

we have over 200 titles available
Catalog upon request
NBM
160 Broadway, Suite 700, East Wing
New York, NY 10038
If ordering by mail add $4 P&H 1st item,
$1 each addt'l

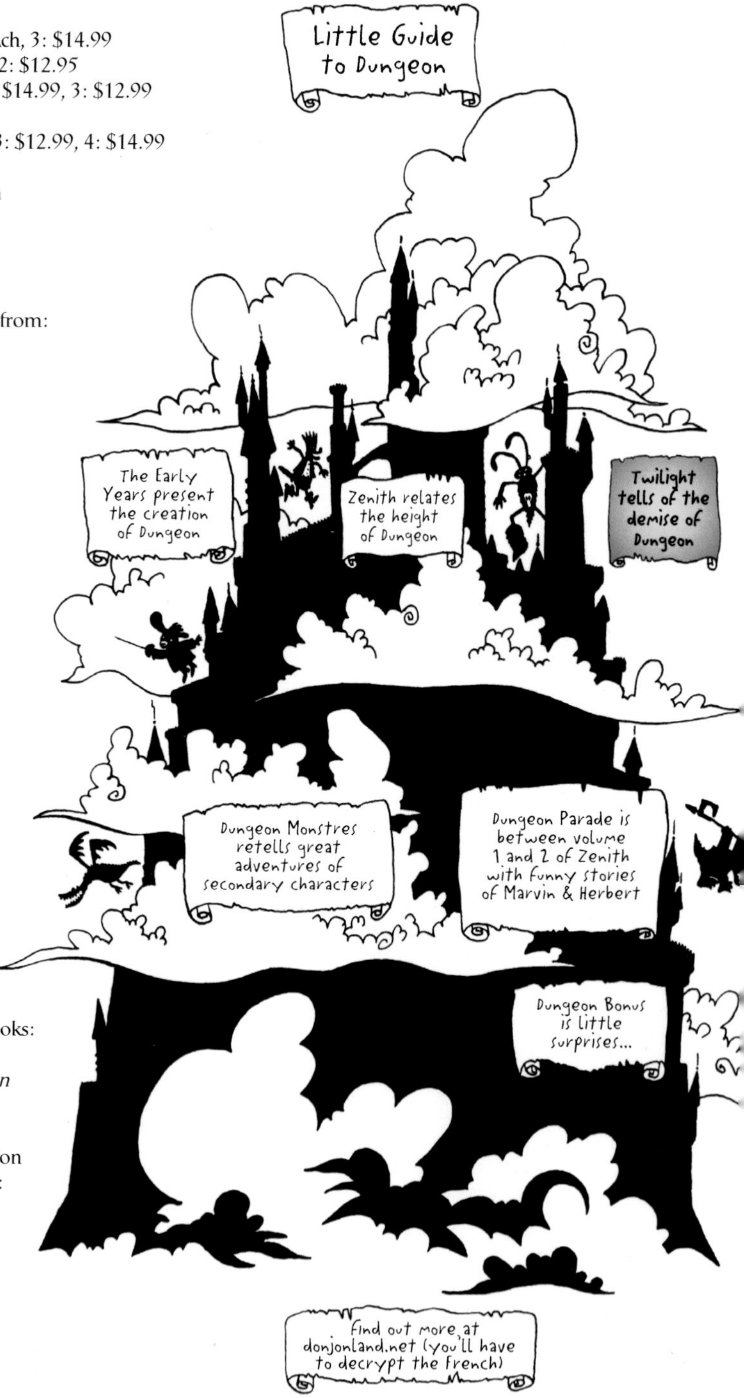
Little Guide to Dungeon
The Early Years present the creation of Dungeon
Zenith relates the height of Dungeon
Twilight tells of the demise of Dungeon
Dungeon Monstres retells great adventures of secondary characters
Dungeon Parade is between volume 1 and 2 of Zenith with funny stories of Marvin & Herbert
Dungeon Bonus is little surprises...
Find out more at donjonland.net (you'll have to decrypt the French)

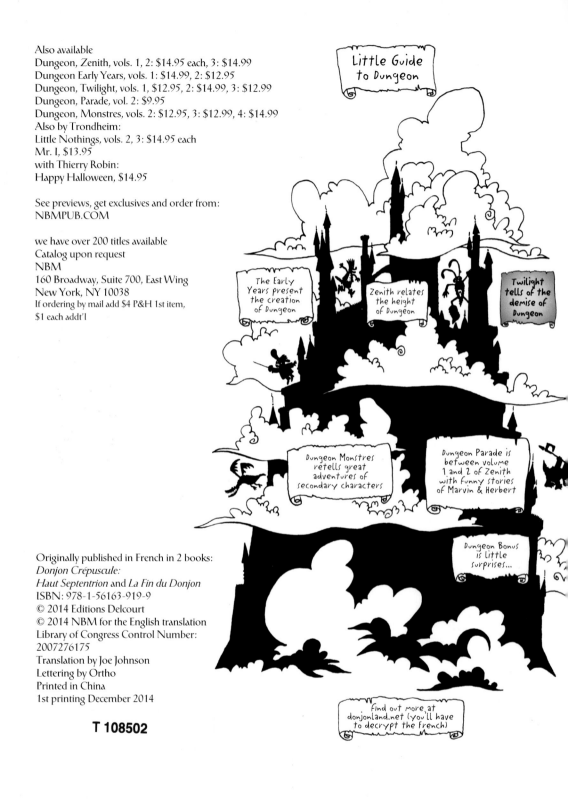

Originally published in French in 2 books:
Donjon Crépuscule:
Haut Septentrion and *La Fin du Donjon*
ISBN: 978-1-56163-919-9

Library of Congress Control Number:
2007276175
Translation by Joe Johnson
Lettering by Ortho
Printed in China
1st printing December 2014

T 108502

HIGH SEPTENTRION

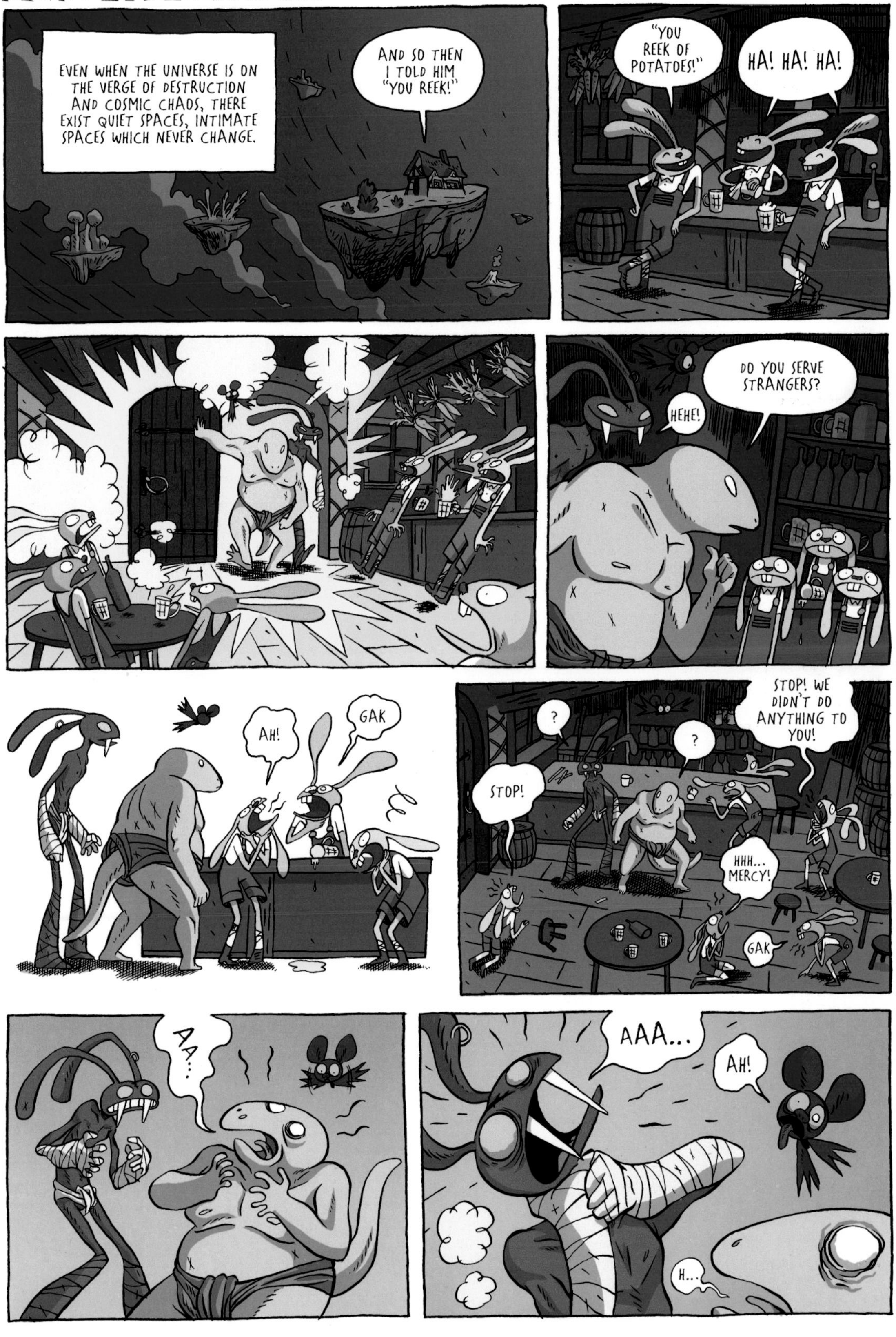

EVEN WHEN THE UNIVERSE IS ON THE VERGE OF DESTRUCTION AND COSMIC CHAOS, THERE EXIST QUIET SPACES, INTIMATE SPACES WHICH NEVER CHANGE.
AND SO THEN I TOLD HIM "YOU REEK!"
"YOU REEK OF POTATOES!"
HA! HA! HA!
HEHE!
DO YOU SERVE STRANGERS?
AH!
GAK
?
?
STOP!
STOP! WE DIDN'T DO ANYTHING TO YOU!
HHH... MERCY!
GAK
AA...
AAA...
AH!
H...

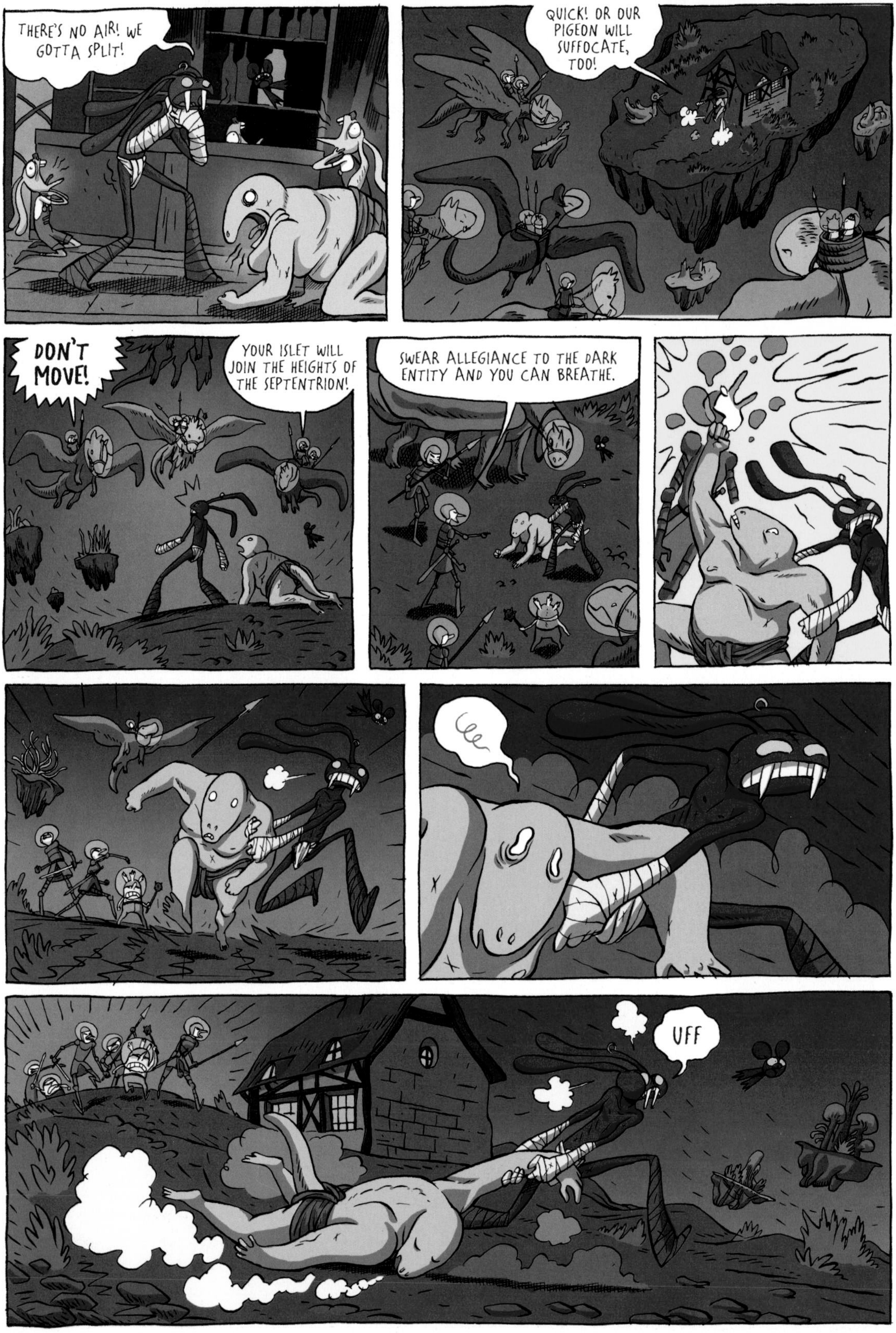
THERE'S NO AIR! WE GOTTA SPLIT!
QUICK! OR OUR PIGEON WILL SUFFOCATE, TOO!
DON'T MOVE!
YOUR ISLET WILL JOIN THE HEIGHTS OF THE SEPTENTRION!
SWEAR ALLEGIANCE TO THE DARK ENTITY AND YOU CAN BREATHE.
UFF

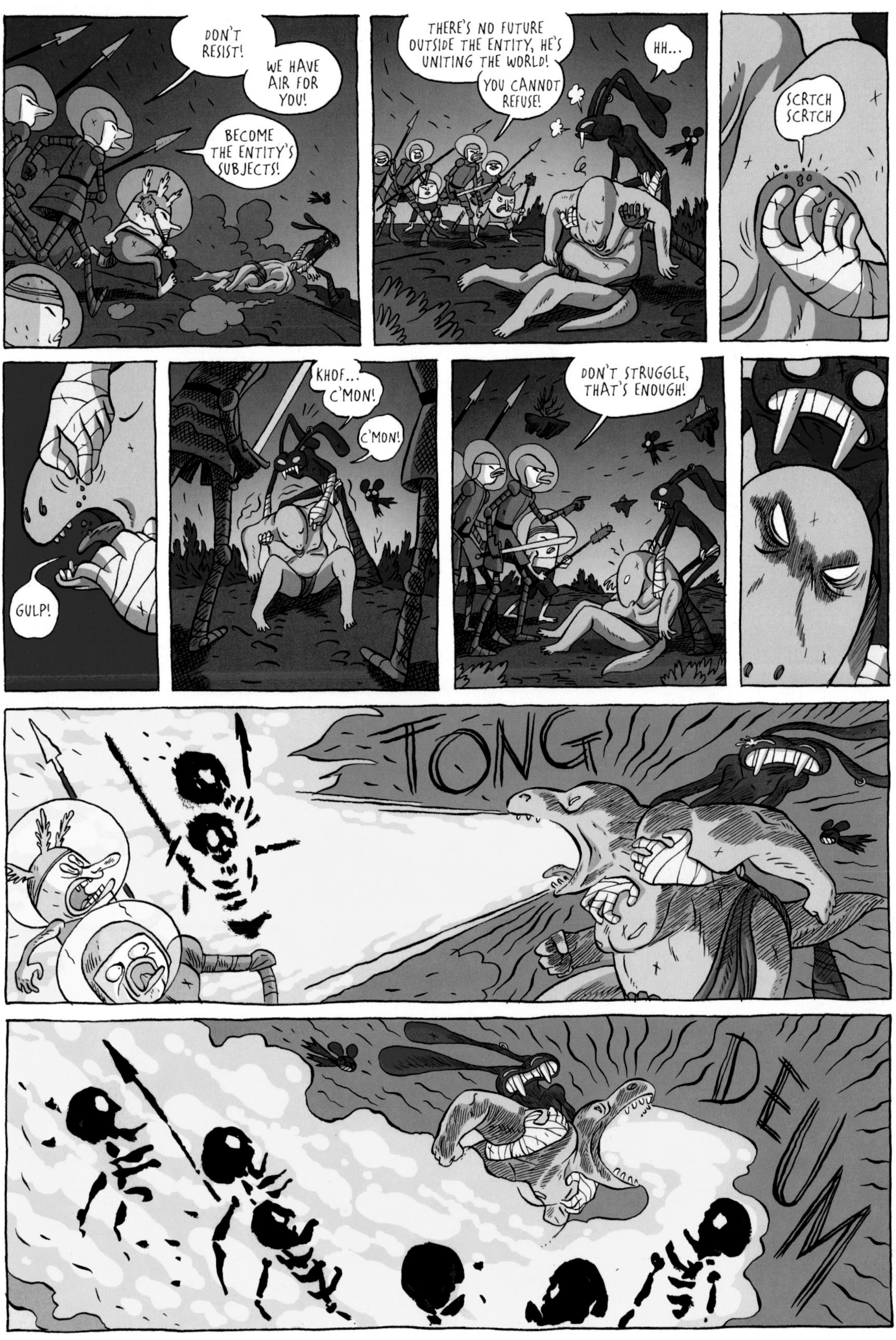
DON'T RESIST!
WE HAVE AIR FOR YOU!
BECOME THE ENTITY'S SUBJECTS!
THERE'S NO FUTURE OUTSIDE THE ENTITY, HE'S UNITING THE WORLD!
YOU CANNOT REFUSE!
HH...
SCRTCH SCRTCH
GULP!
KHOF... C'MON!
C'MON!
DON'T STRUGGLE, THAT'S ENOUGH!
TONG
DEUM

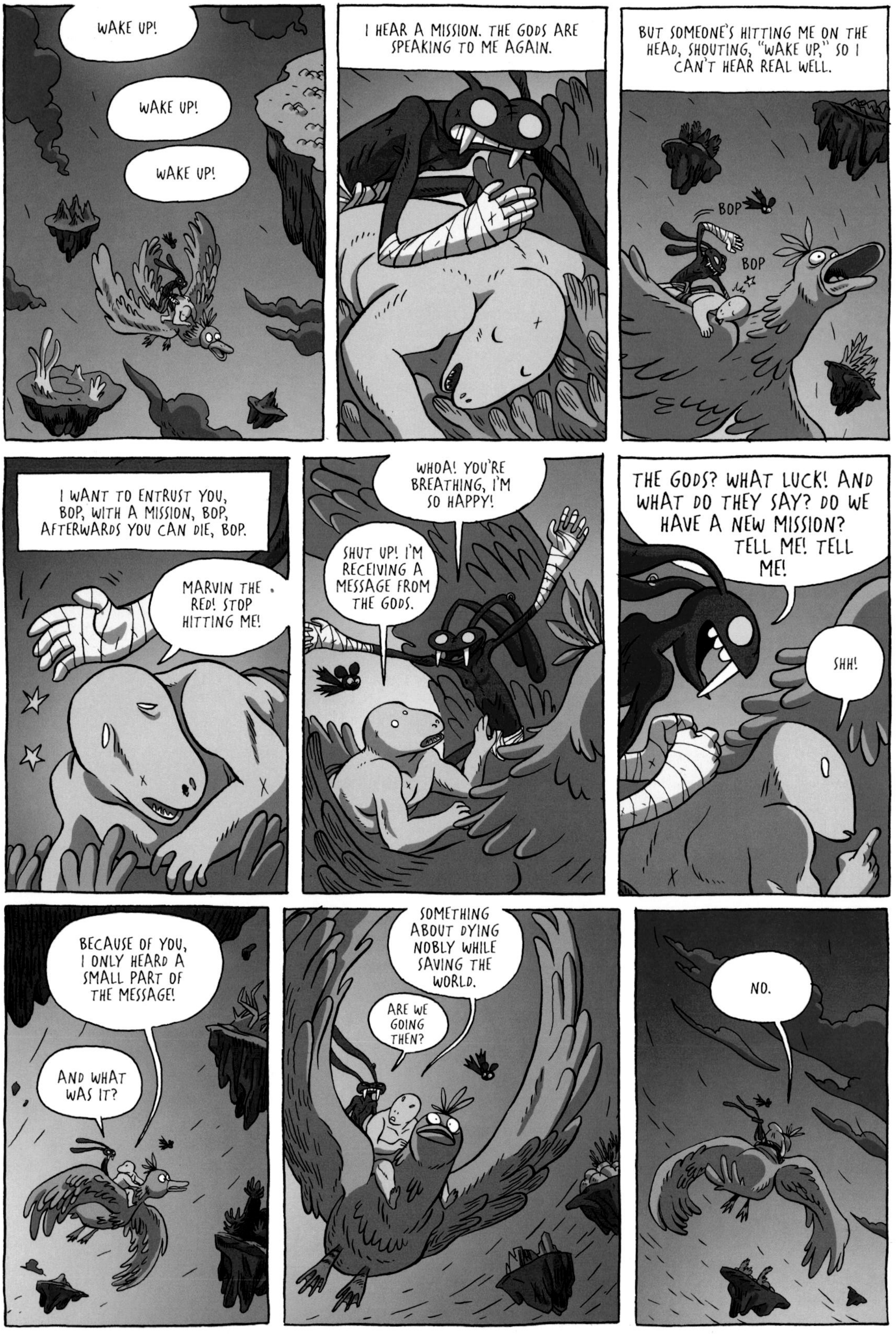
WAKE UP!
WAKE UP!
WAKE UP!
I HEAR A MISSION. THE GODS ARE SPEAKING TO ME AGAIN.
BUT SOMEONE'S HITTING ME ON THE HEAD, SHOUTING, "WAKE UP," SO I CAN'T HEAR REAL WELL.
BOP
BOP
I WANT TO ENTRUST YOU, BOP, WITH A MISSION, BOP, AFTERWARDS YOU CAN DIE, BOP.
MARVIN THE RED! STOP HITTING ME!
WHOA! YOU'RE BREATHING, I'M SO HAPPY!
SHUT UP! I'M RECEIVING A MESSAGE FROM THE GODS.
THE GODS? WHAT LUCK! AND WHAT DO THEY SAY? DO WE HAVE A NEW MISSION? TELL ME! TELL ME!
SHH!
BECAUSE OF YOU, I ONLY HEARD A SMALL PART OF THE MESSAGE!
AND WHAT WAS IT?
SOMETHING ABOUT DYING NOBLY WHILE SAVING THE WORLD.
ARE WE GOING THEN?
NO.

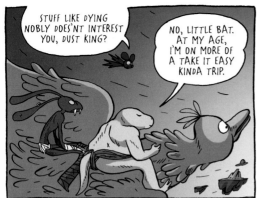

STUFF LIKE DYING NOBLY DOES'NT INTEREST YOU, DUST KING?

NO, LITTLE BAT. AT MY AGE, I'M ON MORE OF A TAKE IT EASY KINDA TRIP.

AH, I UNDERSTAND YOU, DUST KING. I ALWAYS SAY THAT THE...

SAVE THE WORLD AND DIE!

AHH!

UH, WHAT DID I SAY?

YOU WANT US TO FIND AN ISLET TO SET DOWN ON, DUST KING?

YOU UNDERSTAND, LITTLE BAT, HE MAY BE THE DUST KING, BUT HE'S A BIT OF GRANDPA, TOO.

NO! I GOT THE ENTIRE MESSAGE! THERE'S NO TIME TO WASTE! TAKE ME TO ORLONDOH'S.

WE'LL HAVE TO STOP TO LIGHT A FIRE, THEN!

THERE'S NO TIME!

SHLAK

MASTER! TELL US WHAT'S HAPPENING?

MARVIN TO ORLONDOH, MARVIN TO ORLONDOH. IT'S URGENT THAT WE REACH YOU.

YOU MUST OPEN THE DOOR TO THE LAND OF THE DEAD! PREPARE EVERYTHING FOR THE CEREMONY. I'M COMING. DON'T WASTE A SECOND OR THE WORLD WILL BE DESTROYED!

ANY MESSAGES DURING MY ABSENCE, GILBERTO?

NONE AT ALL! AND I HAVEN'T MOVED FROM HERE IN AT LEAST THREE HOURS.

WHEN I TUNE IN TO THE FLAMES, I'M TOTALLY ONTO THEM, MAN.

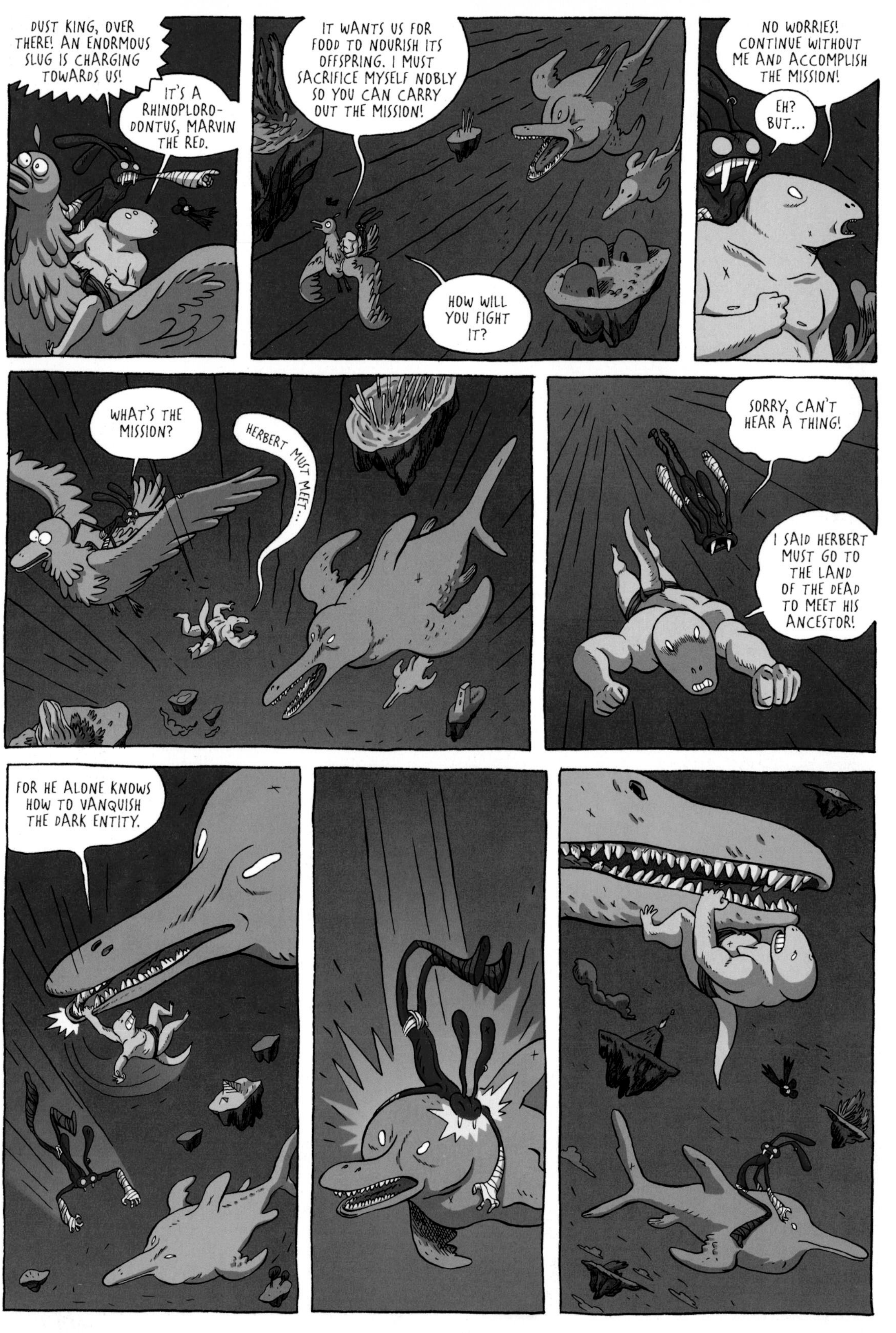
DUST KING, OVER THERE! AN ENORMOUS SLUG IS CHARGING TOWARDS US!
IT'S A RHINOPLORODONTUS, MARVIN THE RED.
IT WANTS US FOR FOOD TO NOURISH ITS OFFSPRING. I MUST SACRIFICE MYSELF NOBLY SO YOU CAN CARRY OUT THE MISSION!
HOW WILL YOU FIGHT IT?
NO WORRIES! CONTINUE WITHOUT ME AND ACCOMPLISH THE MISSION!
EH? BUT...
WHAT'S THE MISSION?
HERBERT MUST MEET...
SORRY, CAN'T HEAR A THING!
I SAID HERBERT MUST GO TO THE LAND OF THE DEAD TO MEET HIS ANCESTOR!
FOR HE ALONE KNOWS HOW TO VANQUISH THE DARK ENTITY.

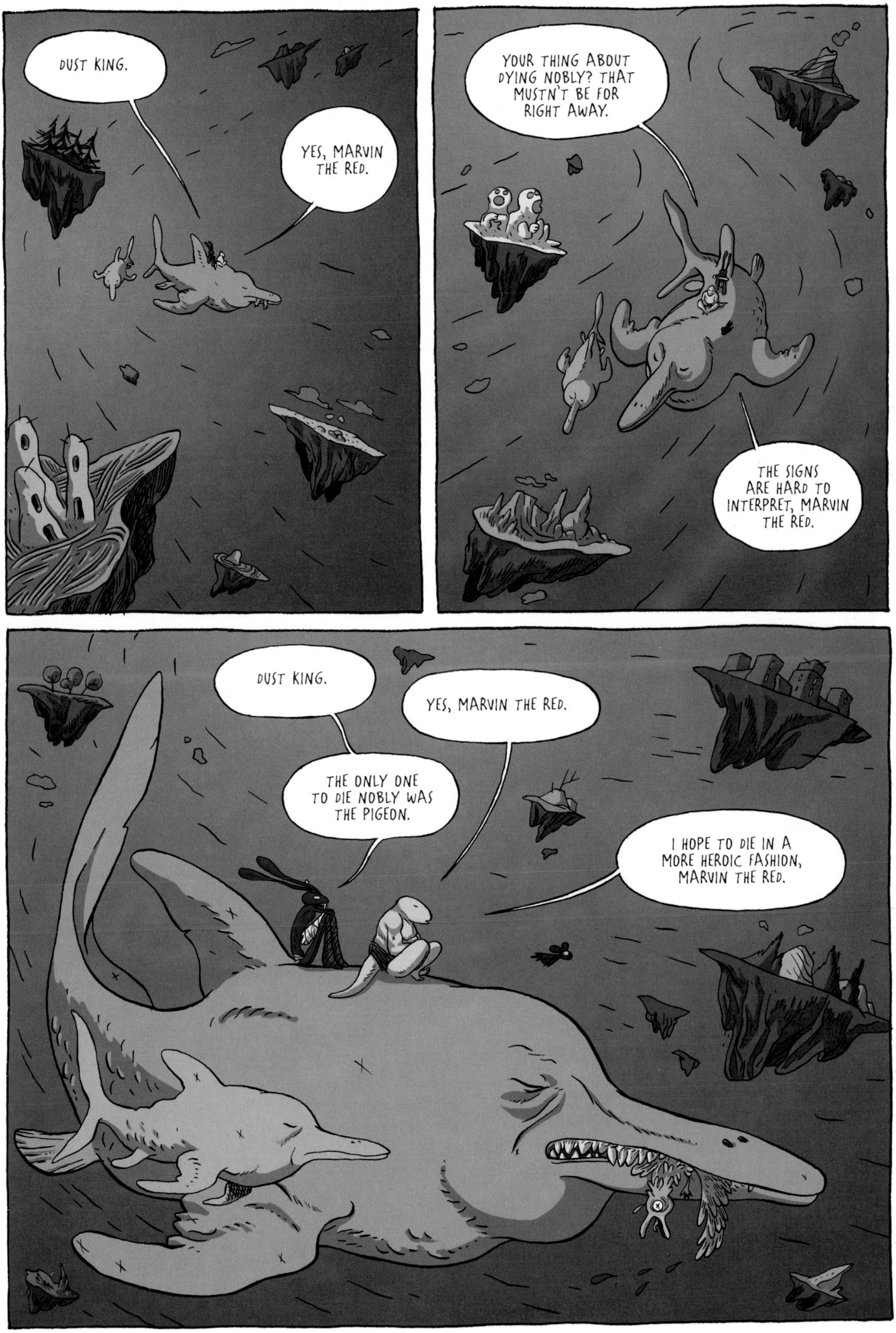
DUST KING.
YES, MARVIN THE RED.
YOUR THING ABOUT DYING NOBLY? THAT MUSTN'T BE FOR RIGHT AWAY.
THE SIGNS ARE HARD TO INTERPRET, MARVIN THE RED.
DUST KING.
THE ONLY ONE TO DIE NOBLY WAS THE PIGEON.
YES, MARVIN THE RED.
I HOPE TO DIE IN A MORE HEROIC FASHION, MARVIN THE RED.

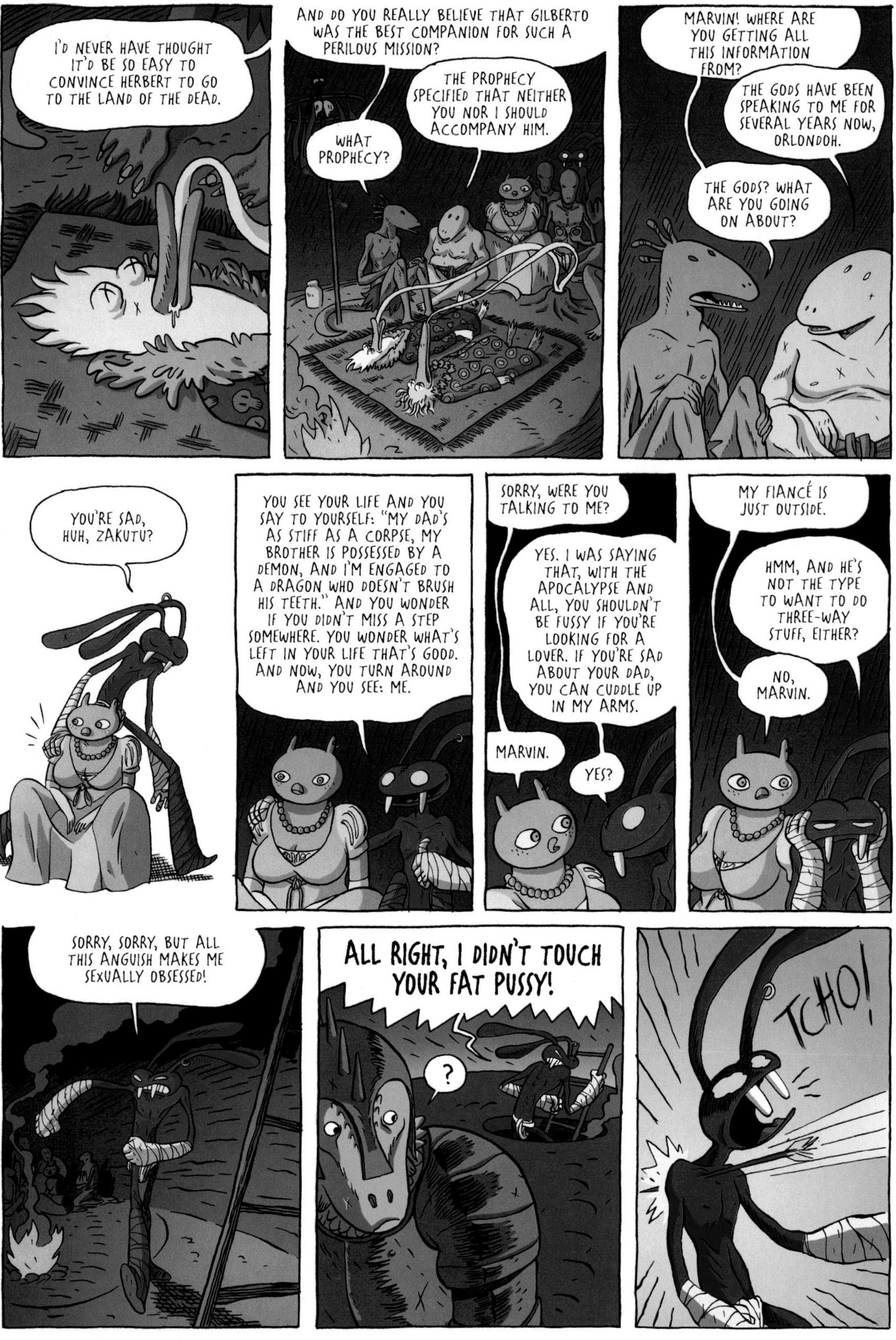
I'D NEVER HAVE THOUGHT IT'D BE SO EASY TO CONVINCE HERBERT TO GO TO THE LAND OF THE DEAD.
AND DO YOU REALLY BELIEVE THAT GILBERTO WAS THE BEST COMPANION FOR SUCH A PERILOUS MISSION?
THE PROPHECY SPECIFIED THAT NEITHER YOU NOR I SHOULD ACCOMPANY HIM.
WHAT PROPHECY?
MARVIN! WHERE ARE YOU GETTING ALL THIS INFORMATION FROM?
THE GODS HAVE BEEN SPEAKING TO ME FOR SEVERAL YEARS NOW, ORLONDOH.
THE GODS? WHAT ARE YOU GOING ON ABOUT?
YOU'RE SAD, HUH, ZAKUTU?
YOU SEE YOUR LIFE AND YOU SAY TO YOURSELF: "MY DAD'S AS STIFF AS A CORPSE, MY BROTHER IS POSSESSED BY A DEMON, AND I'M ENGAGED TO A DRAGON WHO DOESN'T BRUSH HIS TEETH." AND YOU WONDER IF YOU DIDN'T MISS A STEP SOMEWHERE. YOU WONDER WHAT'S LEFT IN YOUR LIFE THAT'S GOOD. AND NOW, YOU TURN AROUND AND YOU SEE: ME.
SORRY, WERE YOU TALKING TO ME?
YES. I WAS SAYING THAT, WITH THE APOCALYPSE AND ALL, YOU SHOULDN'T BE FUSSY IF YOU'RE LOOKING FOR A LOVER. IF YOU'RE SAD ABOUT YOUR DAD, YOU CAN CUDDLE UP IN MY ARMS.
MARVIN.
YES?
MY FIANCÉ IS JUST OUTSIDE.
HMM, AND HE'S NOT THE TYPE TO WANT TO DO THREE-WAY STUFF, EITHER?
NO, MARVIN.
SORRY, SORRY, BUT ALL THIS ANGUISH MAKES ME SEXUALLY OBSESSED!
ALL RIGHT, I DIDN'T TOUCH YOUR FAT PUSSY!
?
TCHO!

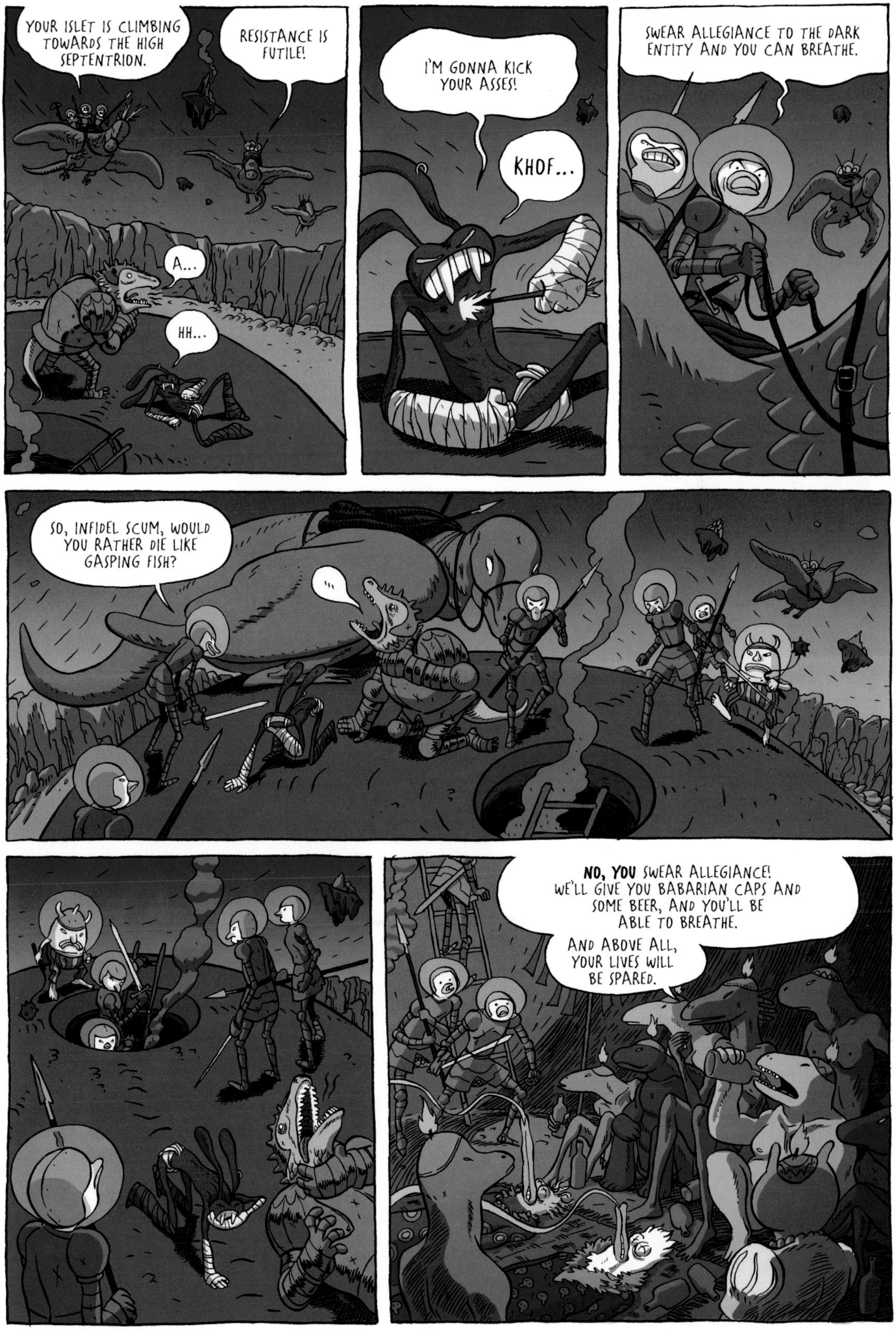

YOUR ISLET IS CLIMBING TOWARDS THE HIGH SEPTENTRION.
RESISTANCE IS FUTILE!
A...
HH...
I'M GONNA KICK YOUR ASSES!
KHOF...
SWEAR ALLEGIANCE TO THE DARK ENTITY AND YOU CAN BREATHE.
SO, INFIDEL SCUM, WOULD YOU RATHER DIE LIKE GASPING FISH?
...
NO, YOU SWEAR ALLEGIANCE! WE'LL GIVE YOU BABARIAN CAPS AND SOME BEER, AND YOU'LL BE ABLE TO BREATHE.
AND ABOVE ALL, YOUR LIVES WILL BE SPARED.

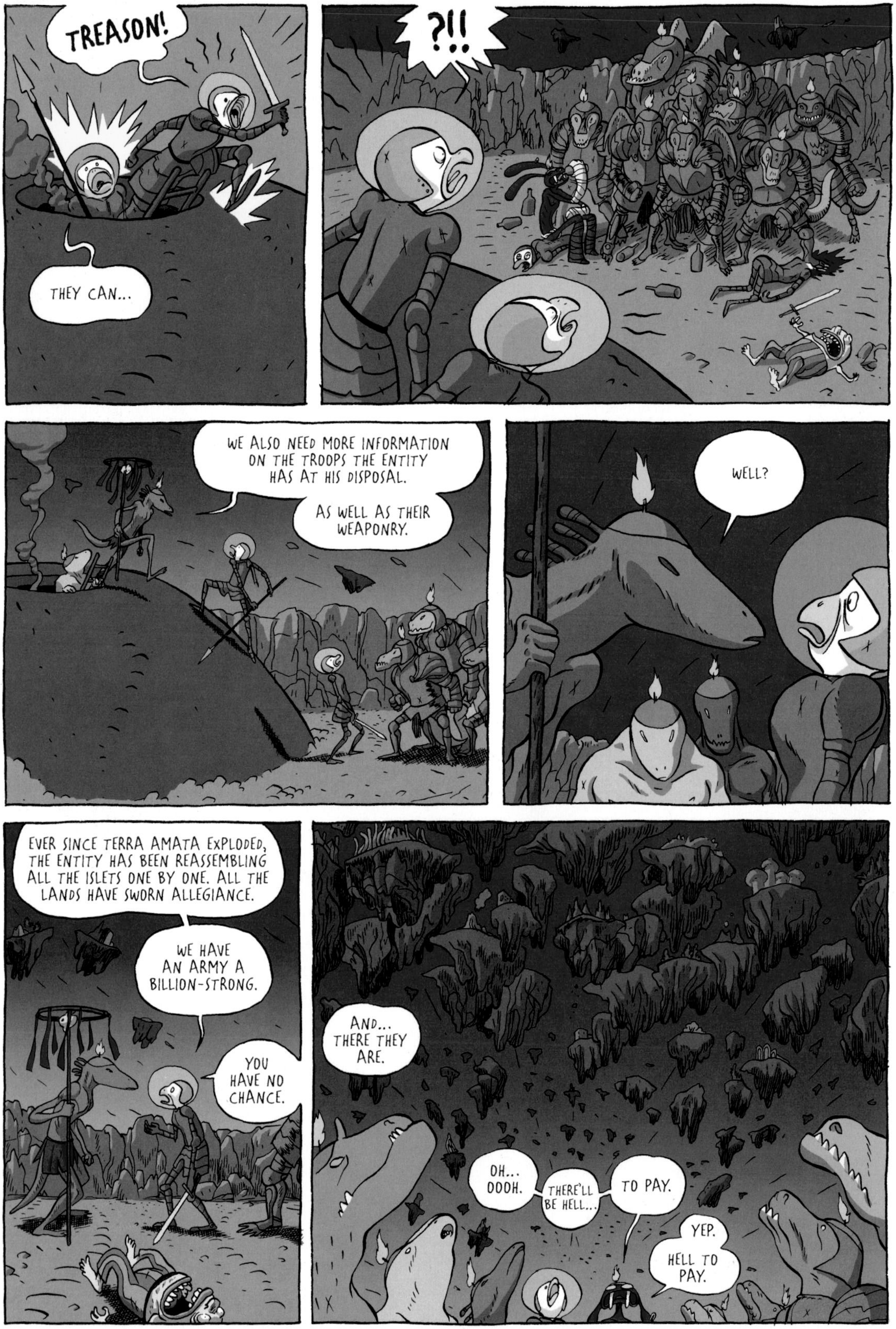
TREASON!
THEY CAN...
?!!
WE ALSO NEED MORE INFORMATION ON THE TROOPS THE ENTITY HAS AT HIS DISPOSAL.
AS WELL AS THEIR WEAPONRY.
WELL?
EVER SINCE TERRA AMATA EXPLODED, THE ENTITY HAS BEEN REASSEMBLING ALL THE ISLETS ONE BY ONE. ALL THE LANDS HAVE SWORN ALLEGIANCE.
WE HAVE AN ARMY A BILLION-STRONG.
YOU HAVE NO CHANCE.
AND... THERE THEY ARE.
OH... OOOH.
THERE'LL BE HELL...
TO PAY.
YEP.
HELL TO PAY.

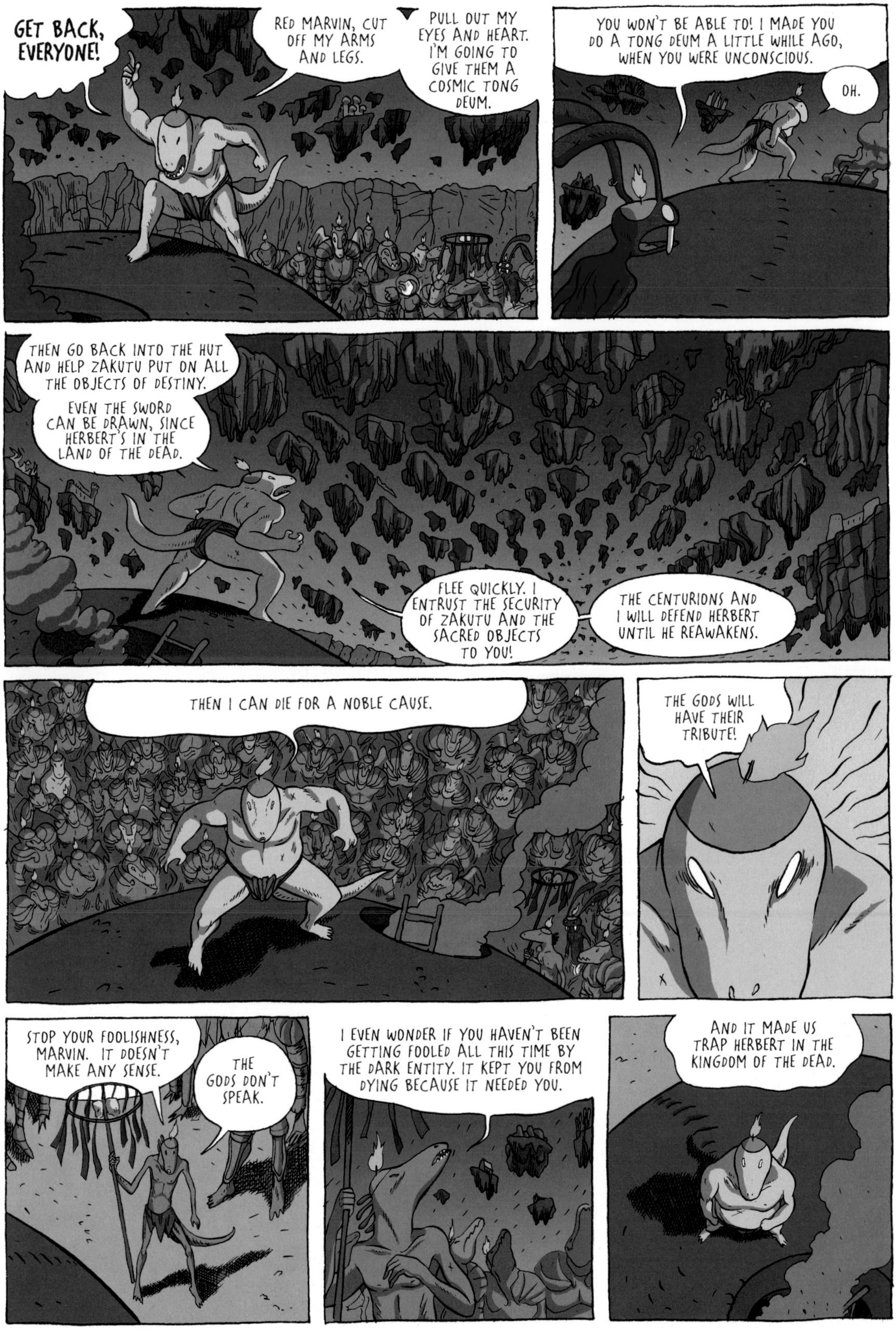
GET BACK, EVERYONE!
RED MARVIN, CUT OFF MY ARMS AND LEGS.
PULL OUT MY EYES AND HEART. I'M GOING TO GIVE THEM A COSMIC TONG DEUM.
YOU WON'T BE ABLE TO! I MADE YOU DO A TONG DEUM A LITTLE WHILE AGO, WHEN YOU WERE UNCONSCIOUS.
OH.
THEN GO BACK INTO THE HUT AND HELP ZAKUTU PUT ON ALL THE OBJECTS OF DESTINY.
EVEN THE SWORD CAN BE DRAWN, SINCE HERBERT'S IN THE LAND OF THE DEAD.
FLEE QUICKLY. I ENTRUST THE SECURITY OF ZAKUTU AND THE SACRED OBJECTS TO YOU!
THE CENTURIONS AND I WILL DEFEND HERBERT UNTIL HE REAWAKENS.
THEN I CAN DIE FOR A NOBLE CAUSE.
THE GODS WILL HAVE THEIR TRIBUTE!
STOP YOUR FOOLISHNESS, MARVIN. IT DOESN'T MAKE ANY SENSE.
THE GODS DON'T SPEAK.
I EVEN WONDER IF YOU HAVEN'T BEEN GETTING FOOLED ALL THIS TIME BY THE DARK ENTITY. IT KEPT YOU FROM DYING BECAUSE IT NEEDED YOU.
AND IT MADE US TRAP HERBERT IN THE KINGDOM OF THE DEAD.

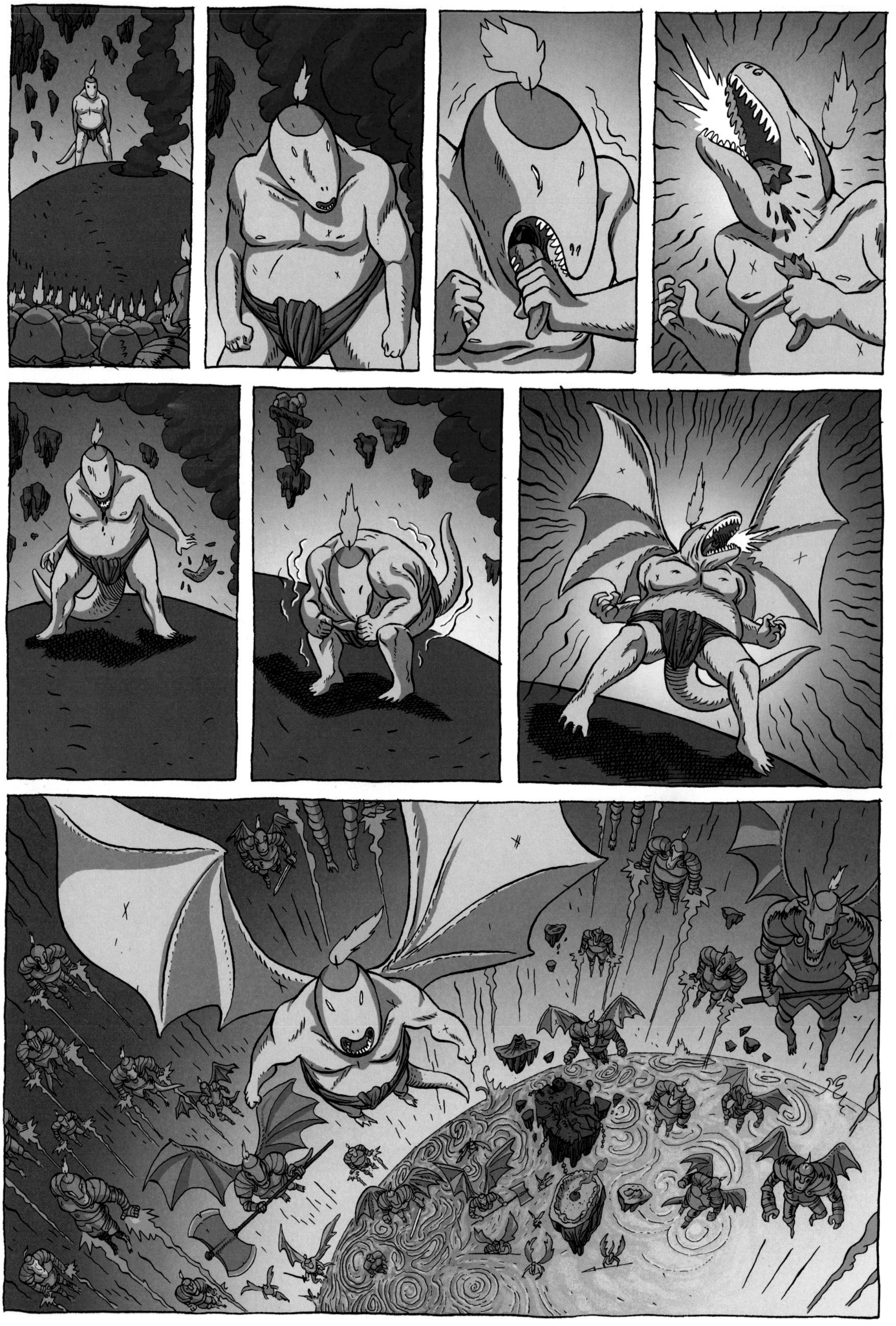

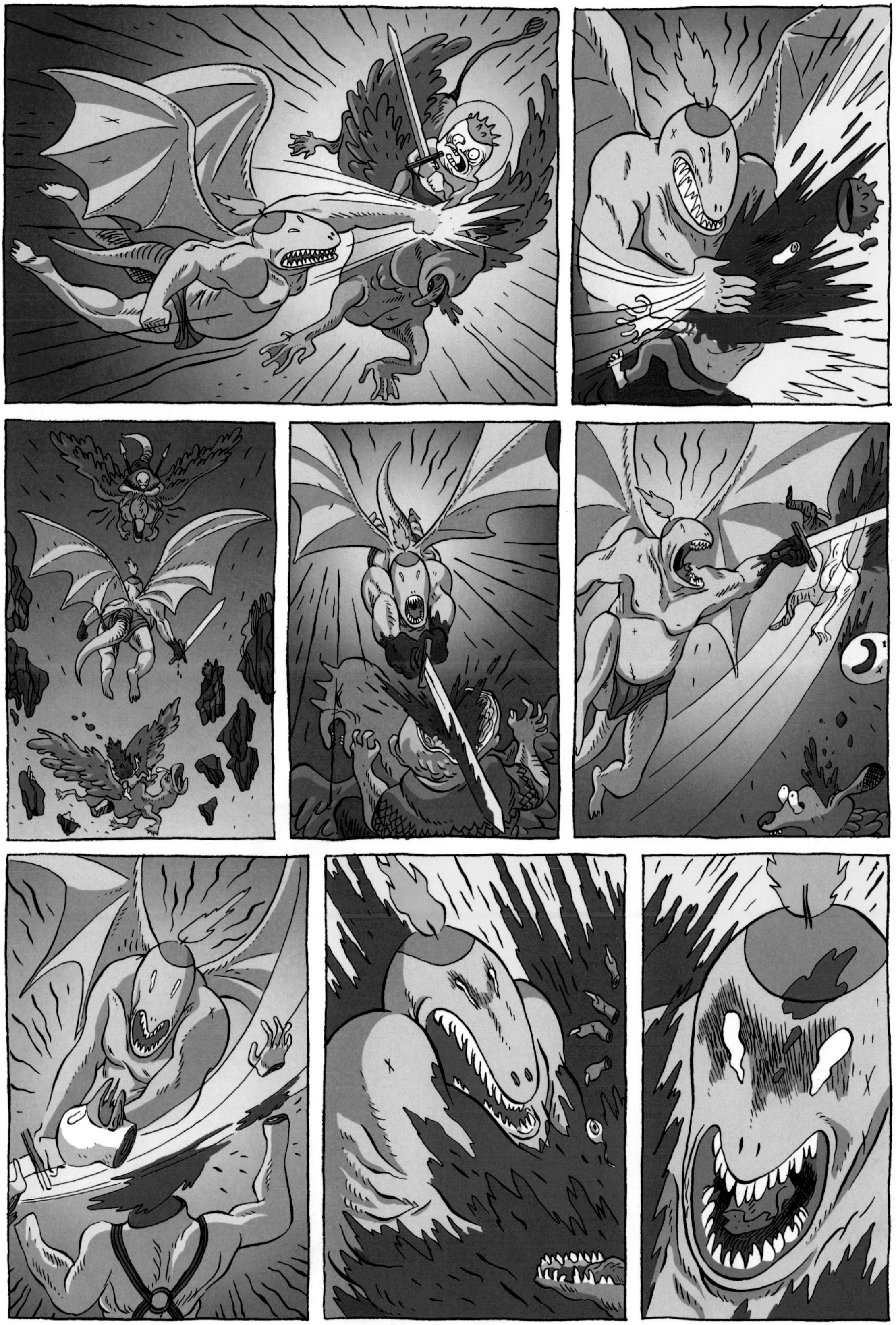

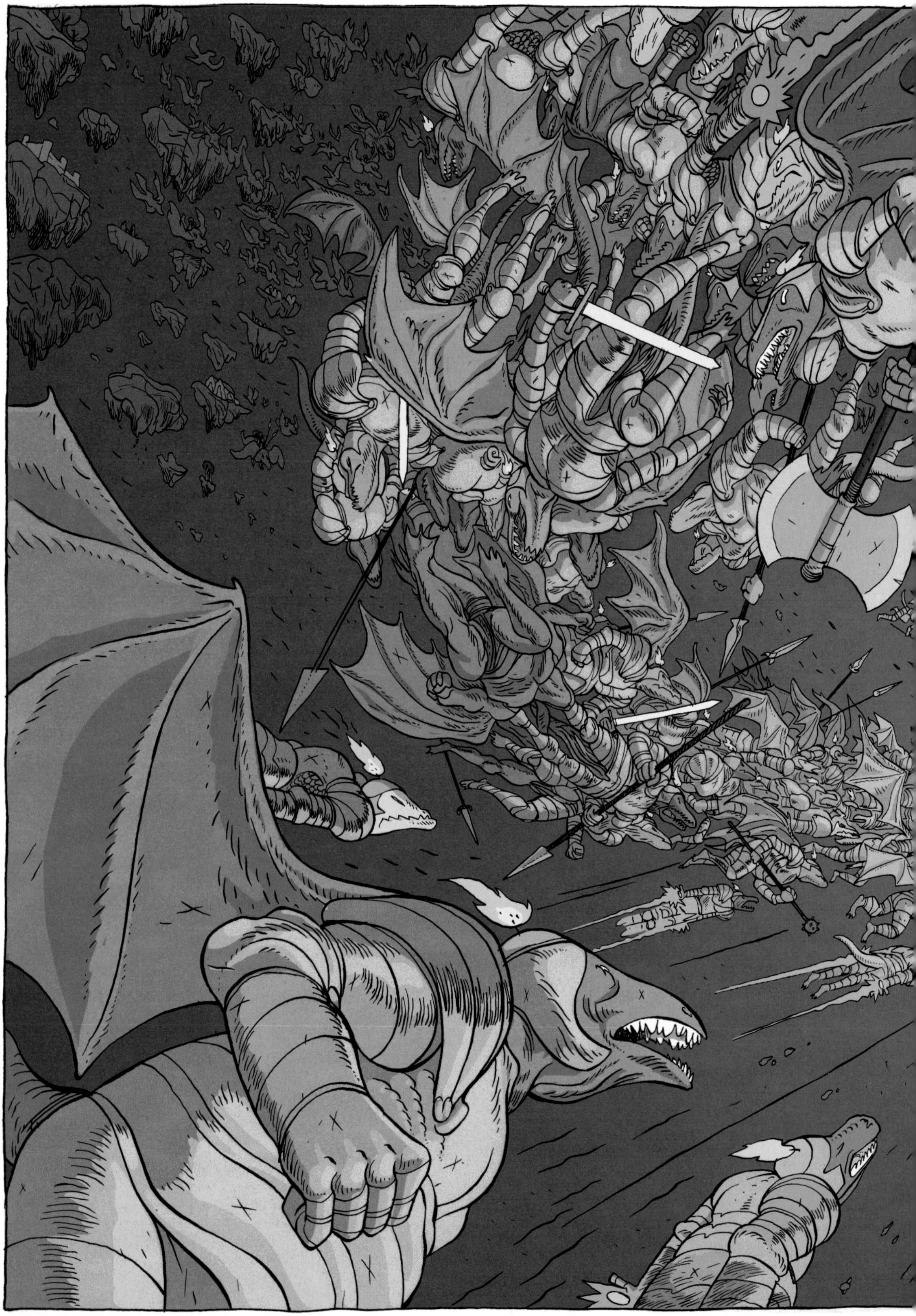

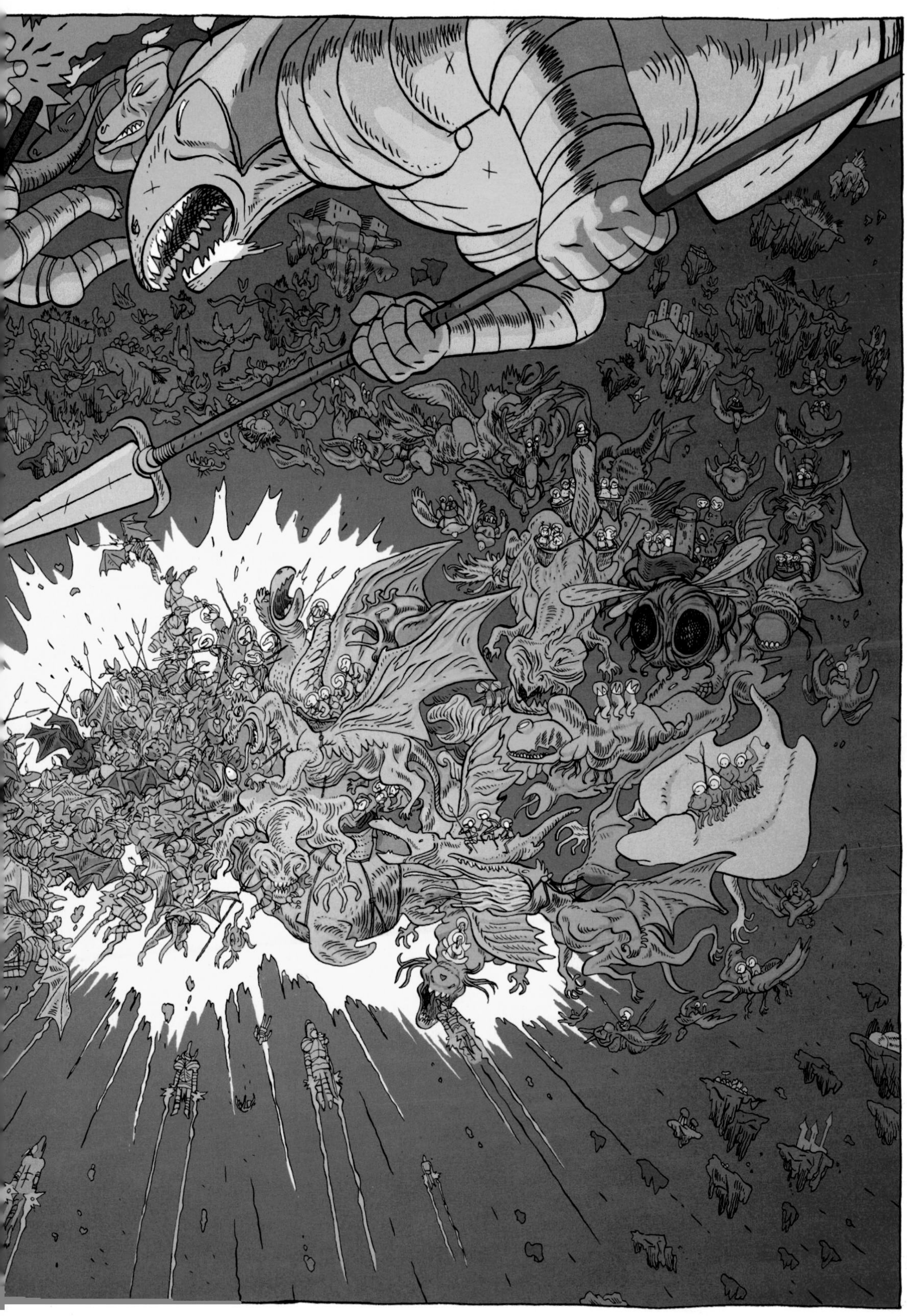

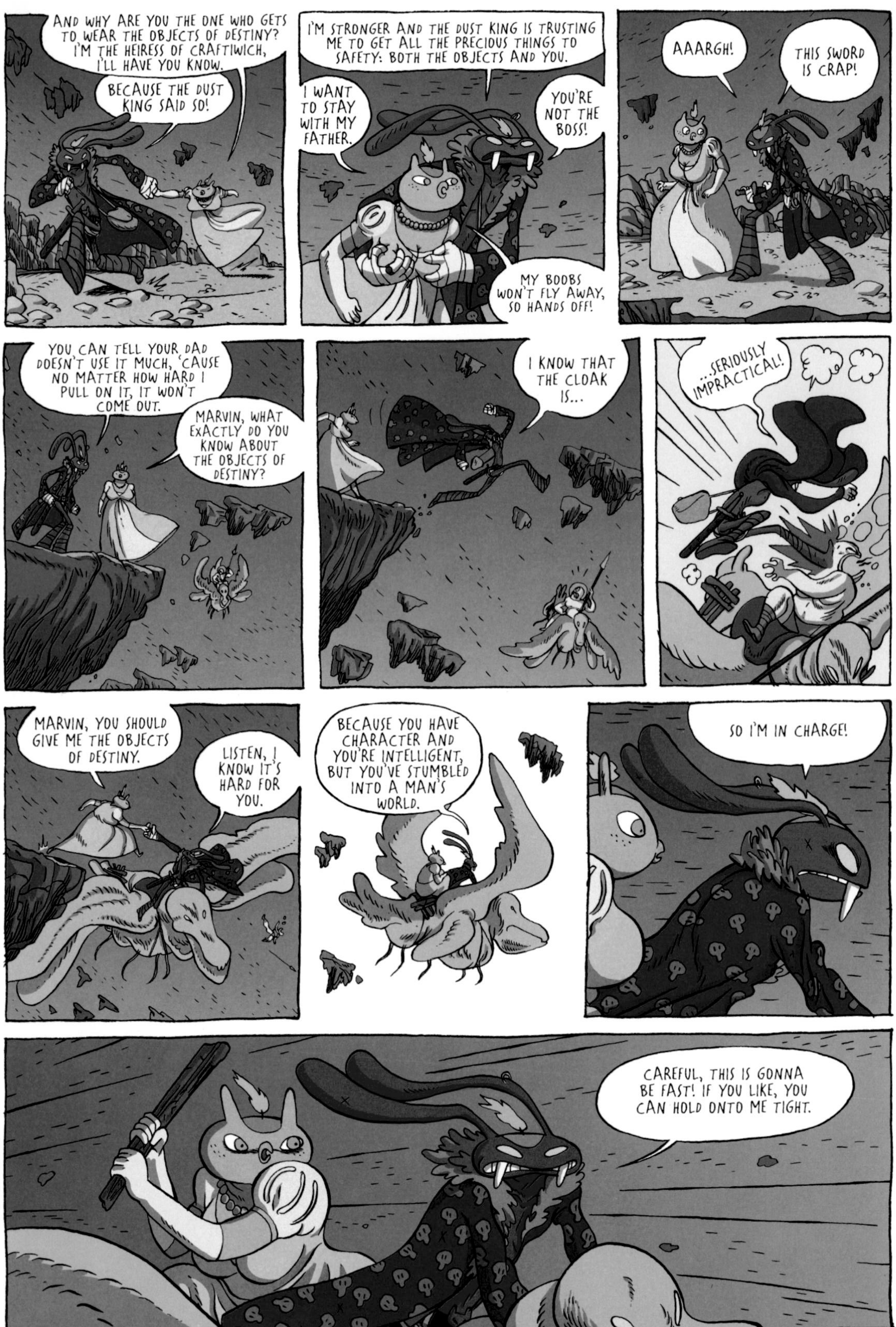
AND WHY ARE YOU THE ONE WHO GETS TO WEAR THE OBJECTS OF DESTINY? I'M THE HEIRESS OF CRAFTIWICH, I'LL HAVE YOU KNOW.
BECAUSE THE DUST KING SAID SO!
I'M STRONGER AND THE DUST KING IS TRUSTING ME TO GET ALL THE PRECIOUS THINGS TO SAFETY: BOTH THE OBJECTS AND YOU.
I WANT TO STAY WITH MY FATHER.
YOU'RE NOT THE BOSS!
MY BOOBS WON'T FLY AWAY, SO HANDS OFF!
AAARGH!
THIS SWORD IS CRAP!
YOU CAN TELL YOUR DAD DOESN'T USE IT MUCH, 'CAUSE NO MATTER HOW HARD I PULL ON IT, IT WON'T COME OUT.
MARVIN, WHAT EXACTLY DO YOU KNOW ABOUT THE OBJECTS OF DESTINY?
I KNOW THAT THE CLOAK IS...
...SERIOUSLY IMPRACTICAL!
MARVIN, YOU SHOULD GIVE ME THE OBJECTS OF DESTINY.
LISTEN, I KNOW IT'S HARD FOR YOU.
BECAUSE YOU HAVE CHARACTER AND YOU'RE INTELLIGENT, BUT YOU'VE STUMBLED INTO A MAN'S WORLD.
SO I'M IN CHARGE!
CAREFUL, THIS IS GONNA BE FAST! IF YOU LIKE, YOU CAN HOLD ONTO ME TIGHT.

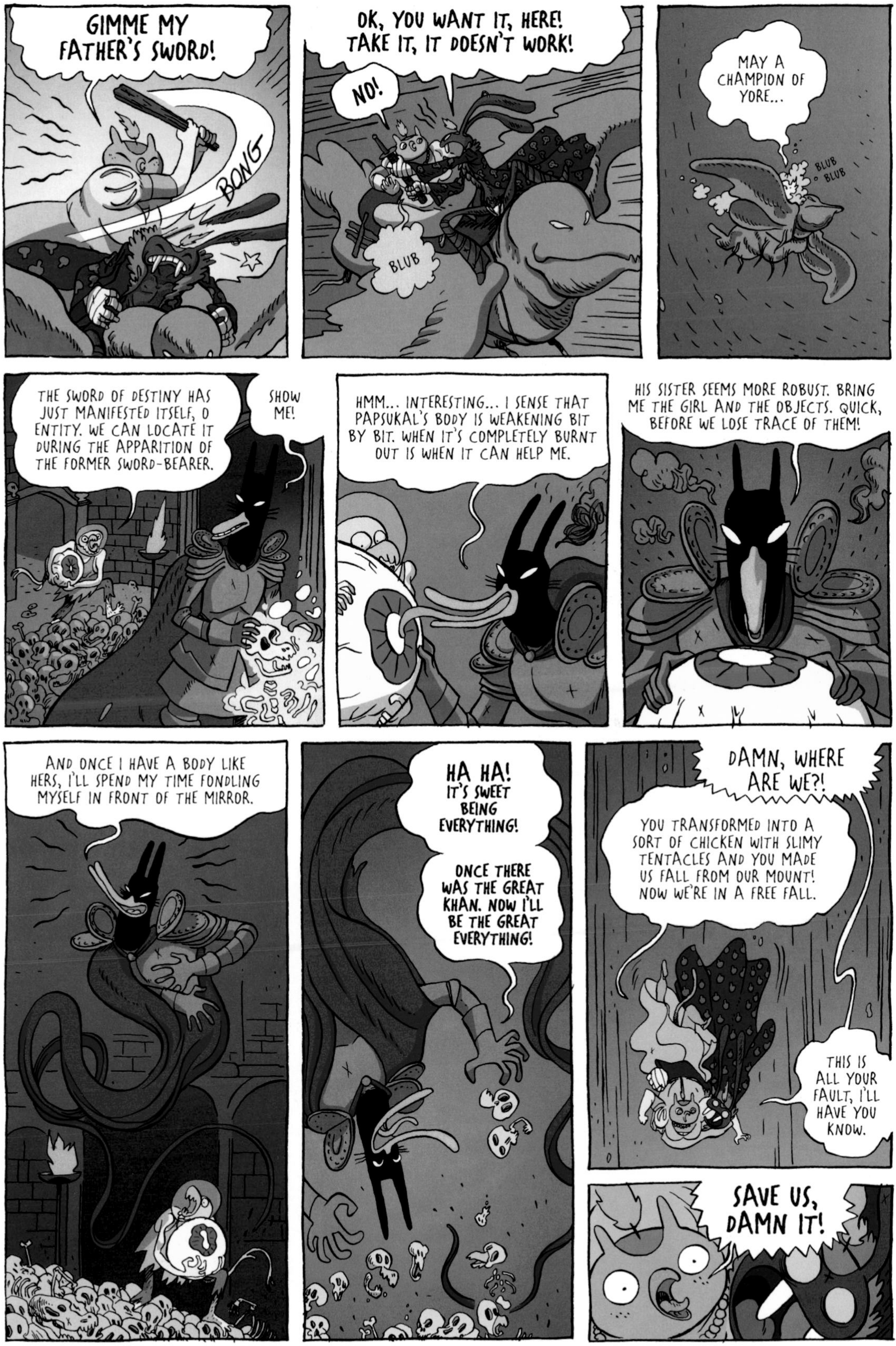
GIMME MY FATHER'S SWORD!
BONG
OK, YOU WANT IT, HERE! TAKE IT, IT DOESN'T WORK!
NO!
BLUB
MAY A CHAMPION OF YORE...
BLUB BLUB
THE SWORD OF DESTINY HAS JUST MANIFESTED ITSELF, O ENTITY. WE CAN LOCATE IT DURING THE APPARITION OF THE FORMER SWORD-BEARER.
SHOW ME!
HMM... INTERESTING... I SENSE THAT PAPSUKAL'S BODY IS WEAKENING BIT BY BIT. WHEN IT'S COMPLETELY BURNT OUT IS WHEN IT CAN HELP ME.
HIS SISTER SEEMS MORE ROBUST. BRING ME THE GIRL AND THE OBJECTS. QUICK, BEFORE WE LOSE TRACE OF THEM!
AND ONCE I HAVE A BODY LIKE HERS, I'LL SPEND MY TIME FONDLING MYSELF IN FRONT OF THE MIRROR.
HA HA! IT'S SWEET BEING EVERYTHING!
ONCE THERE WAS THE GREAT KHAN. NOW I'LL BE THE GREAT EVERYTHING!
DAMN, WHERE ARE WE?!
YOU TRANSFORMED INTO A SORT OF CHICKEN WITH SLIMY TENTACLES AND YOU MADE US FALL FROM OUR MOUNT! NOW WE'RE IN A FREE FALL.
THIS IS ALL YOUR FAULT, I'LL HAVE YOU KNOW.
SAVE US, DAMN IT!

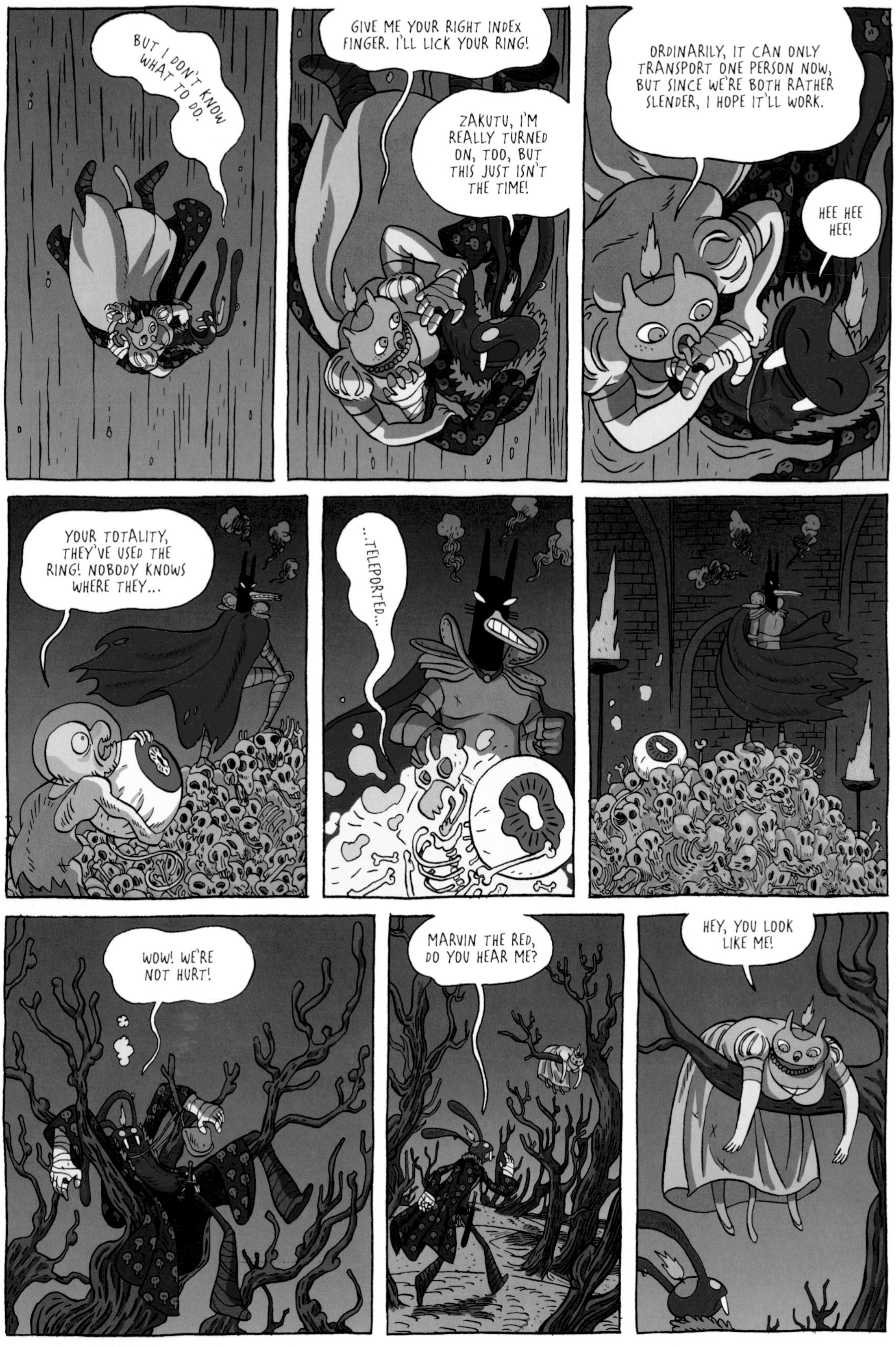
BUT I DON'T KNOW WHAT TO DO.
GIVE ME YOUR RIGHT INDEX FINGER. I'LL LICK YOUR RING!
ZAKUTU, I'M REALLY TURNED ON, TOO, BUT THIS JUST ISN'T THE TIME!
ORDINARILY, IT CAN ONLY TRANSPORT ONE PERSON NOW, BUT SINCE WE'RE BOTH RATHER SLENDER, I HOPE IT'LL WORK.
HEE HEE HEE!
YOUR TOTALITY, THEY'VE USED THE RING! NOBODY KNOWS WHERE THEY...
...TELEPORTED...
WOW! WE'RE NOT HURT!
MARVIN THE RED, DO YOU HEAR ME?
HEY, YOU LOOK LIKE ME!

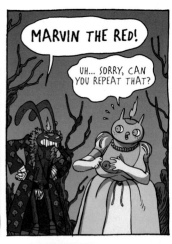

WHOA! THIS IS TOTALLY NUTS! DID YOU SEE? DID YOU SEE? I'M YOU!

HMM, THIS MUST BE AN EFFECT OF THE RING. IT CAN NO LONGER TRANSPORT TWO PEOPLE.

LISTEN I'VE BEEN THINKING. IF THE BABARIAN CAPS AND BOOZE LET US DO WITHOUT THE DARK ENTITY'S SERVICES, WHAT'S THE ONLY GROUP IN THE WORLD THAT'S NOT YET FALLEN UNDER HIS SWAY?

MARVIN THE RED!

UH... SORRY, CAN YOU REPEAT THAT?

KHUH KHOF...

KHOF! THE ALCOHOL IS GETTING SCARCE IN OUR VEINS, MARVIN, WE HAVE TO HIT THE BOTTLE, OR ELSE WE'LL SUFFOCATE!

BUT WHERE ARE WE?

IT DOESN'T MATTER. HOLD MY HAND, WE'RE GOING TO THE BABAR LANDS!

HEY, BUT WHAT WILL WE...

POOF!

...DO THERE?

HEY! DID YOU SEE, I'M MYSELF AGAIN!

HMM, SHOW ME THE RING.

UNDER THE TREE, TWO HUNDRED YARDS AWAY.

POOF!

HEY?! WHY DID YOU DO THAT?!

I'D RATHER THE OBJECTS OF DESTINY BE IN THE HANDS OF A RESPONSIBLE PERSON.

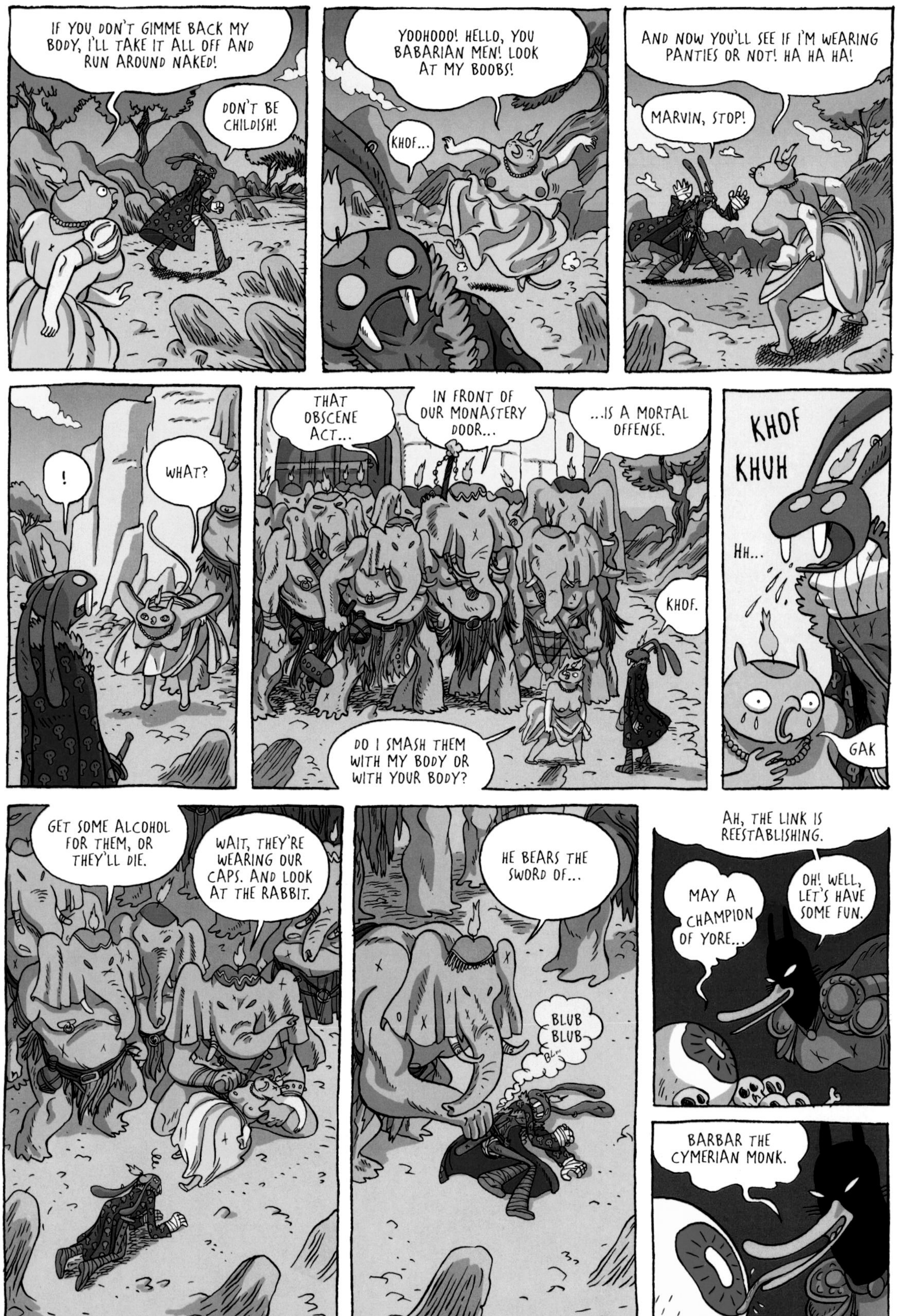
IF YOU DON'T GIMME BACK MY BODY, I'LL TAKE IT ALL OFF AND RUN AROUND NAKED!
DON'T BE CHILDISH!
YOOHOOO! HELLO, YOU BABARIAN MEN! LOOK AT MY BOOBS!
KHOF...
AND NOW YOU'LL SEE IF I'M WEARING PANTIES OR NOT! HA HA HA!
MARVIN, STOP!
!
WHAT?
THAT OBSCENE ACT...
IN FRONT OF OUR MONASTERY DOOR...
...IS A MORTAL OFFENSE.
KHOF.
DO I SMASH THEM WITH MY BODY OR WITH YOUR BODY?
KHOF
KHUH
HH...
GAK
GET SOME ALCOHOL FOR THEM, OR THEY'LL DIE.
WAIT, THEY'RE WEARING OUR CAPS. AND LOOK AT THE RABBIT.
HE BEARS THE SWORD OF...
BLUB BLUB
AH, THE LINK IS REESTABLISHING.
MAY A CHAMPION OF YORE...
OH! WELL, LET'S HAVE SOME FUN.
BARBAR THE CYMERIAN MONK.

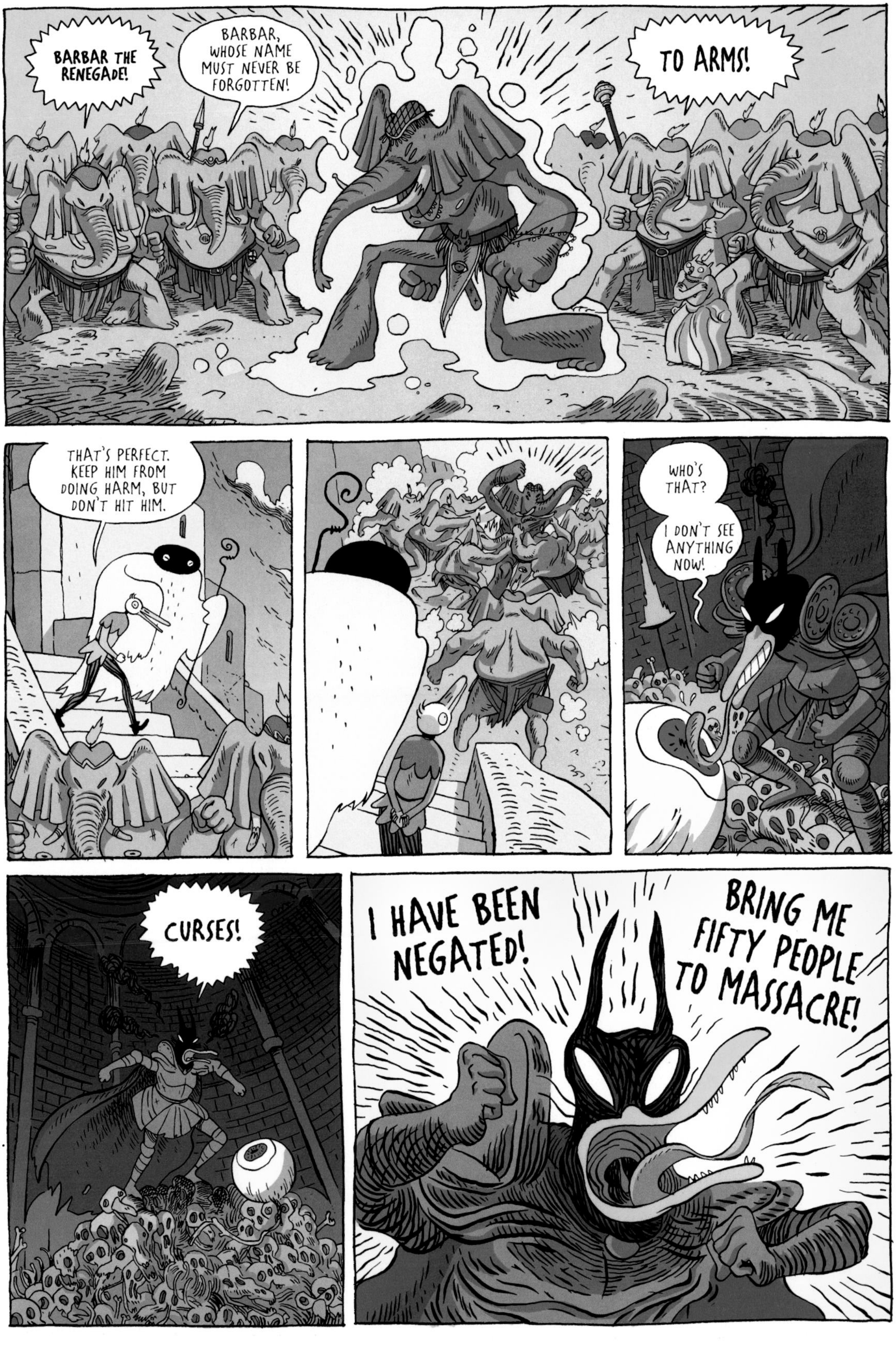

BARBAR THE RENEGADE!
BARBAR, WHOSE NAME MUST NEVER BE FORGOTTEN!
TO ARMS!
THAT'S PERFECT. KEEP HIM FROM DOING HARM, BUT DON'T HIT HIM.
WHO'S THAT?
I DON'T SEE ANYTHING NOW!
CURSES!
I HAVE BEEN NEGATED!
BRING ME FIFTY PEOPLE TO MASSACRE!

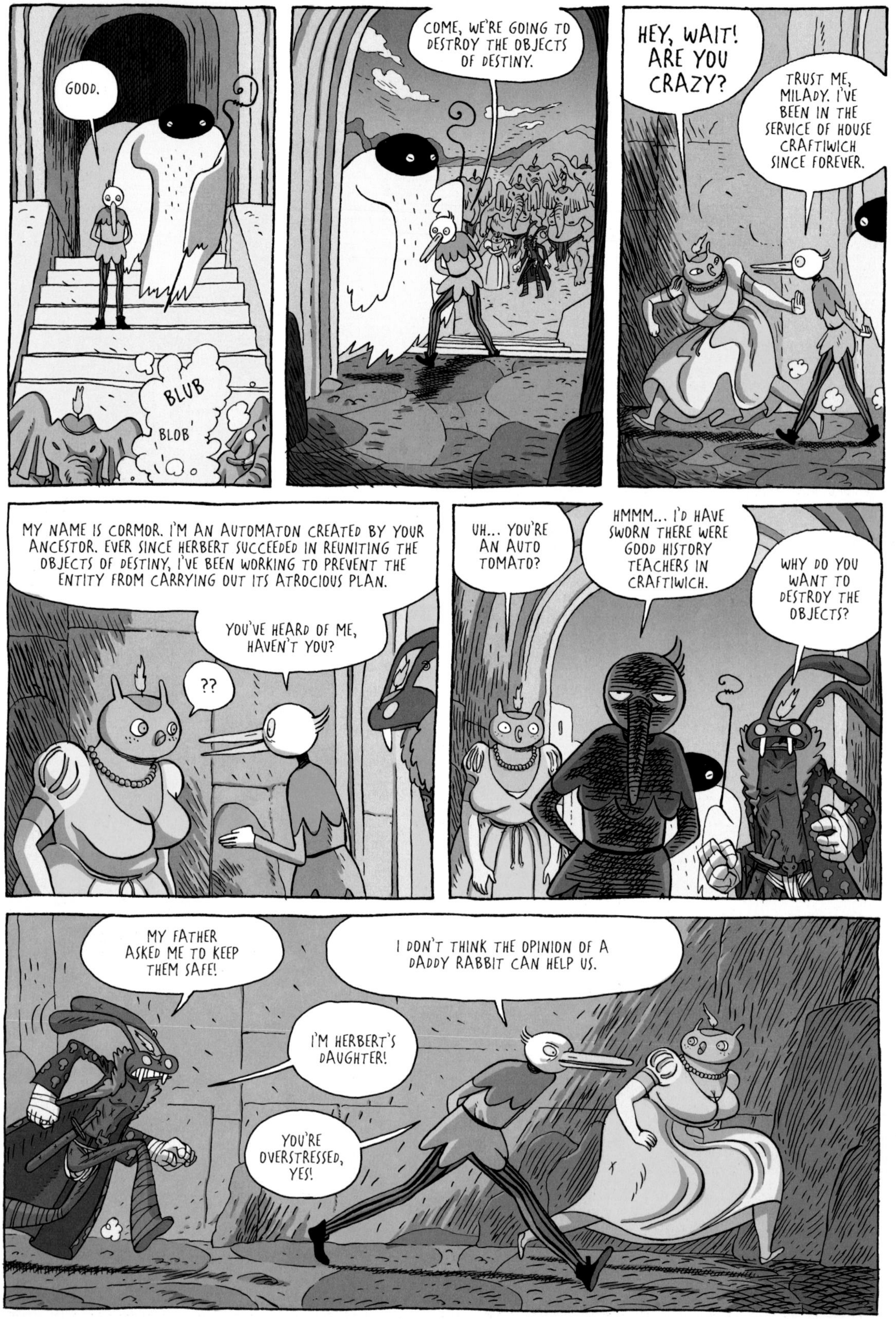
GOOD.
BLUB
BLOB
COME, WE'RE GOING TO DESTROY THE OBJECTS OF DESTINY.
HEY, WAIT! ARE YOU CRAZY?
TRUST ME, MILADY. I'VE BEEN IN THE SERVICE OF HOUSE CRAFTIWICH SINCE FOREVER.
MY NAME IS CORMOR. I'M AN AUTOMATON CREATED BY YOUR ANCESTOR. EVER SINCE HERBERT SUCCEEDED IN REUNITING THE OBJECTS OF DESTINY, I'VE BEEN WORKING TO PREVENT THE ENTITY FROM CARRYING OUT ITS ATROCIOUS PLAN.
YOU'VE HEARD OF ME, HAVEN'T YOU?
??
UH... YOU'RE AN AUTO TOMATO?
HMMM... I'D HAVE SWORN THERE WERE GOOD HISTORY TEACHERS IN CRAFTIWICH.
WHY DO YOU WANT TO DESTROY THE OBJECTS?
MY FATHER ASKED ME TO KEEP THEM SAFE!
I DON'T THINK THE OPINION OF A DADDY RABBIT CAN HELP US.
I'M HERBERT'S DAUGHTER!
YOU'RE OVERSTRESSED, YES!

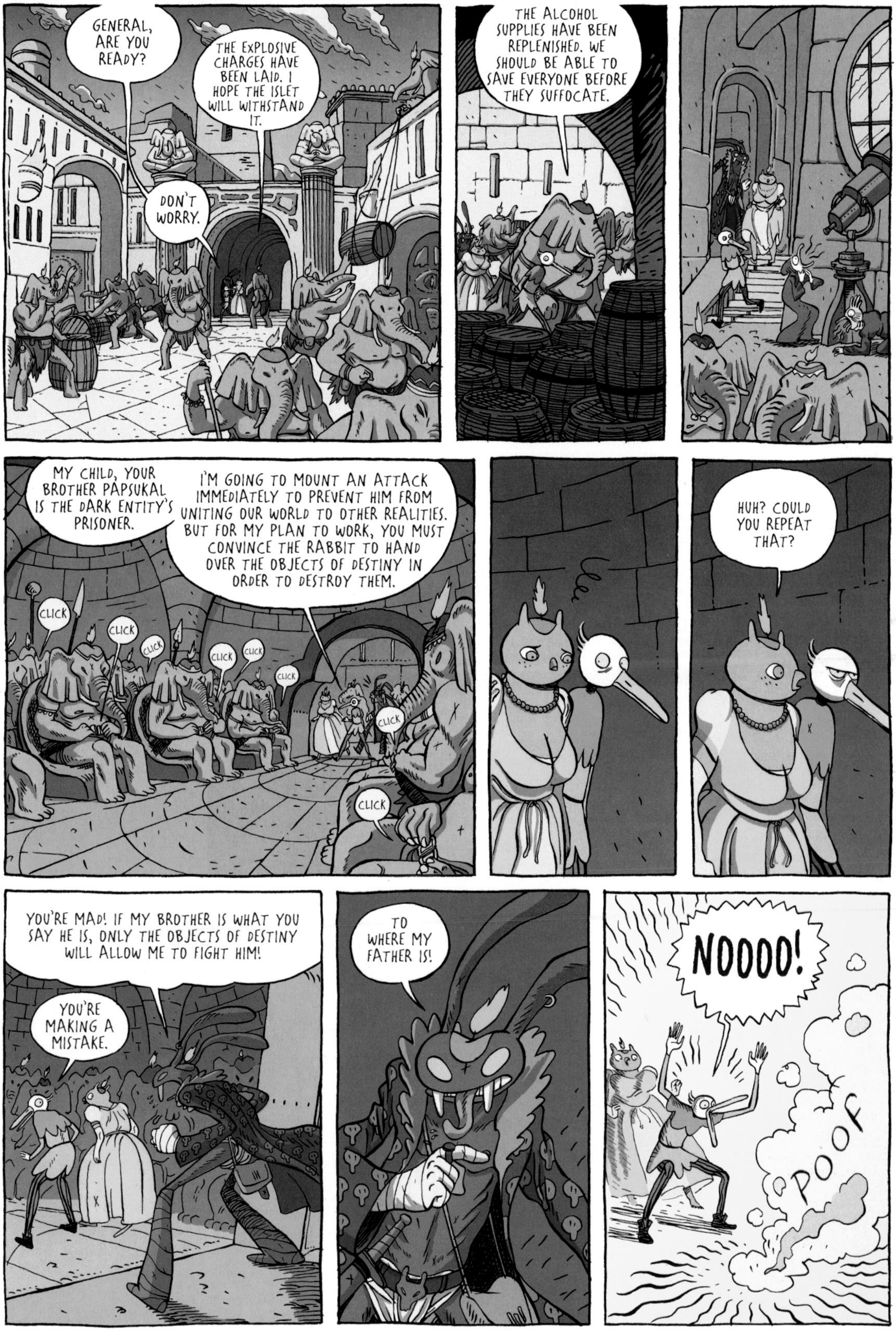
GENERAL, ARE YOU READY?
THE EXPLOSIVE CHARGES HAVE BEEN LAID. I HOPE THE ISLET WILL WITHSTAND IT.
DON'T WORRY.
THE ALCOHOL SUPPLIES HAVE BEEN REPLENISHED. WE SHOULD BE ABLE TO SAVE EVERYONE BEFORE THEY SUFFOCATE.
MY CHILD, YOUR BROTHER PAPSUKAL IS THE DARK ENTITY'S PRISONER.
I'M GOING TO MOUNT AN ATTACK IMMEDIATELY TO PREVENT HIM FROM UNITING OUR WORLD TO OTHER REALITIES. BUT FOR MY PLAN TO WORK, YOU MUST CONVINCE THE RABBIT TO HAND OVER THE OBJECTS OF DESTINY IN ORDER TO DESTROY THEM.
CLICK
CLICK
CLICK
CLICK
CLICK
CLICK
CLICK
CLICK
HUH? COULD YOU REPEAT THAT?
YOU'RE MAD! IF MY BROTHER IS WHAT YOU SAY HE IS, ONLY THE OBJECTS OF DESTINY WILL ALLOW ME TO FIGHT HIM!
YOU'RE MAKING A MISTAKE.
TO WHERE MY FATHER IS!
NOOOO!
POOF

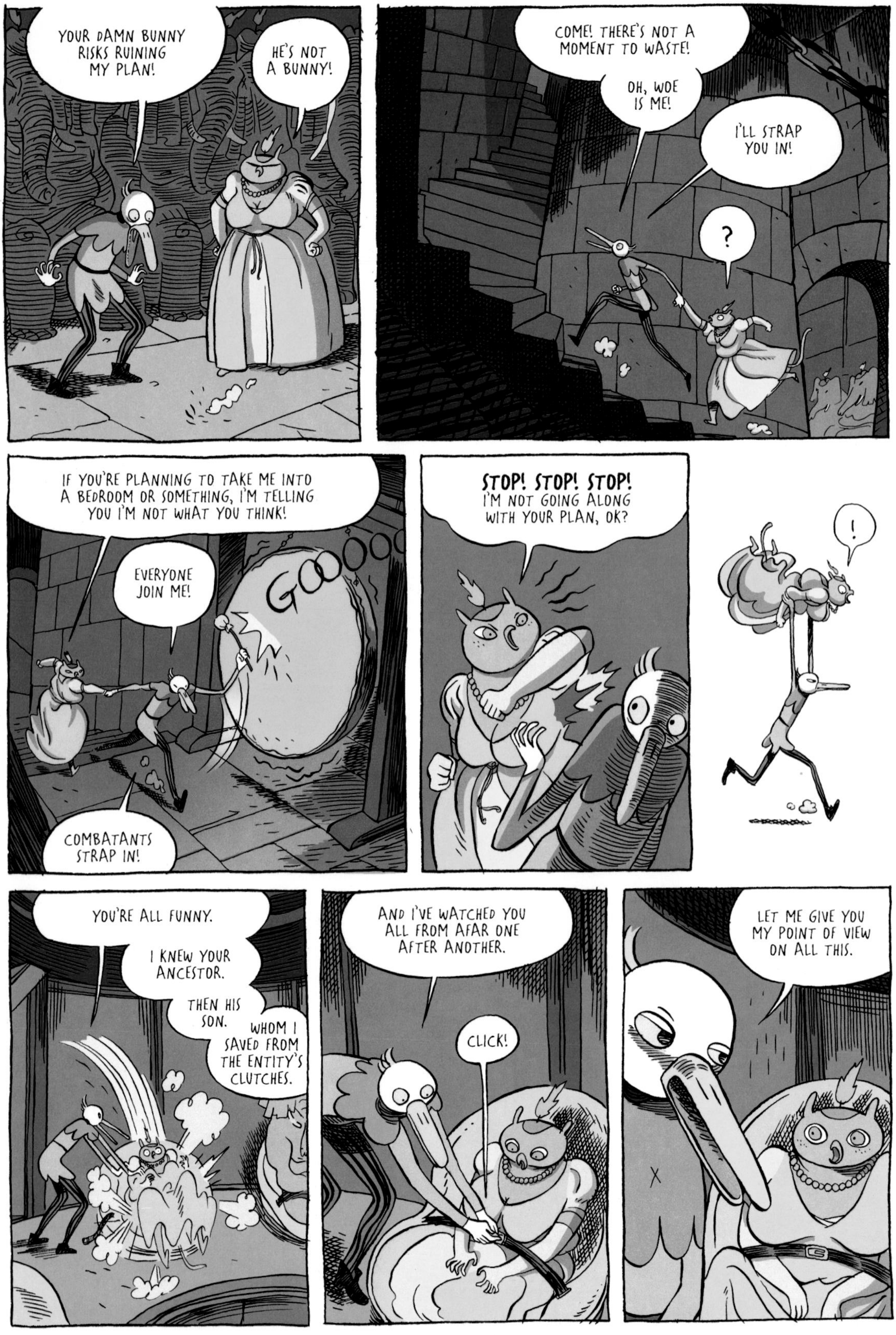
YOUR DAMN BUNNY RISKS RUINING MY PLAN!
HE'S NOT A BUNNY!
COME! THERE'S NOT A MOMENT TO WASTE!
OH, WOE IS ME!
I'LL STRAP YOU IN!
?
IF YOU'RE PLANNING TO TAKE ME INTO A BEDROOM OR SOMETHING, I'M TELLING YOU I'M NOT WHAT YOU THINK!
EVERYONE JOIN ME!
GOOOO
COMBATANTS STRAP IN!
STOP! STOP! STOP! I'M NOT GOING ALONG WITH YOUR PLAN, OK?
!
YOU'RE ALL FUNNY.
I KNEW YOUR ANCESTOR.
THEN HIS SON.
WHOM I SAVED FROM THE ENTITY'S CLUTCHES.
AND I'VE WATCHED YOU ALL FROM AFAR ONE AFTER ANOTHER.
CLICK!
LET ME GIVE YOU MY POINT OF VIEW ON ALL THIS.

WE'RE ALL ANIMATED BY A FIERY ELEMENT—WHEN WE WAKE UP, EVERY DAY, WE "BURN" TO ACT.

COUNTDOWN...

CLICK!

IN MY CASE, IT'S A CARICATURE. BY WAY OF A HEART, I HAVE A FLAME STOLEN FROM A DEMON. I'M A MACHINE SET INTO MOTION THROUGH THE WILLPOWER OF ANOTHER.

ROOF IN WARHEAD MODE.

BUT WHAT ABOUT THE LIVING?

WINDOWS SEALED.

MUNITIONS AND ALCOHOL SECURED.

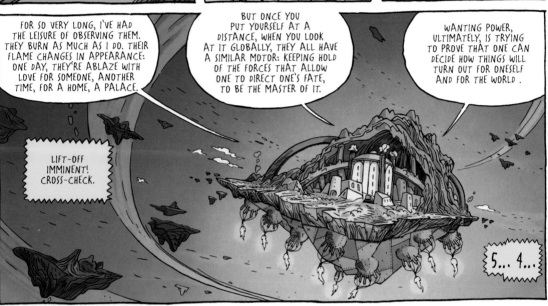

FOR SO VERY LONG, I'VE HAD THE LEISURE OF OBSERVING THEM. THEY BURN AS MUCH AS I DO. THEIR FLAME CHANGES IN APPEARANCE: ONE DAY, THEY'RE ABLAZE WITH LOVE FOR SOMEONE, ANOTHER TIME, FOR A HOME, A PALACE.

BUT ONCE YOU PUT YOURSELF AT A DISTANCE, WHEN YOU LOOK AT IT GLOBALLY, THEY ALL HAVE A SIMILAR MOTOR: KEEPING HOLD OF THE FORCES THAT ALLOW ONE TO DIRECT ONE'S FATE, TO BE THE MASTER OF IT.

WANTING POWER, ULTIMATELY, IS TRYING TO PROVE THAT ONE CAN DECIDE HOW THINGS WILL TURN OUT FOR ONESELF AND FOR THE WORLD.

LIFT-OFF IMMINENT! CROSS-CHECK.

5... 4...

IS THAT POSSIBLE?

3...

SAY, WHY ARE YOUR BUDDIES COUNTING BACKWARDS?

I'VE SEEN THEM FIGHT FOR SO LONG FOR OBJECTS OF POWER, WITHOUT UNDERSTANDING THE PROFOUND NATURE OF THE TOOLS THEY'RE USING.

2

DO YOU SMELL SOMETHING BURNING?

THE "OBJECTS OF DESTINY" TO FIGHT AGAINST THE "DARK ENTITY."

1

OK. LET ME GET OUT OF HERE!

IDIOTS! THE ENTITY'S THE ONE WHO CREATED THOSE OBJECTS!

BLAST OFF!

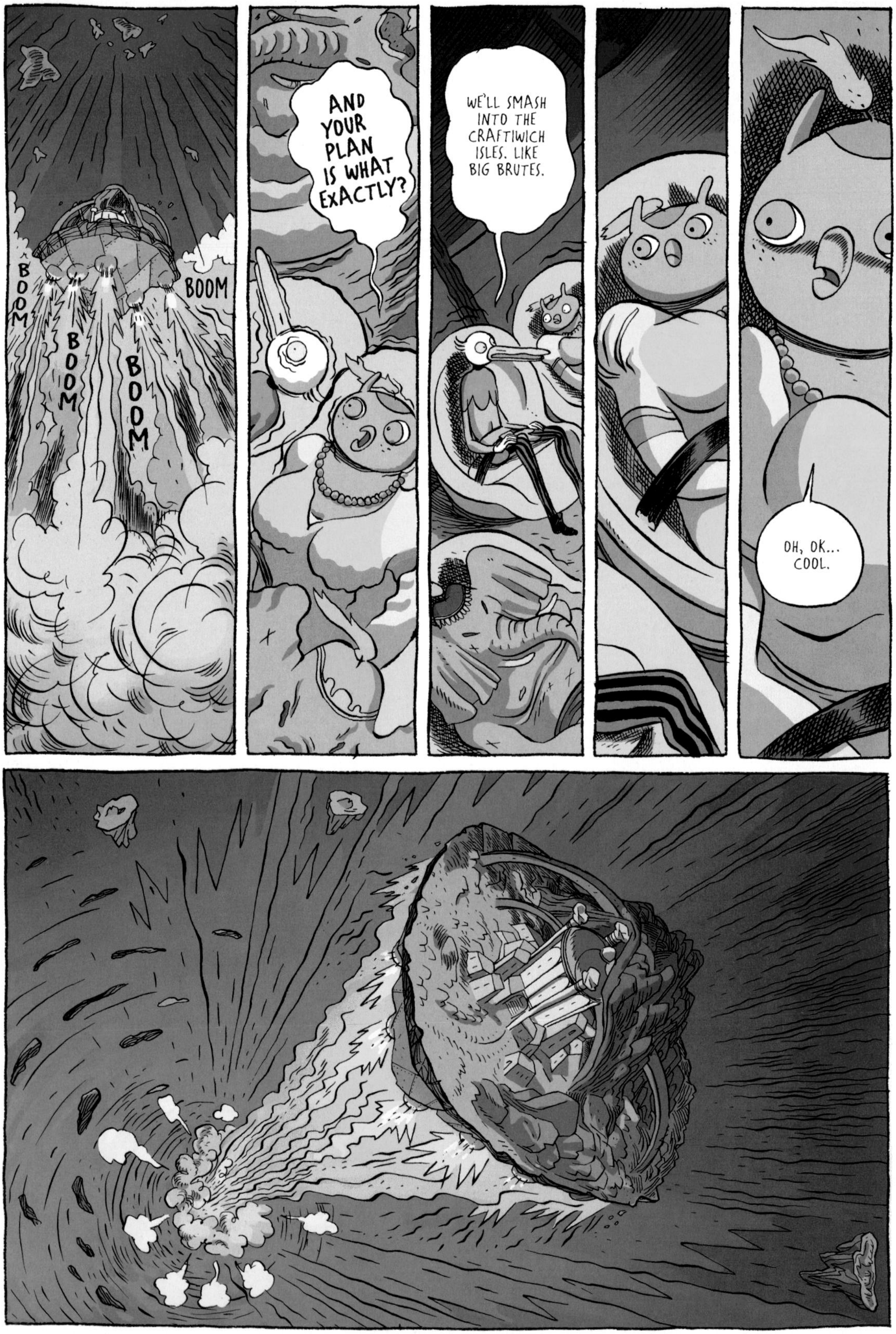
BOOM
BOOM
BOOM
BOOM
AND YOUR PLAN IS WHAT EXACTLY?
WE'LL SMASH INTO THE CRAFTIWICH ISLES. LIKE BIG BRUTES.
OH, OK... COOL.

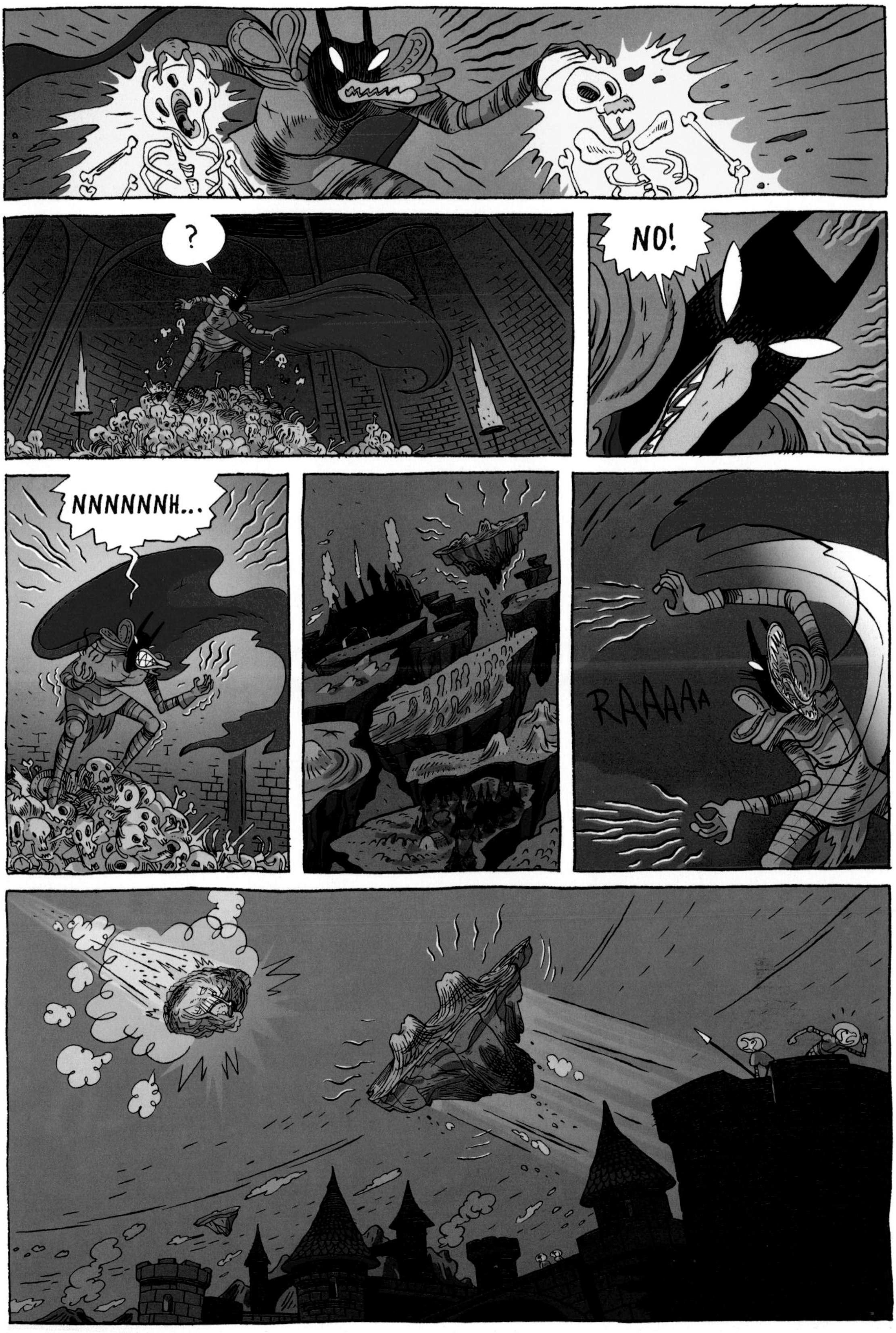
?
NO!
NNNNNNH...
RAAAAA

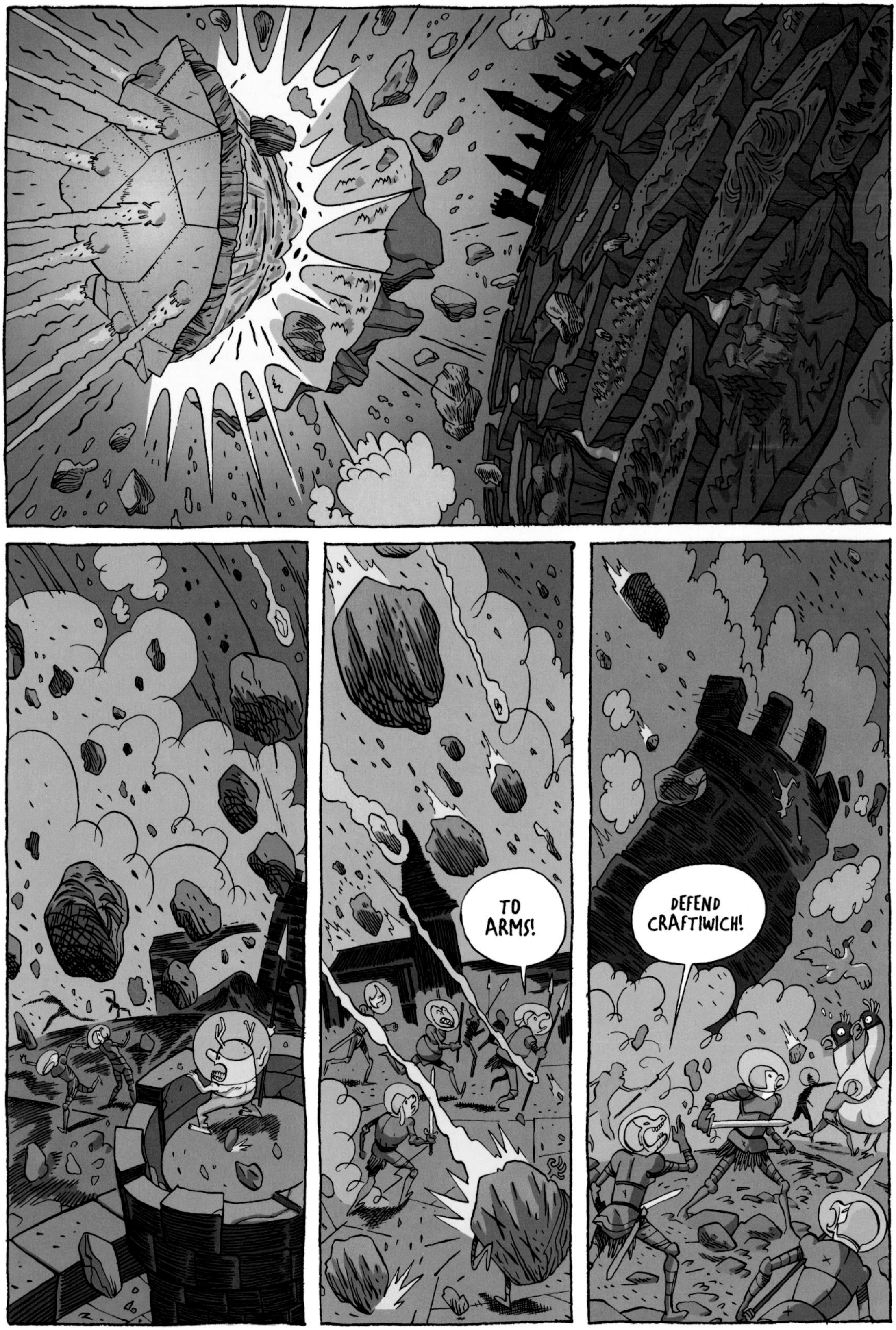
TO ARMS!
DEFEND CRAFTIWICH!

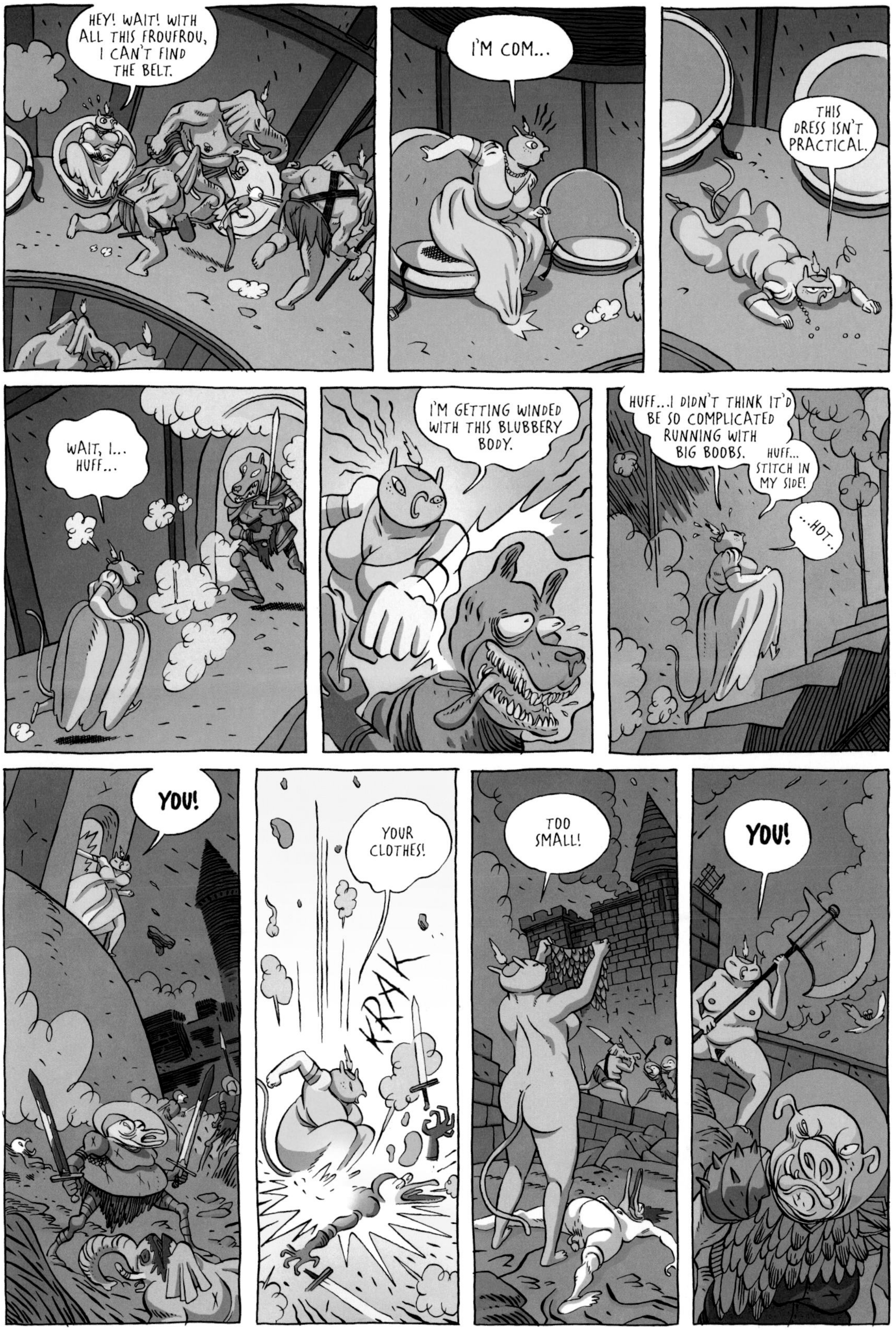

HEY! WAIT! WITH ALL THIS FROUFROU, I CAN'T FIND THE BELT.
I'M COM...
THIS DRESS ISN'T PRACTICAL.
WAIT, I... HUFF...
I'M GETTING WINDED WITH THIS BLUBBERY BODY.
HUFF... I DIDN'T THINK IT'D BE SO COMPLICATED RUNNING WITH BIG BOOBS.
HUFF... STITCH IN MY SIDE!
...HOT...
YOU!
YOUR CLOTHES!
KRAK
TOO SMALL!
YOU!

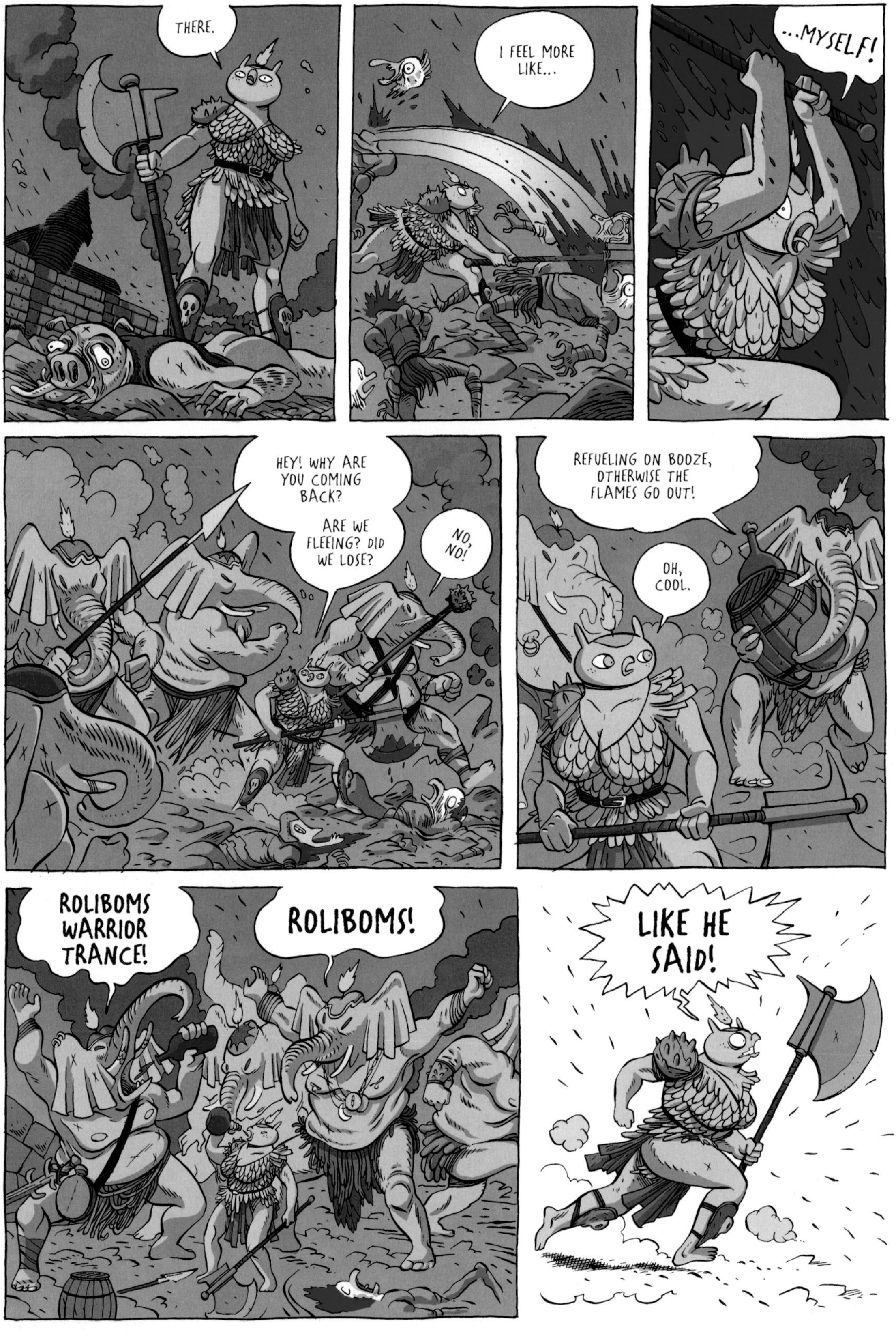
THERE.
I FEEL MORE LIKE...
...MYSELF!
HEY! WHY ARE YOU COMING BACK?
ARE WE FLEEING? DID WE LOSE?
NO, NO!
REFUELING ON BOOZE, OTHERWISE THE FLAMES GO OUT!
OH, COOL.
ROLIBOMS WARRIOR TRANCE!
ROLIBOMS!
LIKE HE SAID!

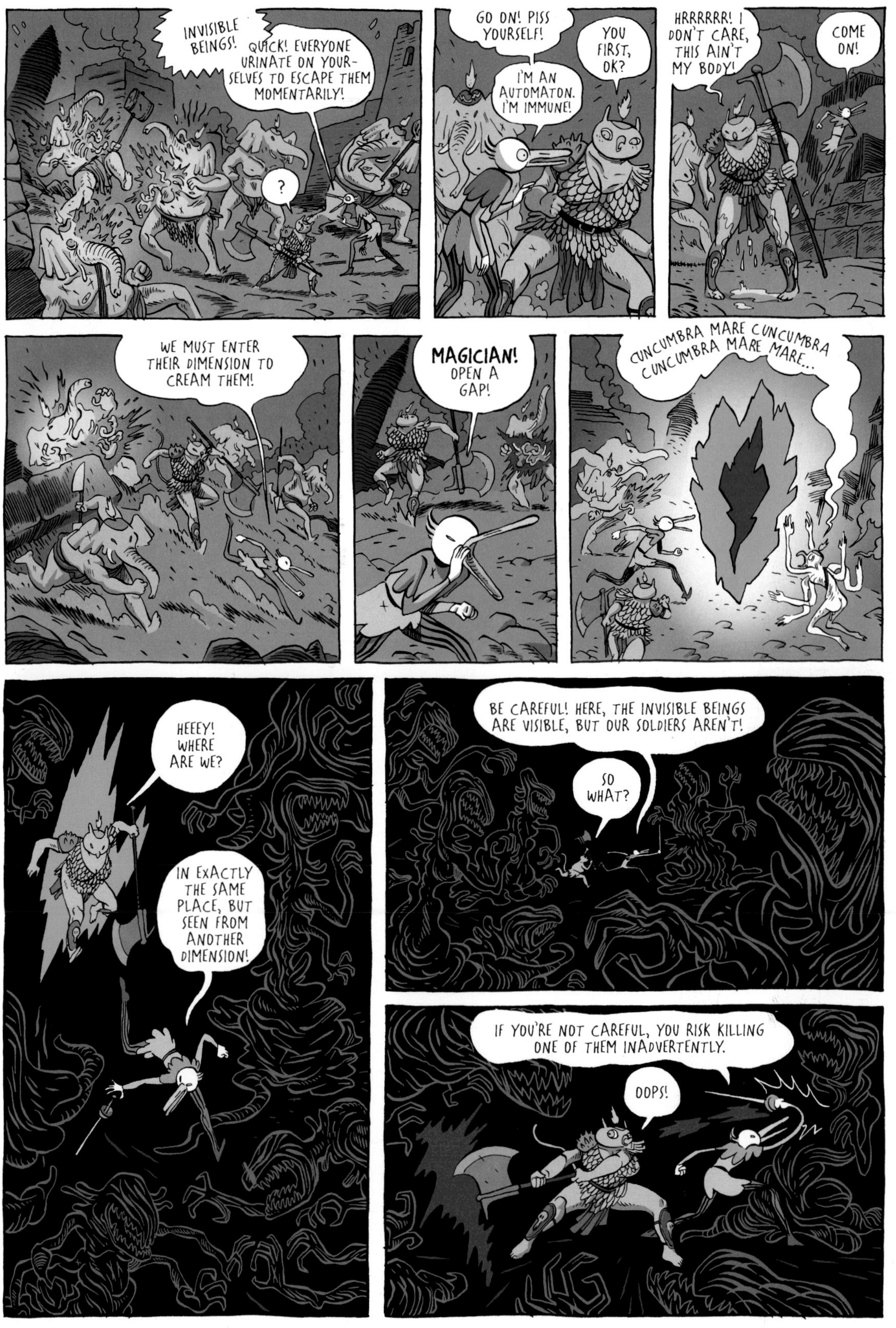
INVISIBLE BEINGS!
QUICK! EVERYONE URINATE ON YOURSELVES TO ESCAPE THEM MOMENTARILY!
?
GO ON! PISS YOURSELF!
I'M AN AUTOMATON. I'M IMMUNE!
YOU FIRST, OK?
HRRRRRR! I DON'T CARE, THIS AIN'T MY BODY!
COME ON!
WE MUST ENTER THEIR DIMENSION TO CREAM THEM!
MAGICIAN! OPEN A GAP!
CUNCUMBRA MARE CUNCUMBRA CUNCUMBRA MARE MARE...
HEEEY! WHERE ARE WE?
IN EXACTLY THE SAME PLACE, BUT SEEN FROM ANOTHER DIMENSION!
BE CAREFUL! HERE, THE INVISIBLE BEINGS ARE VISIBLE, BUT OUR SOLDIERS AREN'T!
SO WHAT?
IF YOU'RE NOT CAREFUL, YOU RISK KILLING ONE OF THEM INADVERTENTLY.
OOPS!

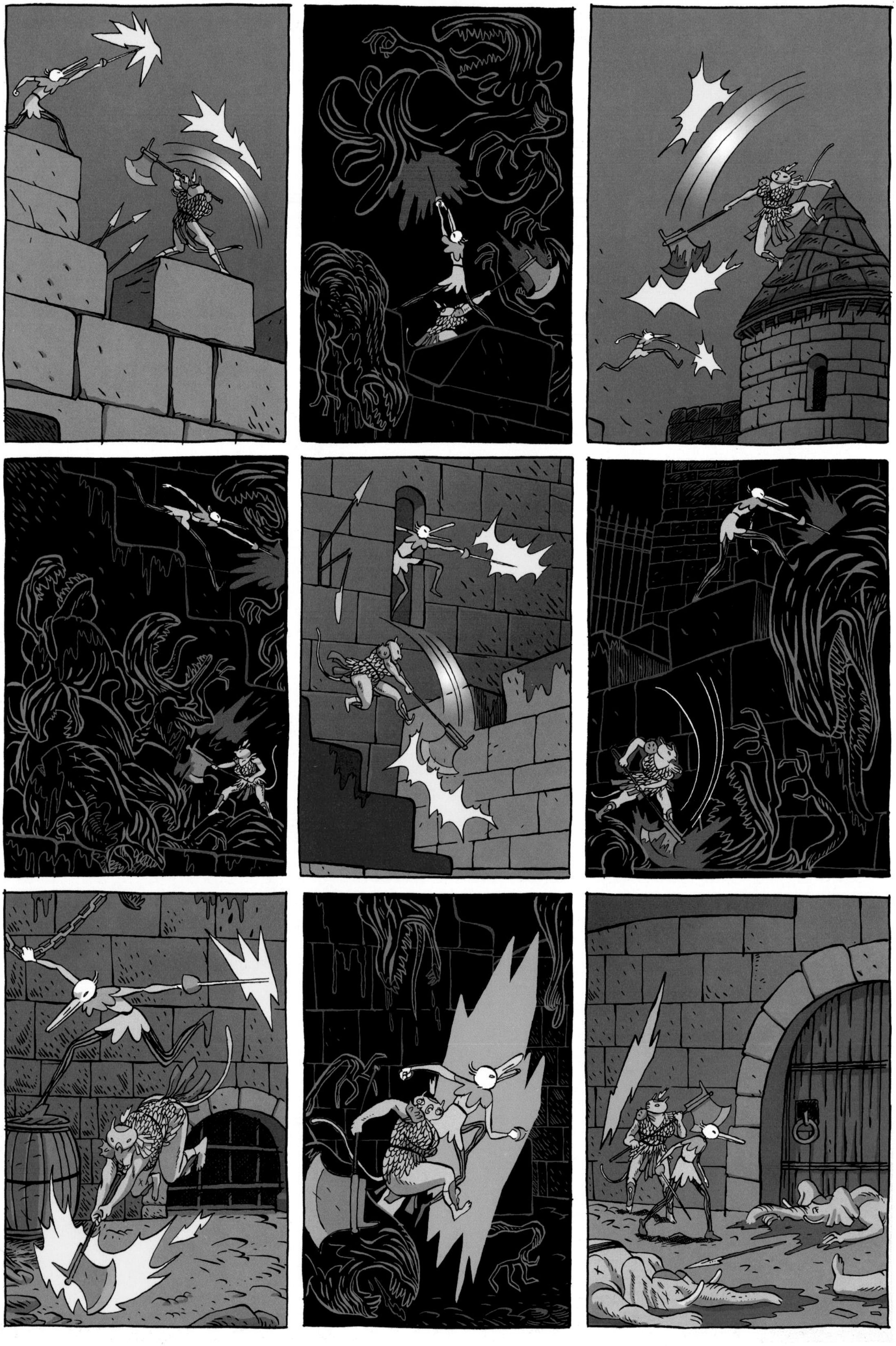

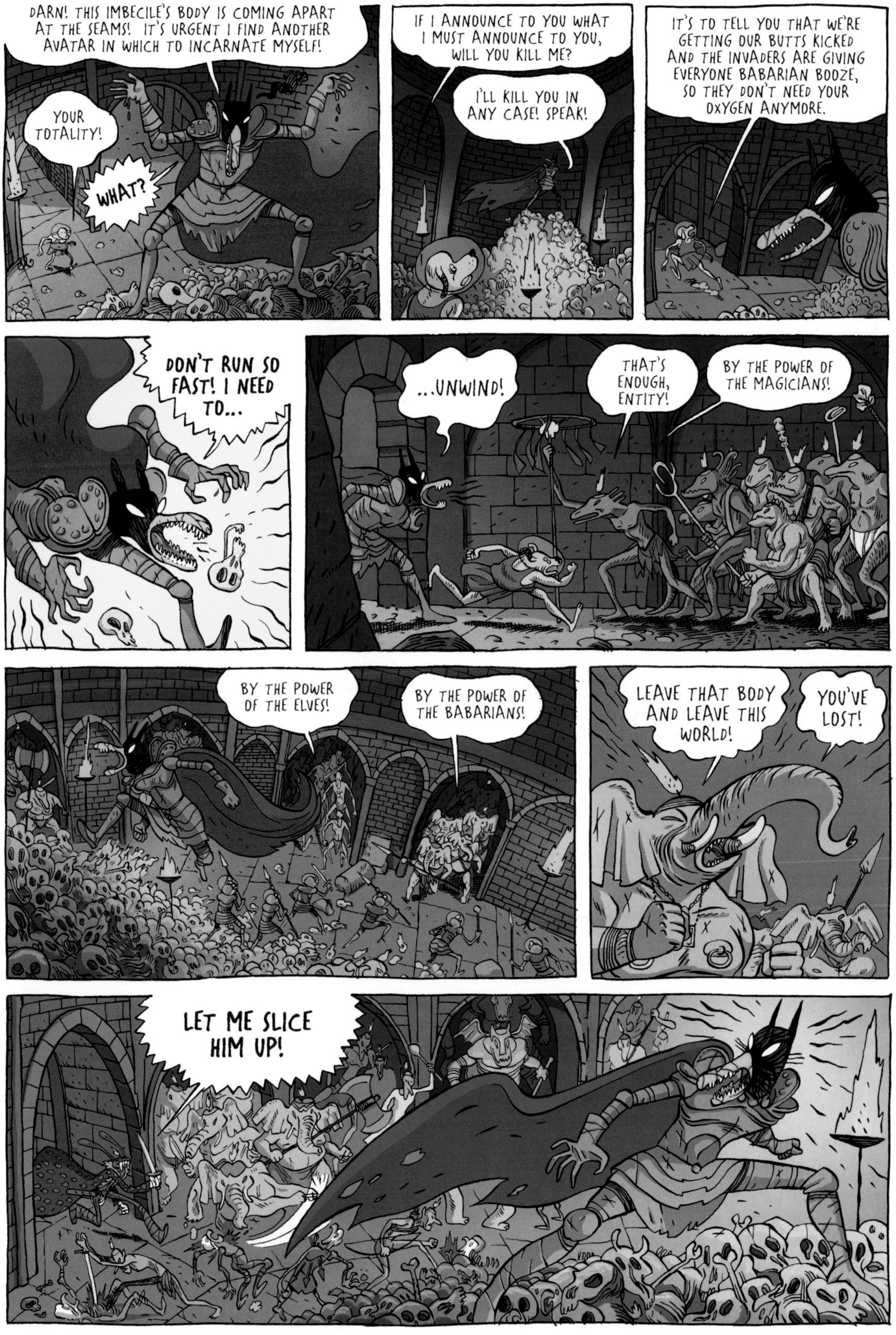
DARN! THIS IMBECILE'S BODY IS COMING APART AT THE SEAMS! IT'S URGENT I FIND ANOTHER AVATAR IN WHICH TO INCARNATE MYSELF!
YOUR TOTALITY!
WHAT?
IF I ANNOUNCE TO YOU WHAT I MUST ANNOUNCE TO YOU, WILL YOU KILL ME?
I'LL KILL YOU IN ANY CASE! SPEAK!
IT'S TO TELL YOU THAT WE'RE GETTING OUR BUTTS KICKED AND THE INVADERS ARE GIVING EVERYONE BABARIAN BOOZE, SO THEY DON'T NEED YOUR OXYGEN ANYMORE.
DON'T RUN SO FAST! I NEED TO...
...UNWIND!
THAT'S ENOUGH, ENTITY!
BY THE POWER OF THE MAGICIANS!
BY THE POWER OF THE ELVES!
BY THE POWER OF THE BABARIANS!
LEAVE THAT BODY AND LEAVE THIS WORLD!
YOU'VE LOST!
LET ME SLICE HIM UP!

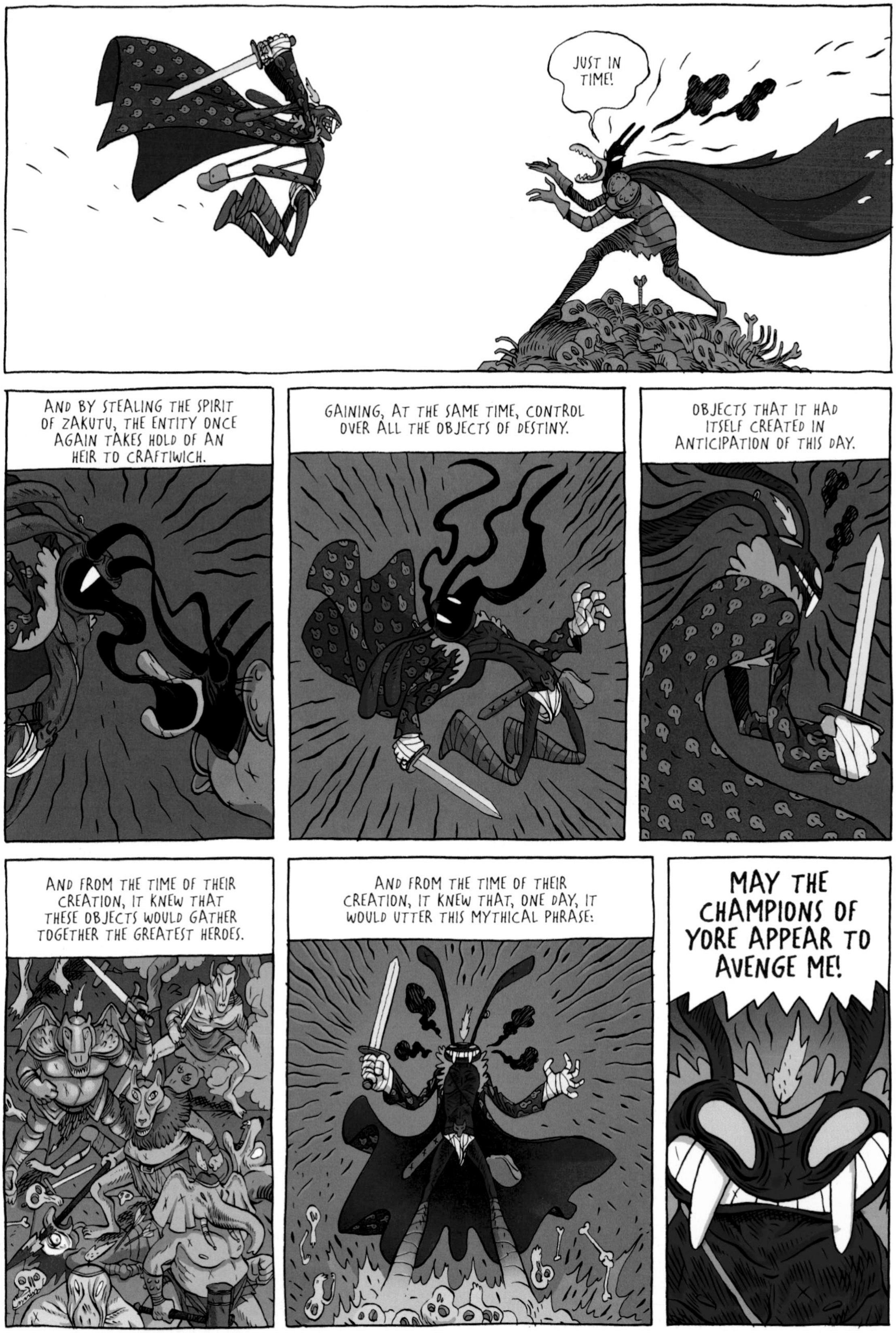
JUST IN TIME!
AND BY STEALING THE SPIRIT OF ZAKUTU, THE ENTITY ONCE AGAIN TAKES HOLD OF AN HEIR TO CRAFTIWICH.
GAINING, AT THE SAME TIME, CONTROL OVER ALL THE OBJECTS OF DESTINY.
OBJECTS THAT IT HAD ITSELF CREATED IN ANTICIPATION OF THIS DAY.
AND FROM THE TIME OF THEIR CREATION, IT KNEW THAT THESE OBJECTS WOULD GATHER TOGETHER THE GREATEST HEROES.
AND FROM THE TIME OF THEIR CREATION, IT KNEW THAT, ONE DAY, IT WOULD UTTER THIS MYTHICAL PHRASE:
MAY THE CHAMPIONS OF YORE APPEAR TO AVENGE ME!

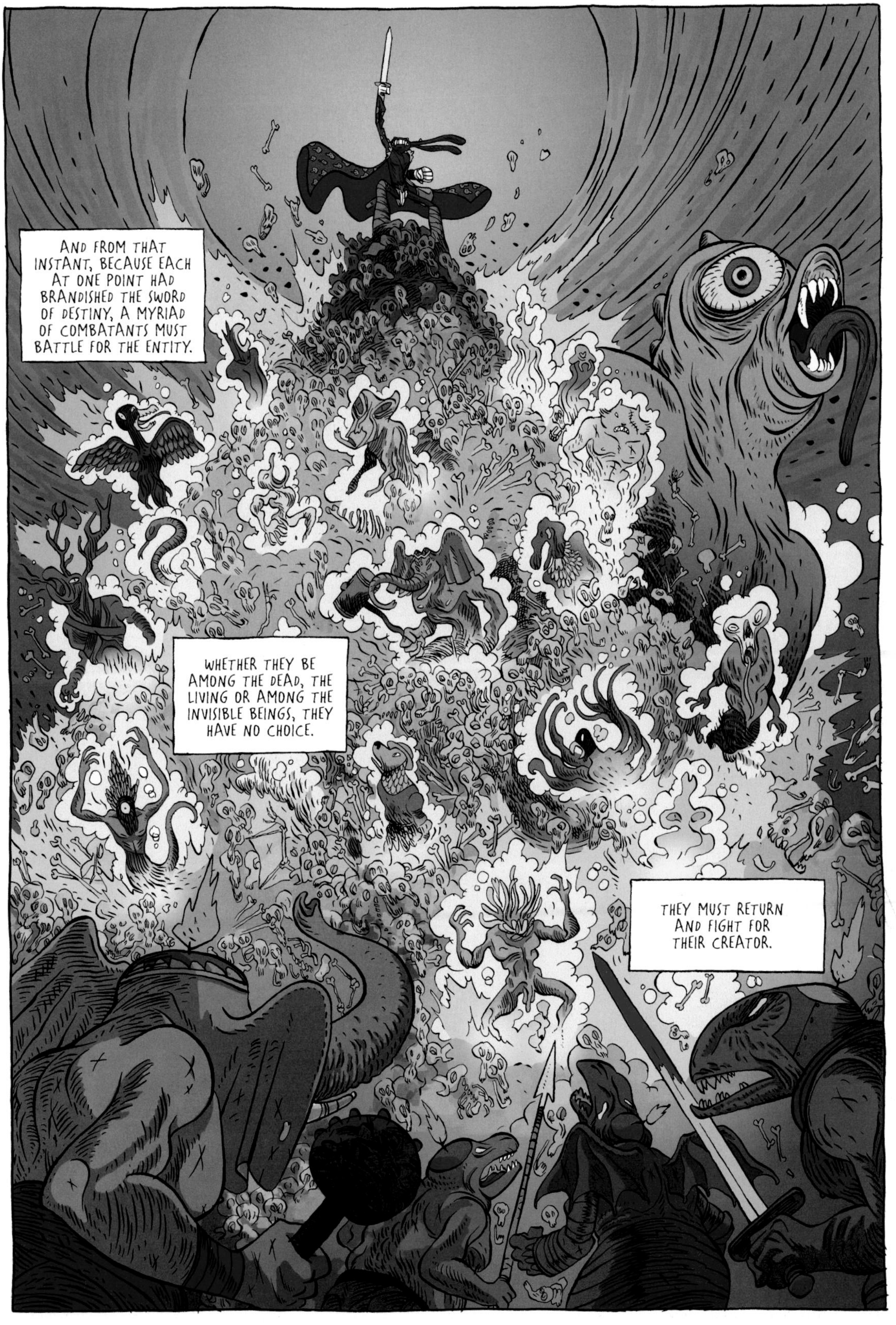
AND FROM THAT INSTANT, BECAUSE EACH AT ONE POINT HAD BRANDISHED THE SWORD OF DESTINY, A MYRIAD OF COMBATANTS MUST BATTLE FOR THE ENTITY.
WHETHER THEY BE AMONG THE DEAD, THE LIVING OR AMONG THE INVISIBLE BEINGS, THEY HAVE NO CHOICE.
THEY MUST RETURN AND FIGHT FOR THEIR CREATOR.

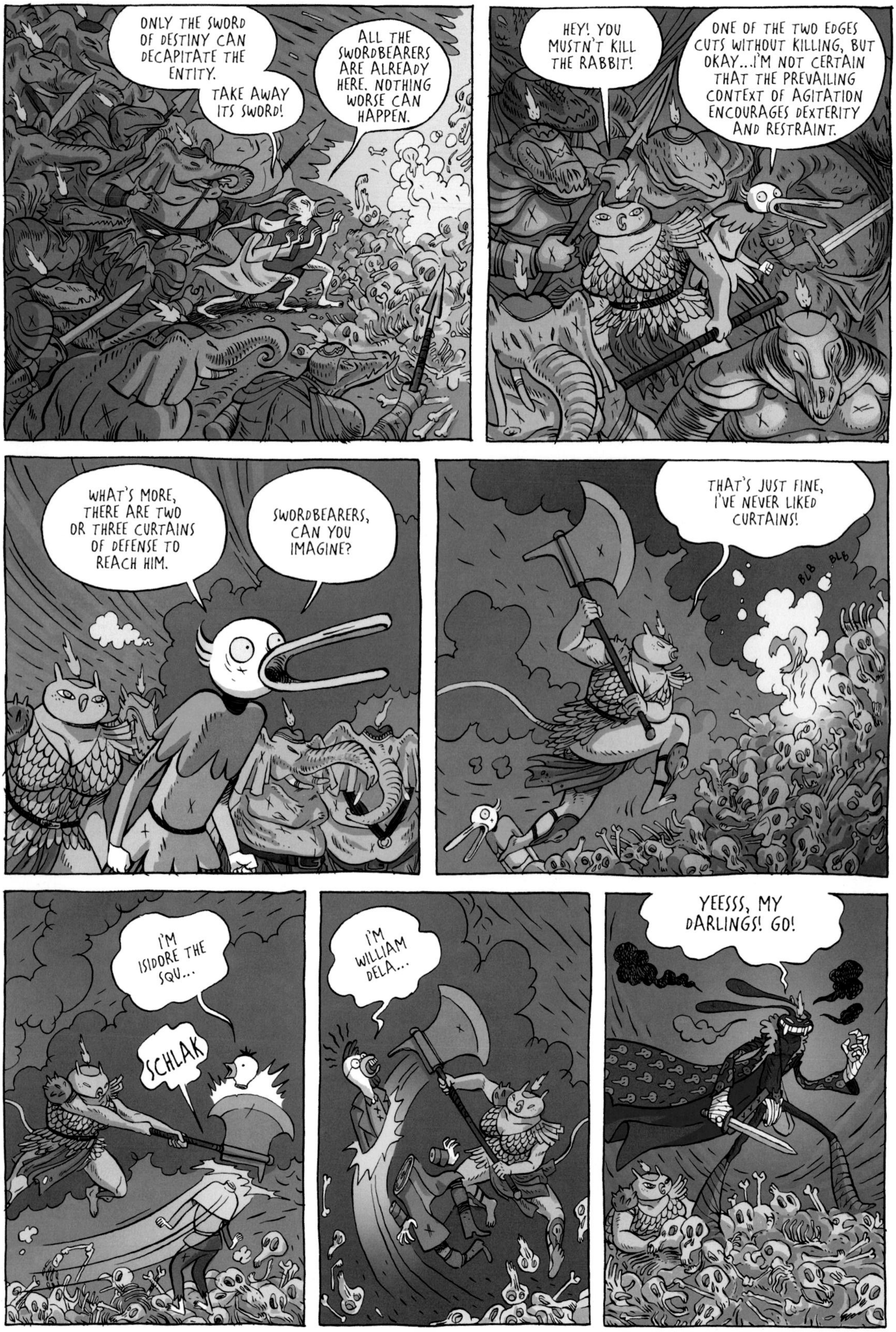
ONLY THE SWORD OF DESTINY CAN DECAPITATE THE ENTITY.
TAKE AWAY ITS SWORD!
ALL THE SWORDBEARERS ARE ALREADY HERE. NOTHING WORSE CAN HAPPEN.
HEY! YOU MUSTN'T KILL THE RABBIT!
ONE OF THE TWO EDGES CUTS WITHOUT KILLING, BUT OKAY...I'M NOT CERTAIN THAT THE PREVAILING CONTEXT OF AGITATION ENCOURAGES DEXTERITY AND RESTRAINT.
WHAT'S MORE, THERE ARE TWO OR THREE CURTAINS OF DEFENSE TO REACH HIM.
SWORDBEARERS, CAN YOU IMAGINE?
THAT'S JUST FINE, I'VE NEVER LIKED CURTAINS!
BLB BLB
I'M ISIDORE THE SQU...
SCHLAK
I'M WILLIAM DELA...
YEESSS, MY DARLINGS! GO!

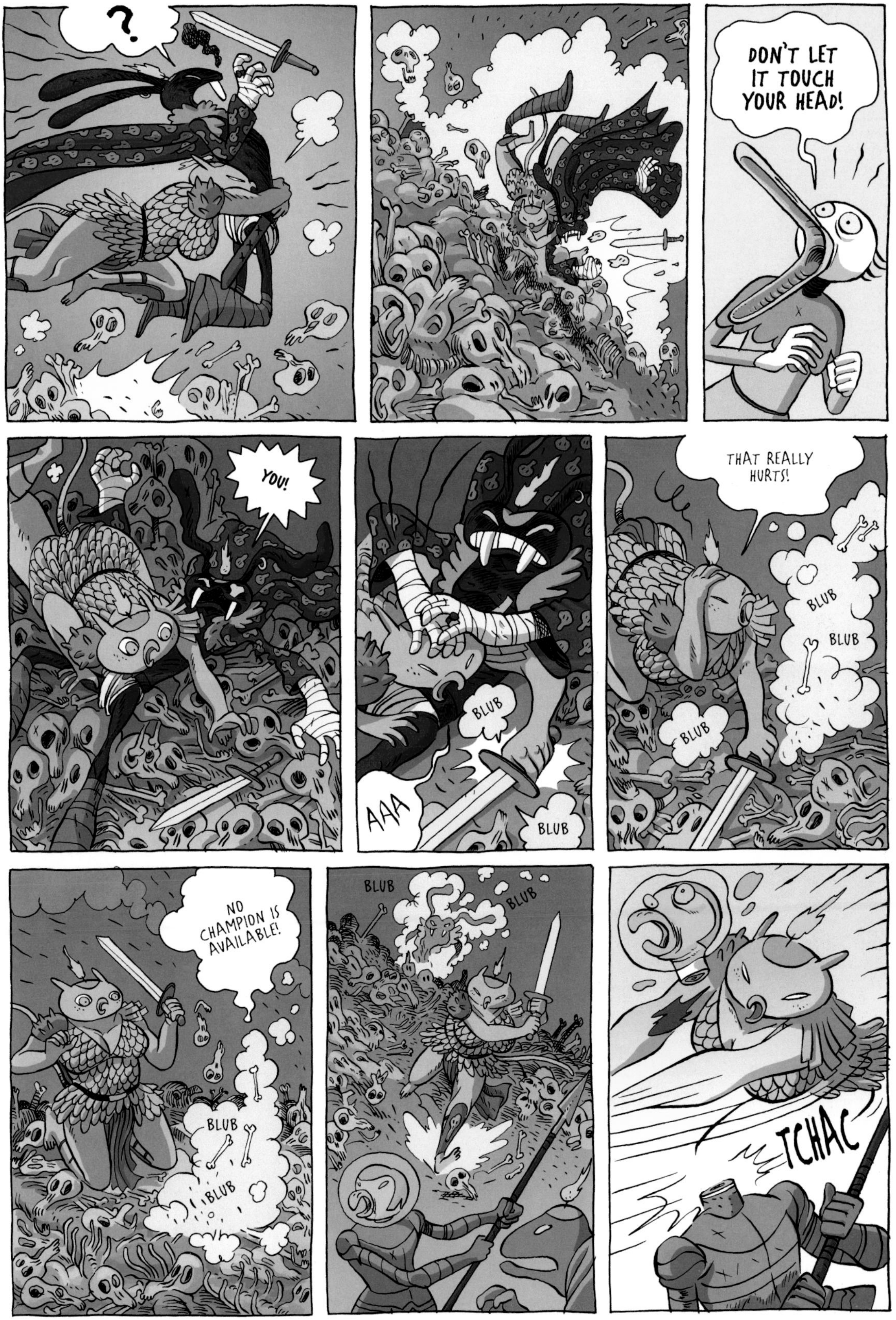
?
DON'T LET IT TOUCH YOUR HEAD!
YOU!
BLUB
AAA
BLUB
THAT REALLY HURTS!
BLUB
BLUB
BLUB
NO CHAMPION IS AVAILABLE!
BLUB
BLUB
BLUB
BLUB
TCHAC

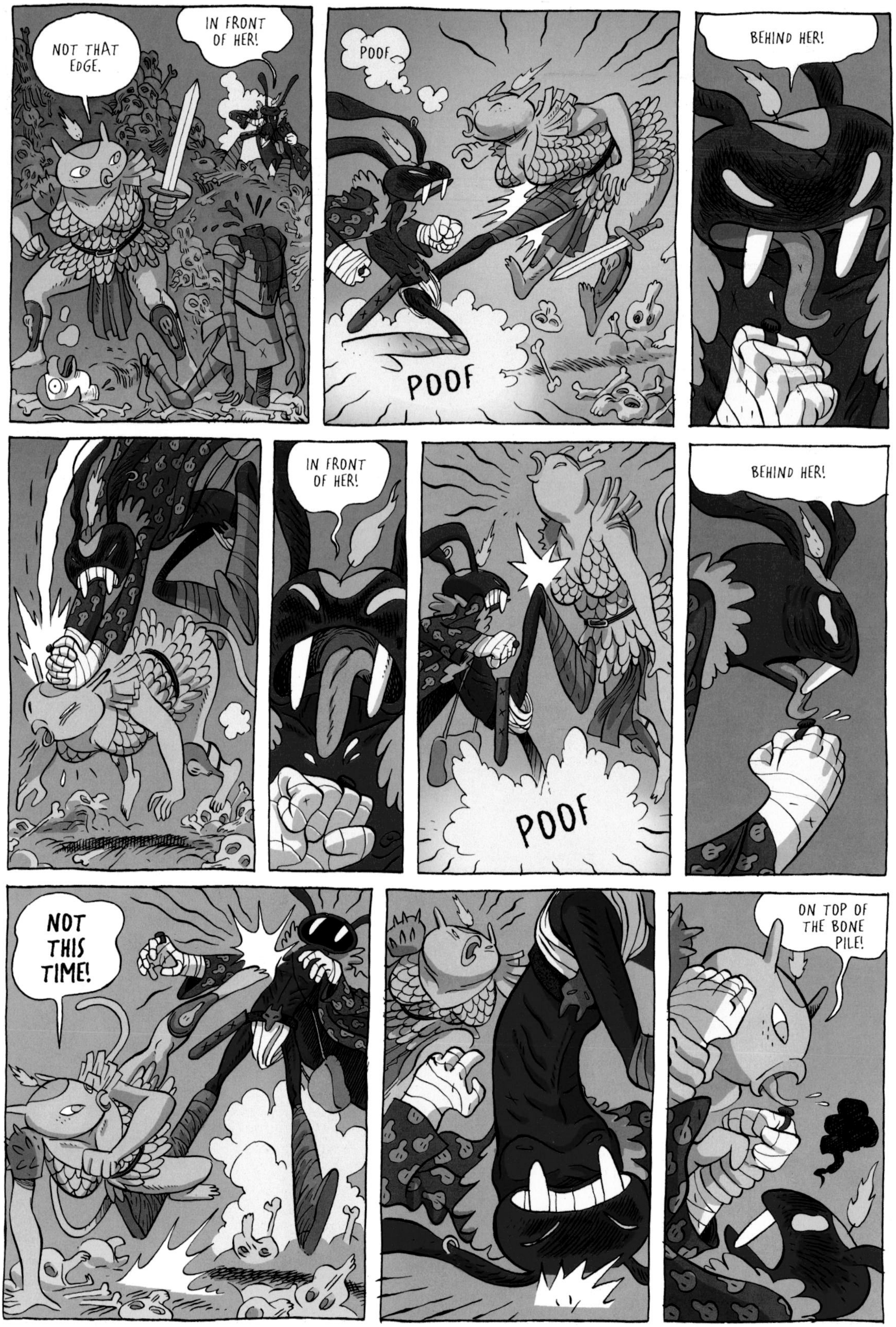
NOT THAT EDGE.
IN FRONT OF HER!
POOF
POOF
BEHIND HER!
IN FRONT OF HER!
POOF
BEHIND HER!
NOT THIS TIME!
ON TOP OF THE BONE PILE!

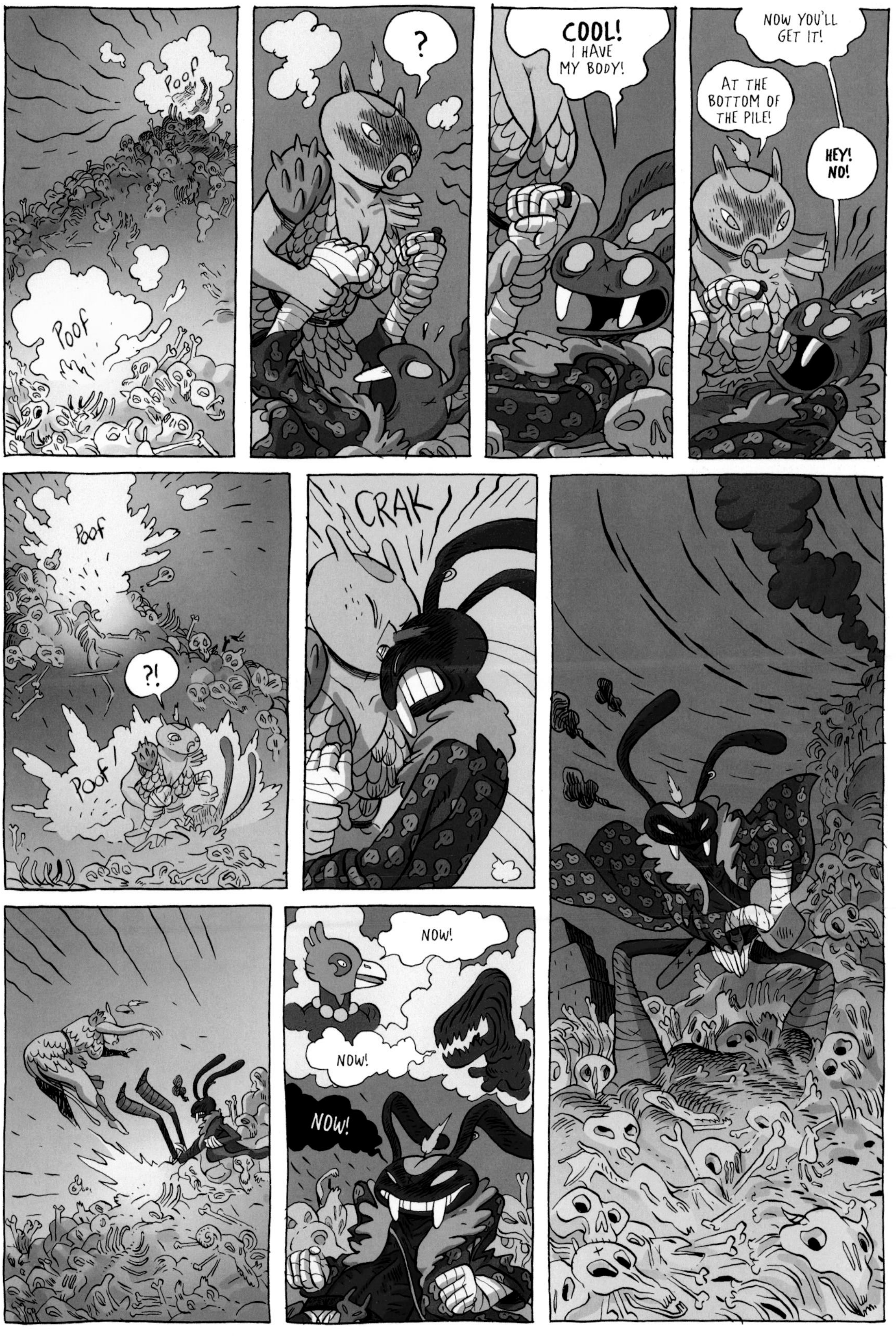
Poof
Poof
?
COOL! I HAVE MY BODY!
NOW YOU'LL GET IT!
AT THE BOTTOM OF THE PILE!
HEY! NO!
Poof
?!
Poof!
CRAK
NOW!
NOW!
NOW!

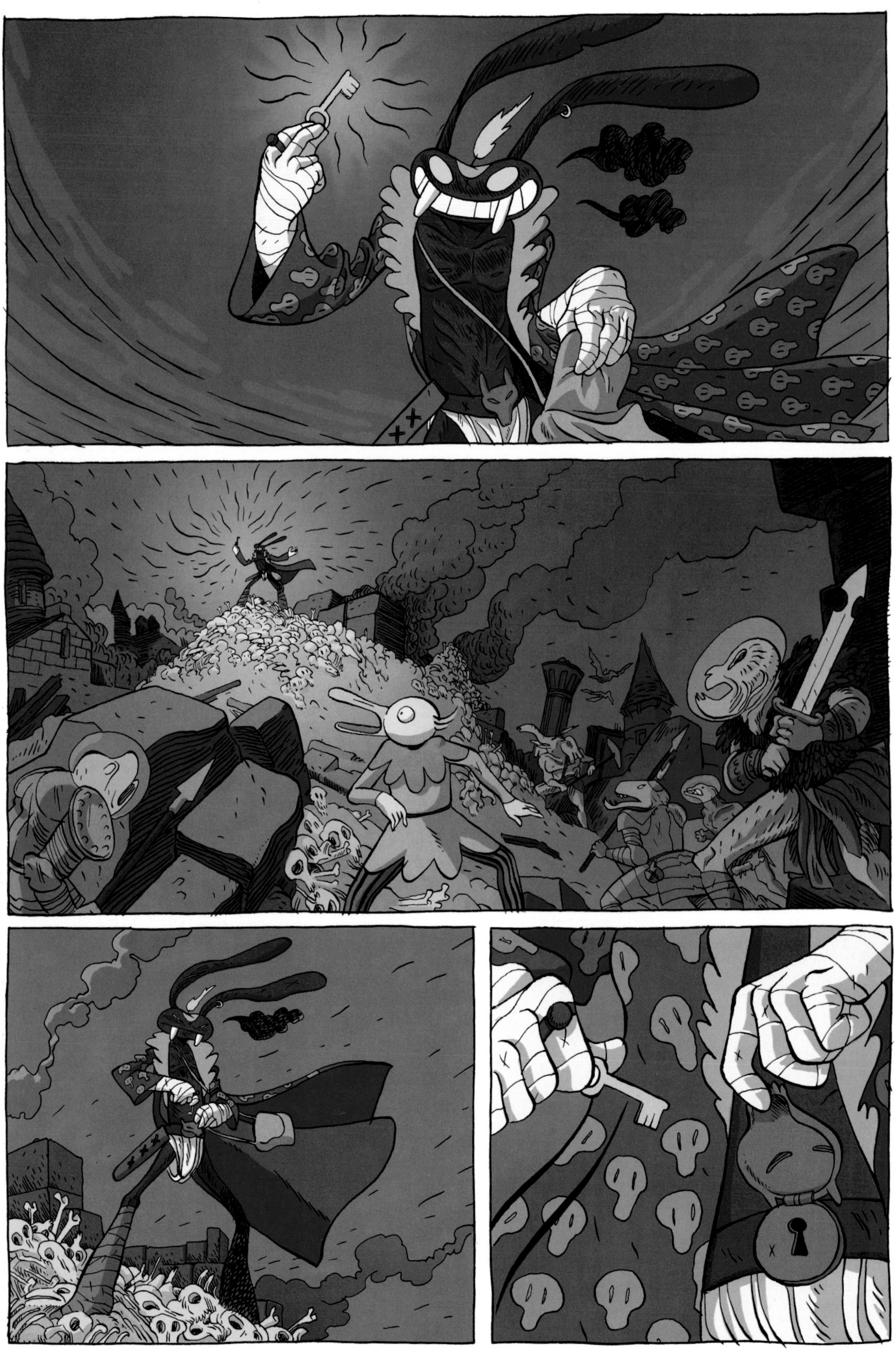

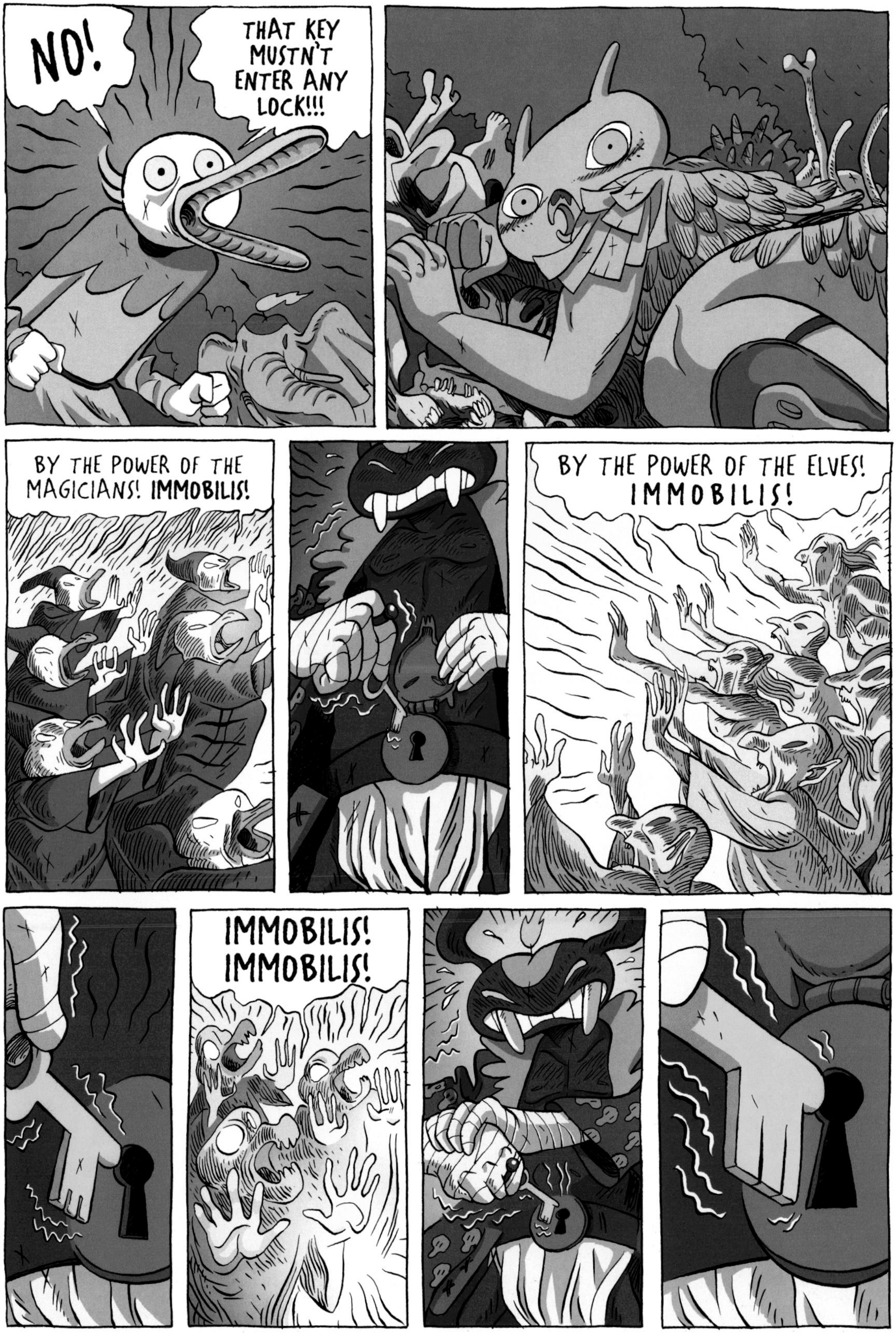
NO!
THAT KEY MUSTN'T ENTER ANY LOCK!!!
BY THE POWER OF THE MAGICIANS! IMMOBILIS!
BY THE POWER OF THE ELVES! IMMOBILIS!
IMMOBILIS! IMMOBILIS!

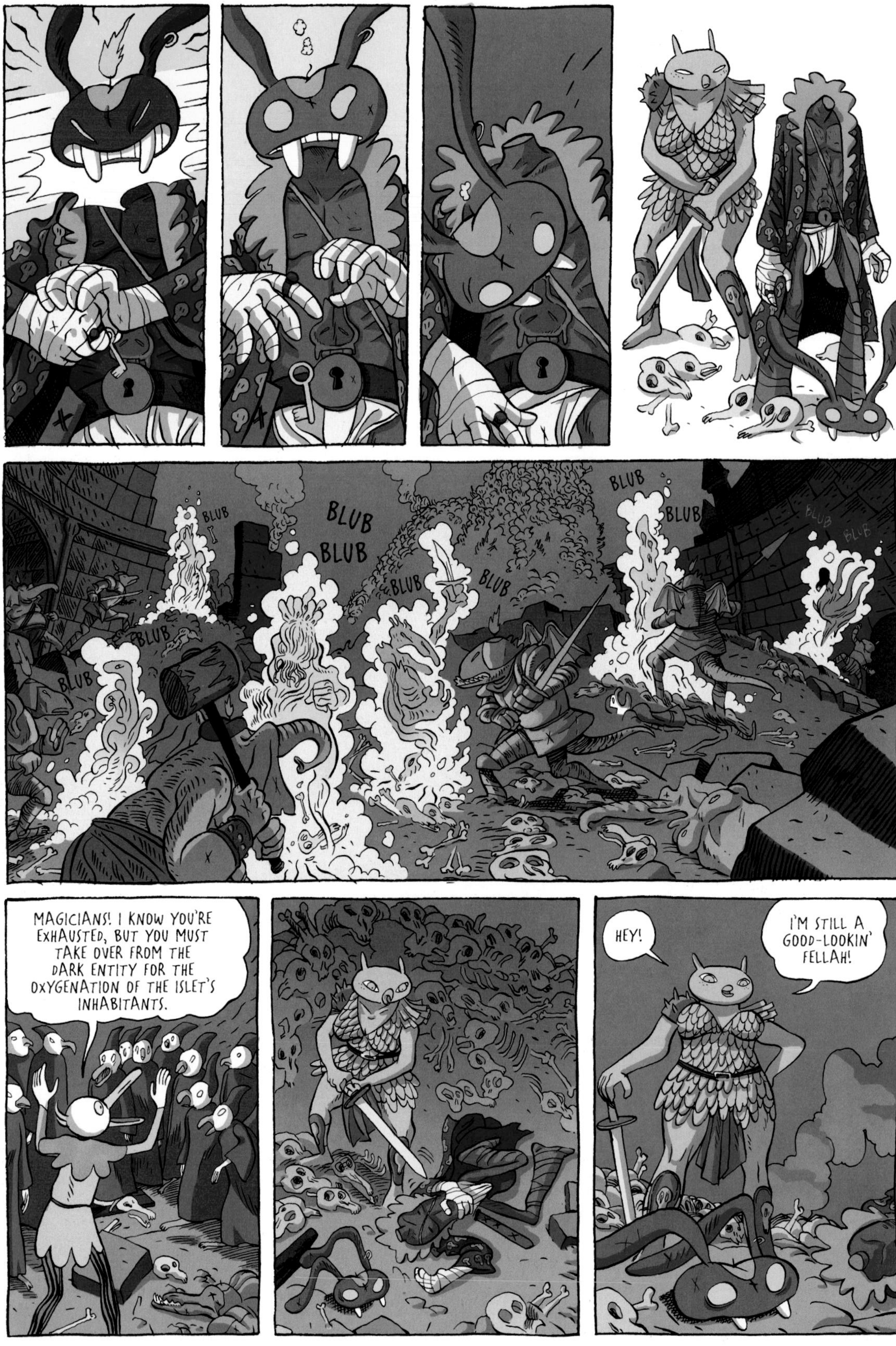
BLUB
BLUB
BLUB
BLUB
BLUB
BLUB
BLUB
BLUB
BLUB
BLUB
BLUB
MAGICIANS! I KNOW YOU'RE EXHAUSTED, BUT YOU MUST TAKE OVER FROM THE DARK ENTITY FOR THE OXYGENATION OF THE ISLET'S INHABITANTS.
HEY!
I'M STILL A GOOD-LOOKIN' FELLAH!

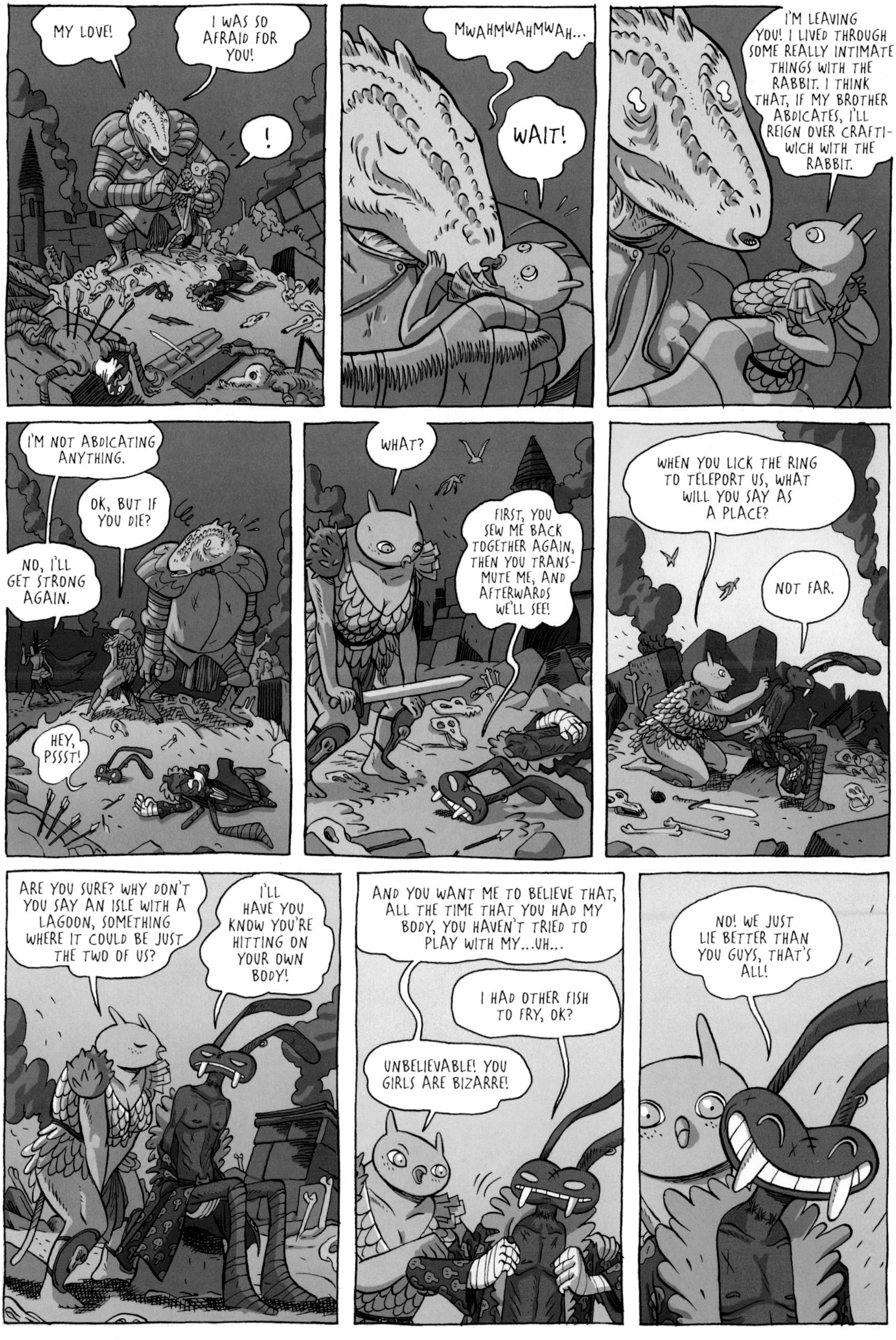
MY LOVE!
I WAS SO AFRAID FOR YOU!
!
MWAHMWAHMWAH...
WAIT!
I'M LEAVING YOU! I LIVED THROUGH SOME REALLY INTIMATE THINGS WITH THE RABBIT. I THINK THAT, IF MY BROTHER ABDICATES, I'LL REIGN OVER CRAFTIWICH WITH THE RABBIT.
I'M NOT ABDICATING ANYTHING.
OK, BUT IF YOU DIE?
NO, I'LL GET STRONG AGAIN.
HEY, PSSST!
WHAT?
FIRST, YOU SEW ME BACK TOGETHER AGAIN, THEN YOU TRANSMUTE ME, AND AFTERWARDS WE'LL SEE!
WHEN YOU LICK THE RING TO TELEPORT US, WHAT WILL YOU SAY AS A PLACE?
NOT FAR.
ARE YOU SURE? WHY DON'T YOU SAY AN ISLE WITH A LAGOON, SOMETHING WHERE IT COULD BE JUST THE TWO OF US?
I'LL HAVE YOU KNOW YOU'RE HITTING ON YOUR OWN BODY!
AND YOU WANT ME TO BELIEVE THAT, ALL THE TIME THAT YOU HAD MY BODY, YOU HAVEN'T TRIED TO PLAY WITH MY...UH...
I HAD OTHER FISH TO FRY, OK?
UNBELIEVABLE! YOU GIRLS ARE BIZARRE!
NO! WE JUST LIE BETTER THAN YOU GUYS, THAT'S ALL!

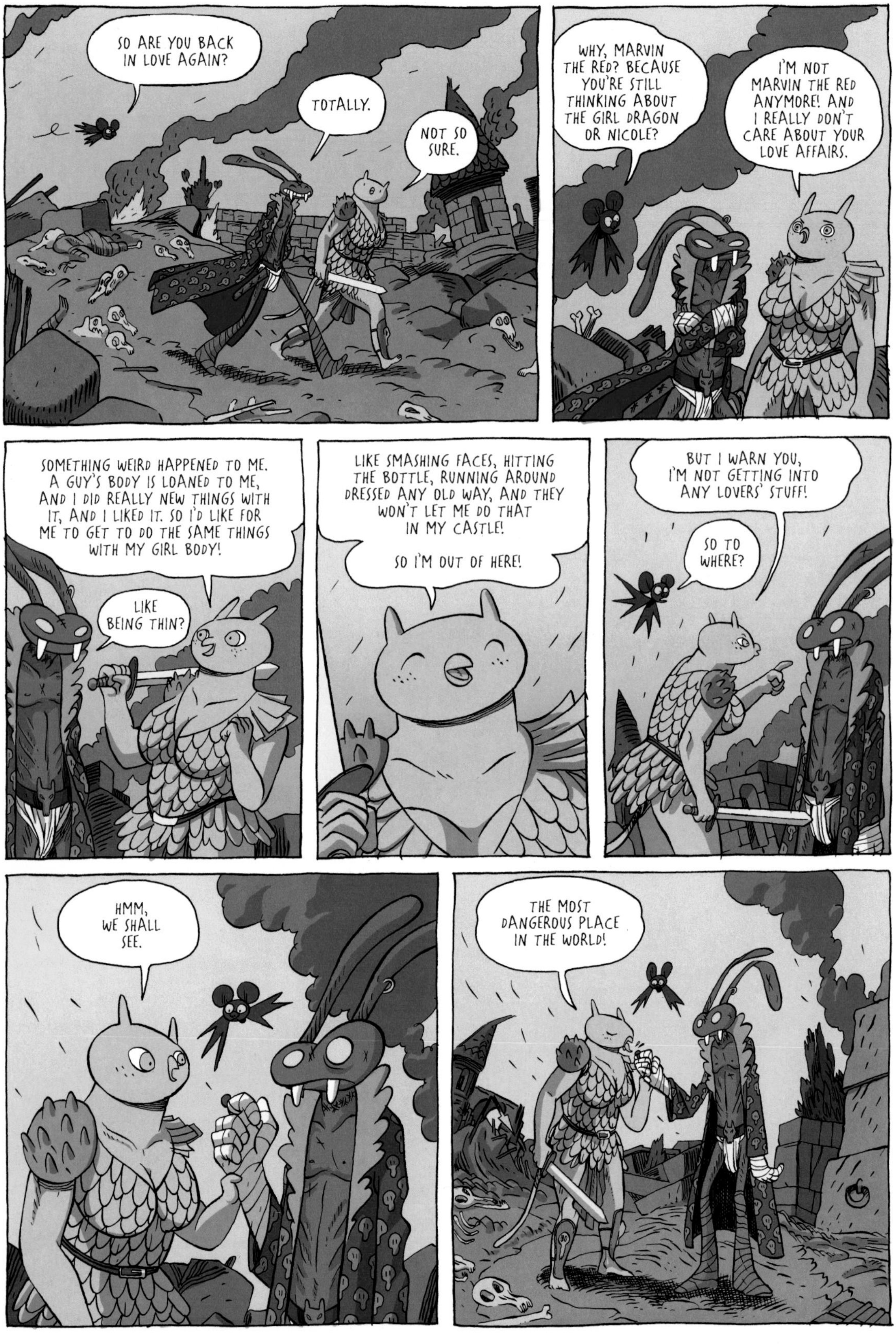
SO ARE YOU BACK IN LOVE AGAIN?
TOTALLY.
NOT SO SURE.
WHY, MARVIN THE RED? BECAUSE YOU'RE STILL THINKING ABOUT THE GIRL DRAGON OR NICOLE?
I'M NOT MARVIN THE RED ANYMORE! AND I REALLY DON'T CARE ABOUT YOUR LOVE AFFAIRS.
SOMETHING WEIRD HAPPENED TO ME. A GUY'S BODY IS LOANED TO ME, AND I DID REALLY NEW THINGS WITH IT, AND I LIKED IT. SO I'D LIKE FOR ME TO GET TO DO THE SAME THINGS WITH MY GIRL BODY!
LIKE BEING THIN?
LIKE SMASHING FACES, HITTING THE BOTTLE, RUNNING AROUND DRESSED ANY OLD WAY, AND THEY WON'T LET ME DO THAT IN MY CASTLE!
SO I'M OUT OF HERE!
BUT I WARN YOU, I'M NOT GETTING INTO ANY LOVERS' STUFF!
SO TO WHERE?
HMM, WE SHALL SEE.
THE MOST DANGEROUS PLACE IN THE WORLD!

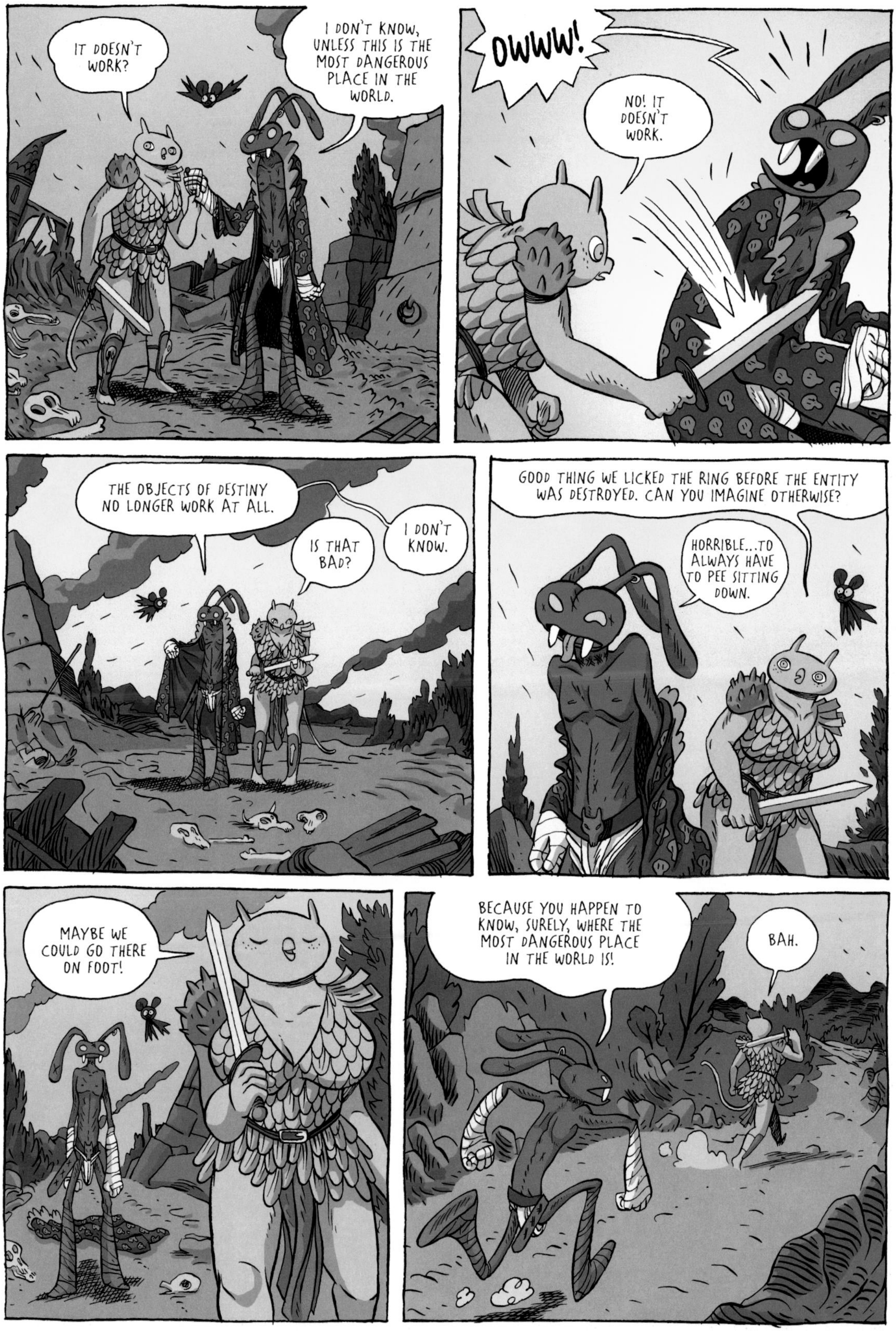
IT DOESN'T WORK?
I DON'T KNOW, UNLESS THIS IS THE MOST DANGEROUS PLACE IN THE WORLD.
OWWW!
NO! IT DOESN'T WORK.
THE OBJECTS OF DESTINY NO LONGER WORK AT ALL.
IS THAT BAD?
I DON'T KNOW.
GOOD THING WE LICKED THE RING BEFORE THE ENTITY WAS DESTROYED. CAN YOU IMAGINE OTHERWISE?
HORRIBLE...TO ALWAYS HAVE TO PEE SITTING DOWN.
MAYBE WE COULD GO THERE ON FOOT!
BECAUSE YOU HAPPEN TO KNOW, SURELY, WHERE THE MOST DANGEROUS PLACE IN THE WORLD IS!
BAH.

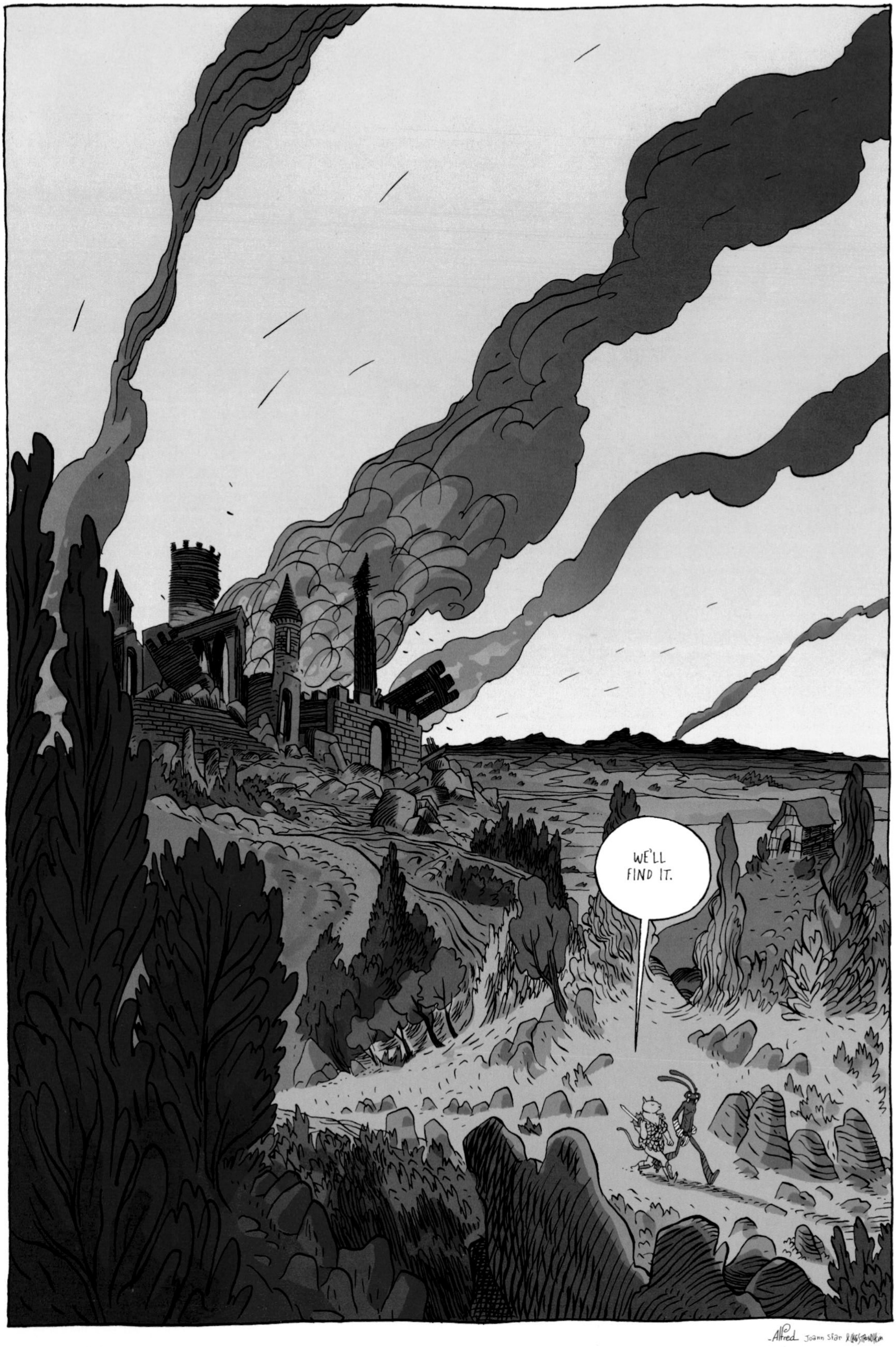
WE'LL FIND IT.

Alfred Joann Sfar

THE END OF DUNGEON

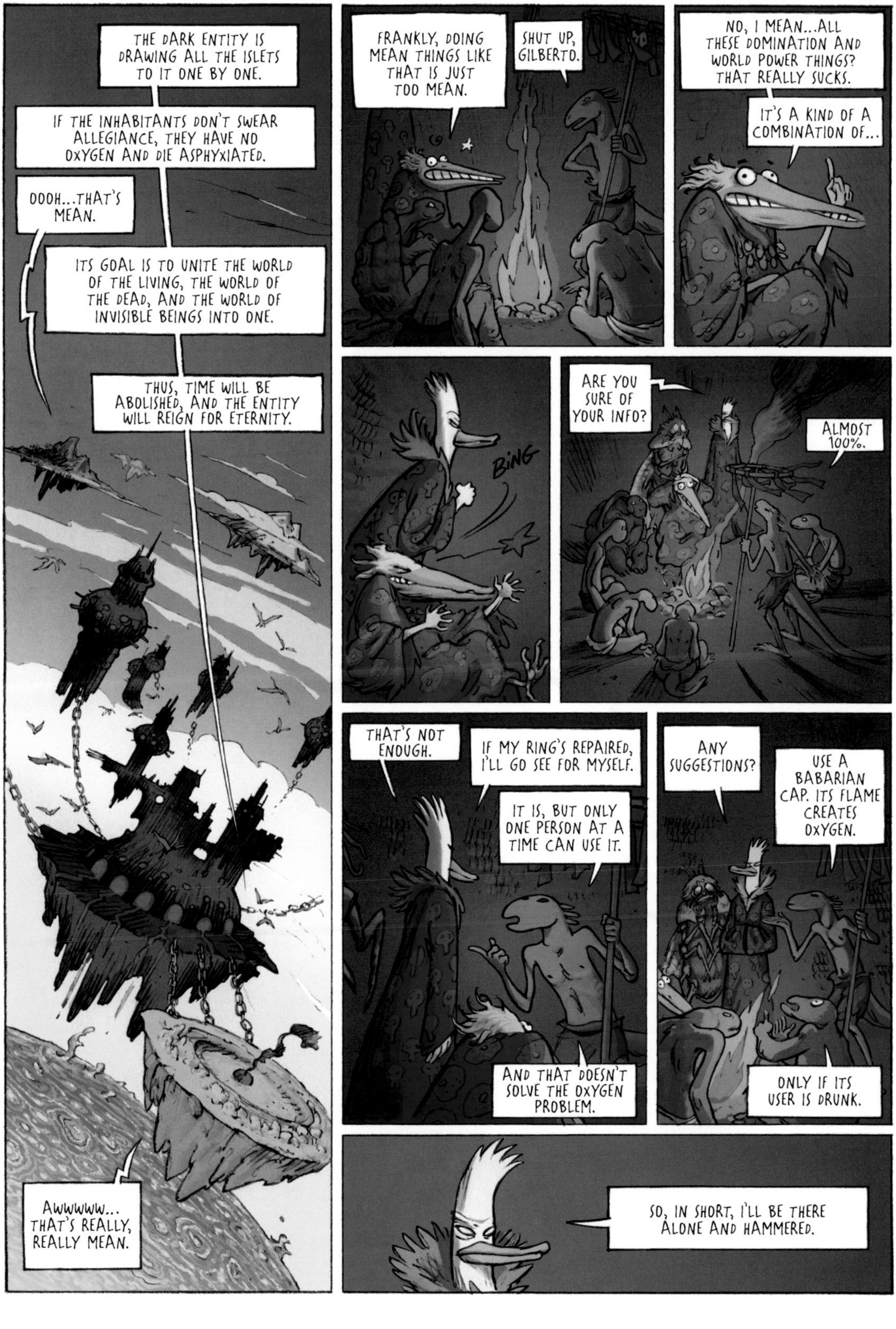
THE DARK ENTITY IS DRAWING ALL THE ISLETS TO IT ONE BY ONE.
IF THE INHABITANTS DON'T SWEAR ALLEGIANCE, THEY HAVE NO OXYGEN AND DIE ASPHYXIATED.
OOOH...THAT'S MEAN.
ITS GOAL IS TO UNITE THE WORLD OF THE LIVING, THE WORLD OF THE DEAD, AND THE WORLD OF INVISIBLE BEINGS INTO ONE.
THUS, TIME WILL BE ABOLISHED, AND THE ENTITY WILL REIGN FOR ETERNITY.
AWWWWW... THAT'S REALLY, REALLY MEAN.
FRANKLY, DOING MEAN THINGS LIKE THAT IS JUST TOO MEAN.
SHUT UP, GILBERTO.
NO, I MEAN...ALL THESE DOMINATION AND WORLD POWER THINGS? THAT REALLY SUCKS.
IT'S A KIND OF A COMBINATION OF...
BING
ARE YOU SURE OF YOUR INFO?
ALMOST 100%.
THAT'S NOT ENOUGH.
IF MY RING'S REPAIRED, I'LL GO SEE FOR MYSELF.
IT IS, BUT ONLY ONE PERSON AT A TIME CAN USE IT.
AND THAT DOESN'T SOLVE THE OXYGEN PROBLEM.
ANY SUGGESTIONS?
USE A BABARIAN CAP. ITS FLAME CREATES OXYGEN.
ONLY IF ITS USER IS DRUNK.
SO, IN SHORT, I'LL BE THERE ALONE AND HAMMERED.

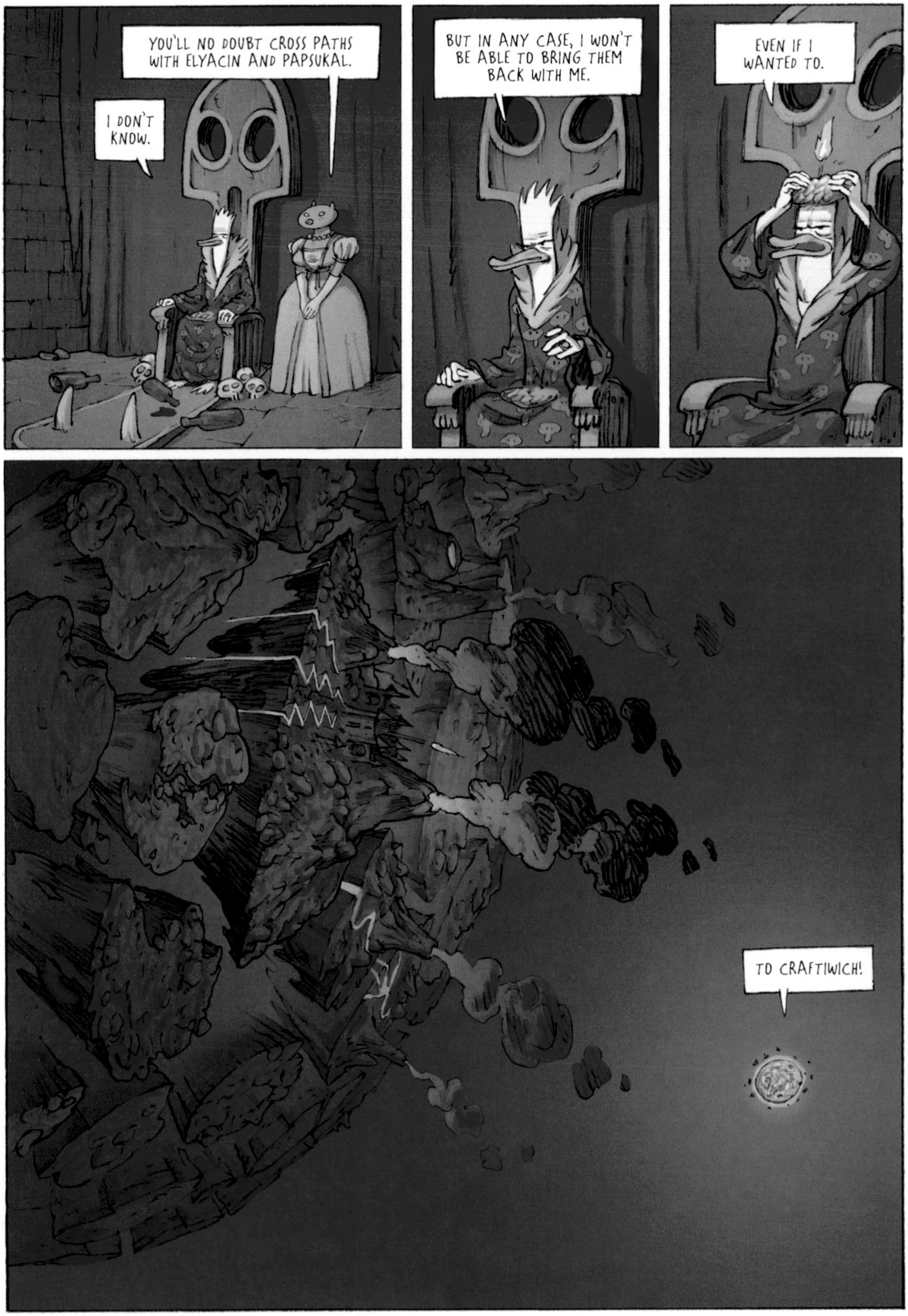
YOU'LL NO DOUBT CROSS PATHS WITH ELYACIN AND PAPSUKAL.
I DON'T KNOW.
BUT IN ANY CASE, I WON'T BE ABLE TO BRING THEM BACK WITH ME.
EVEN IF I WANTED TO.
TO CRAFTIWICH!

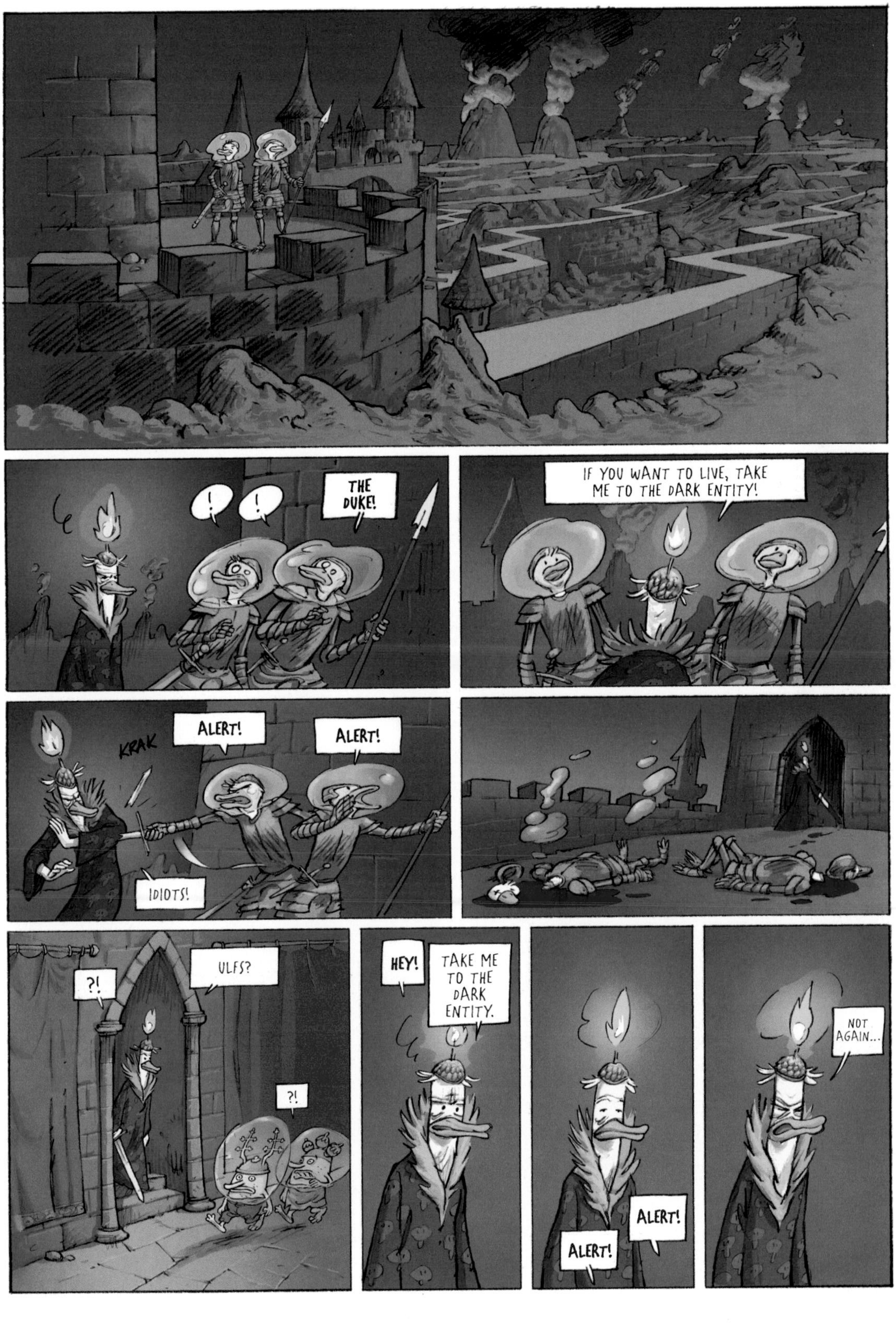
!
!
THE DUKE!
IF YOU WANT TO LIVE, TAKE ME TO THE DARK ENTITY!
KRAK
ALERT!
ALERT!
IDIOTS!
?!
ULFS?
?!
HEY!
TAKE ME TO THE DARK ENTITY.
ALERT!
ALERT!
NOT AGAIN...

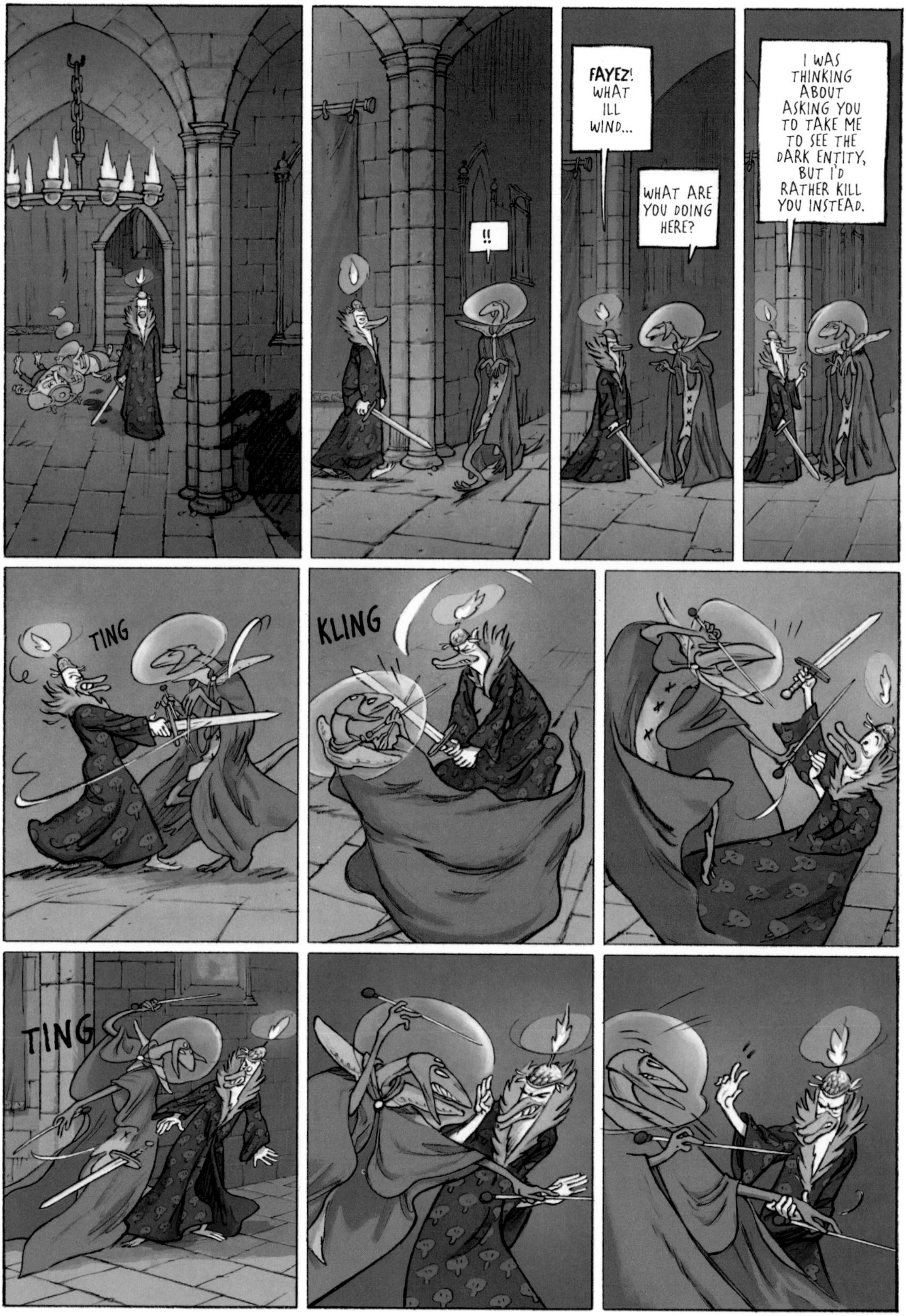
!!
FAYEZ! WHAT ILL WIND...
WHAT ARE YOU DOING HERE?
I WAS THINKING ABOUT ASKING YOU TO TAKE ME TO SEE THE DARK ENTITY, BUT I'D RATHER KILL YOU INSTEAD.
TING
KLING
TING

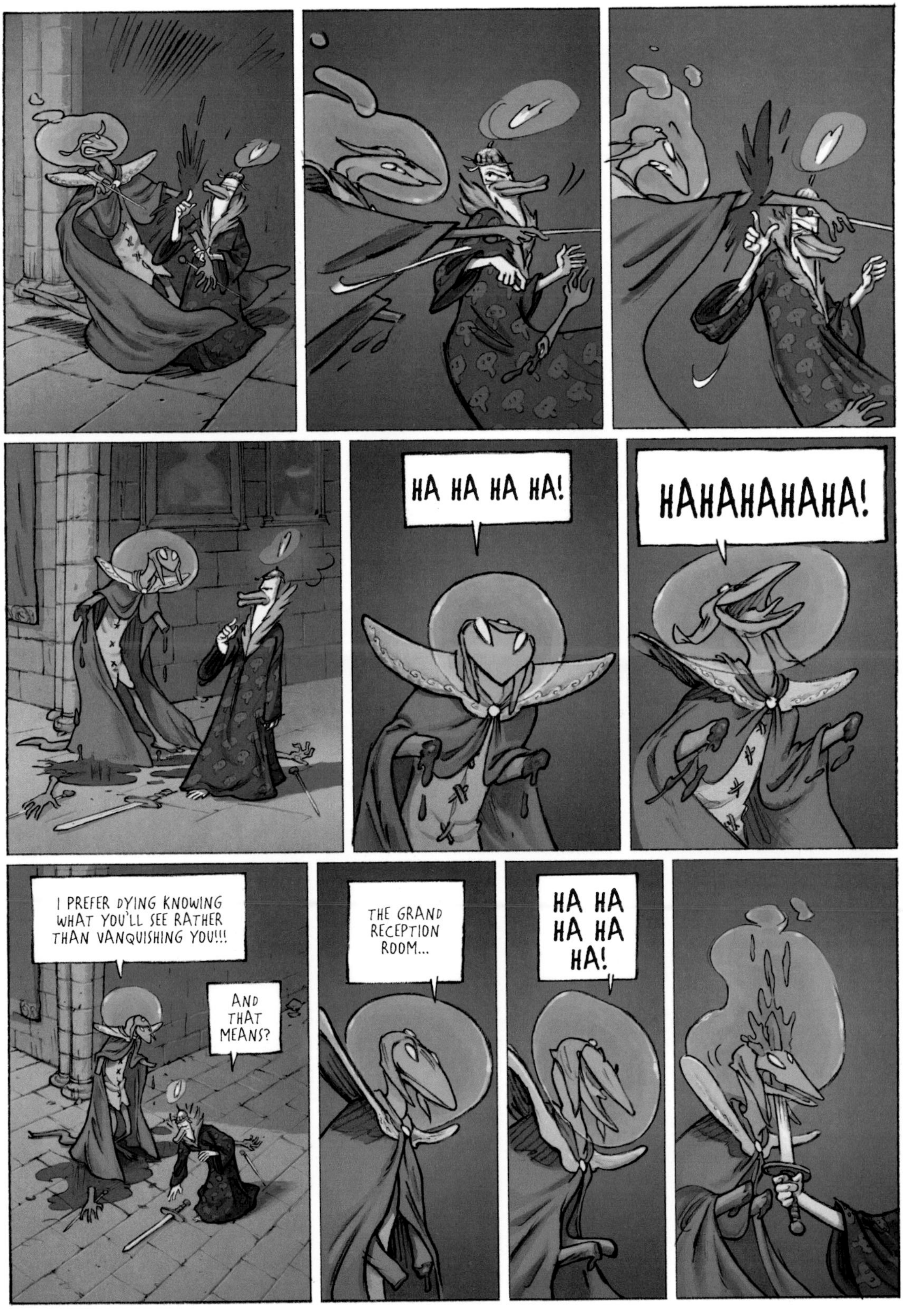
HA HA HA HA!
HAHAHAHAHA!
I PREFER DYING KNOWING WHAT YOU'LL SEE RATHER THAN VANQUISHING YOU!!!
AND THAT MEANS?
THE GRAND RECEPTION ROOM...
HA HA HA HA HA!

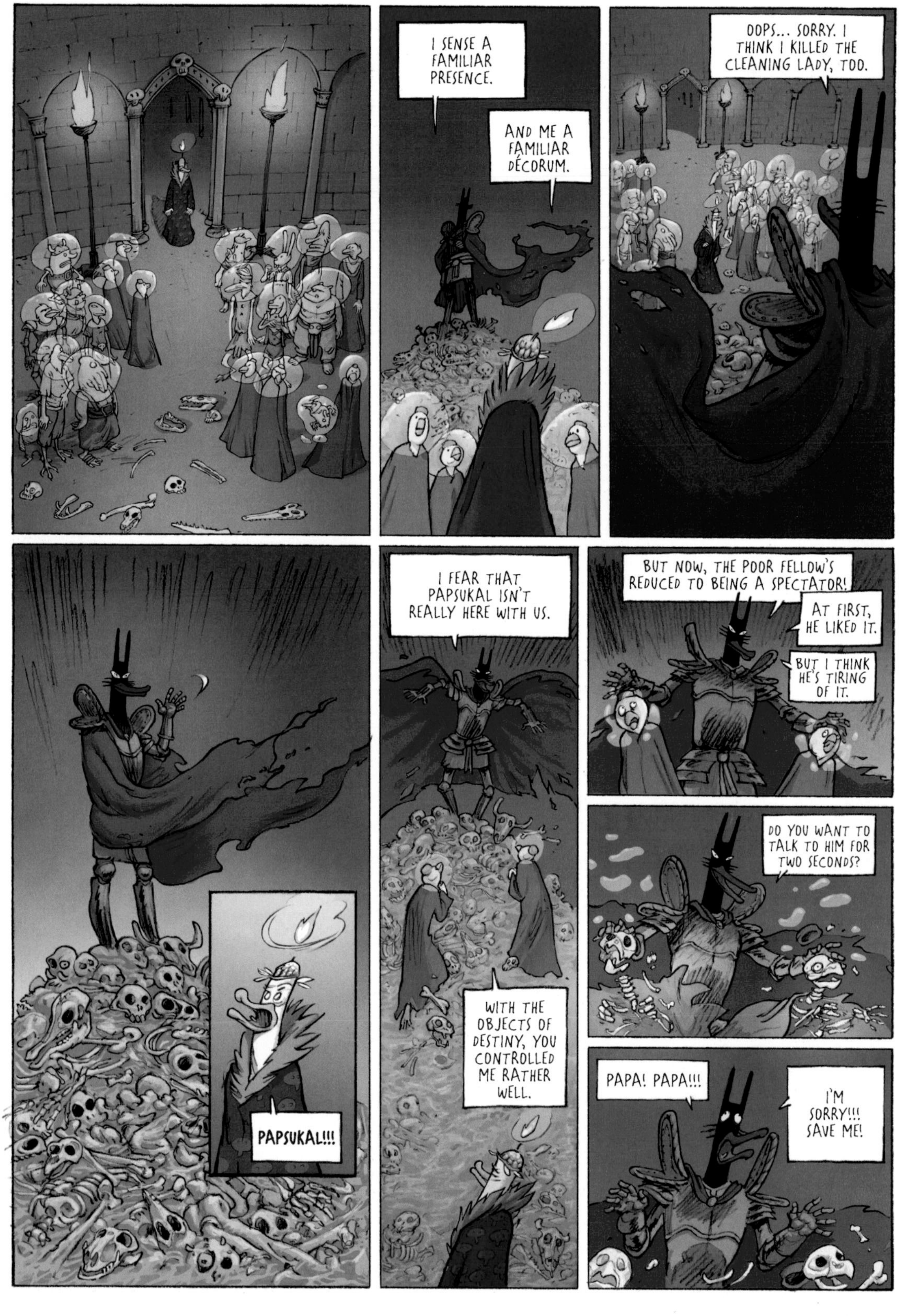
I SENSE A FAMILIAR PRESENCE.
AND ME A FAMILIAR DÉCORUM.
OOPS... SORRY. I THINK I KILLED THE CLEANING LADY, TOO.
PAPSUKAL!!!
I FEAR THAT PAPSUKAL ISN'T REALLY HERE WITH US.
WITH THE OBJECTS OF DESTINY, YOU CONTROLLED ME RATHER WELL.
BUT NOW, THE POOR FELLOW'S REDUCED TO BEING A SPECTATOR!
AT FIRST, HE LIKED IT.
BUT I THINK HE'S TIRING OF IT.
DO YOU WANT TO TALK TO HIM FOR TWO SECONDS?
PAPA! PAPA!!!
I'M SORRY!!! SAVE ME!

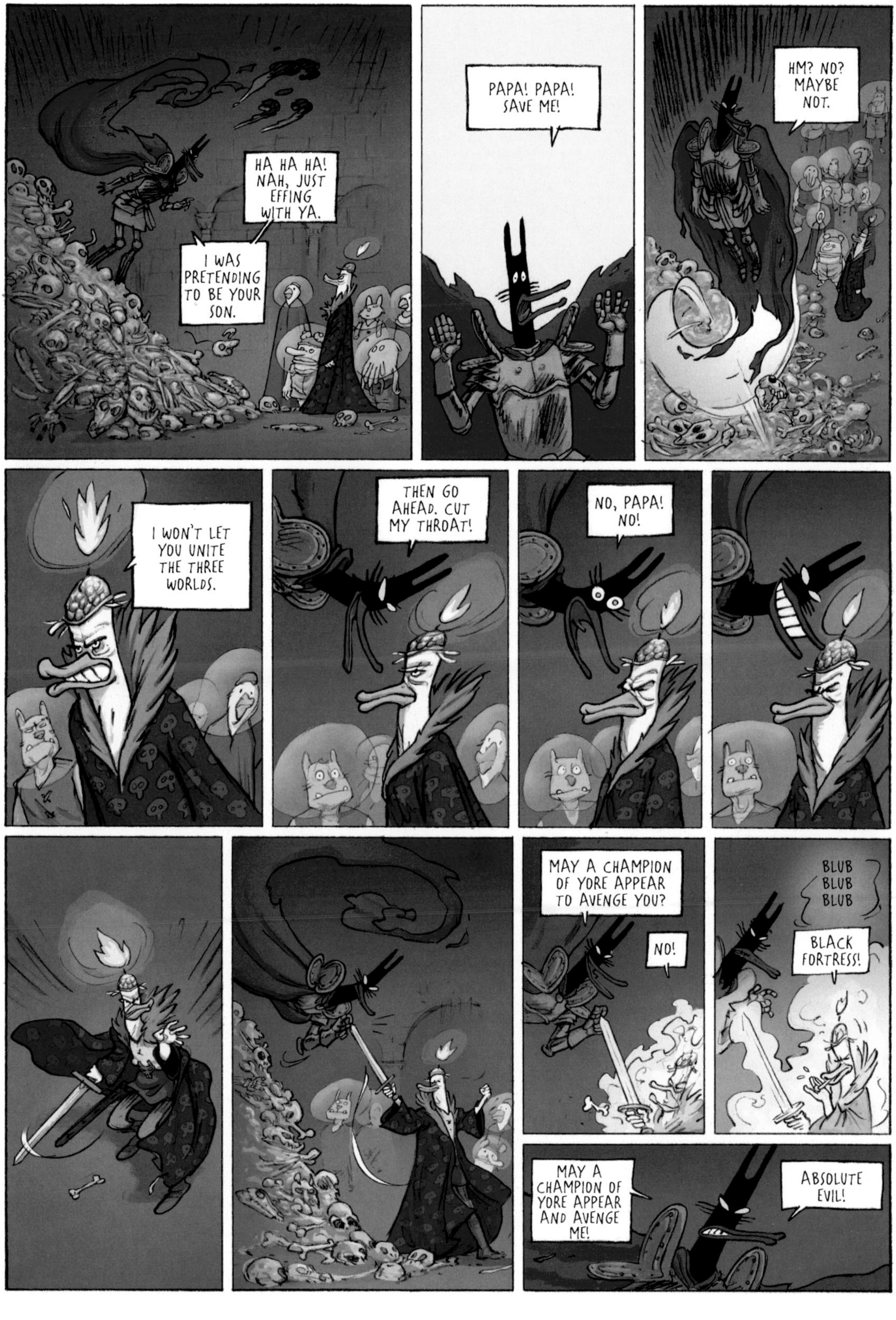
HA HA HA! NAH, JUST EFFING WITH YA.
I WAS PRETENDING TO BE YOUR SON.
PAPA! PAPA! SAVE ME!
HM? NO? MAYBE NOT.
I WON'T LET YOU UNITE THE THREE WORLDS.
THEN GO AHEAD. CUT MY THROAT!
NO, PAPA! NO!
MAY A CHAMPION OF YORE APPEAR TO AVENGE YOU?
NO!
BLUB BLUB BLUB
BLACK FORTRESS!
MAY A CHAMPION OF YORE APPEAR AND AVENGE ME!
ABSOLUTE EVIL!

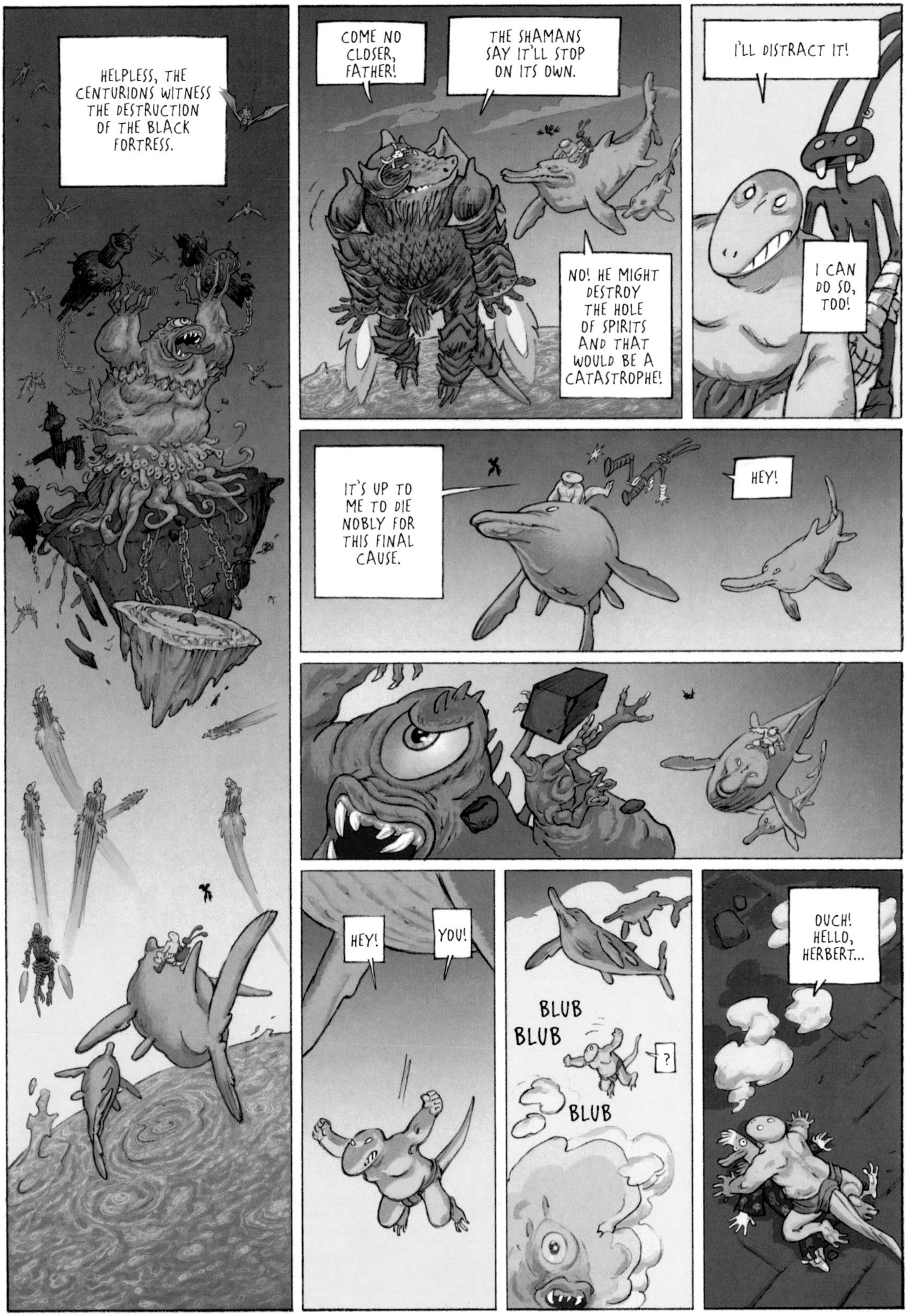
HELPLESS, THE CENTURIONS WITNESS THE DESTRUCTION OF THE BLACK FORTRESS.
COME NO CLOSER, FATHER!
THE SHAMANS SAY IT'LL STOP ON ITS OWN.
NO! HE MIGHT DESTROY THE HOLE OF SPIRITS AND THAT WOULD BE A CATASTROPHE!
I'LL DISTRACT IT!
I CAN DO SO, TOO!
IT'S UP TO ME TO DIE NOBLY FOR THIS FINAL CAUSE.
HEY!
HEY!
YOU!
BLUB
BLUB
?
BLUB
OUCH! HELLO, HERBERT...

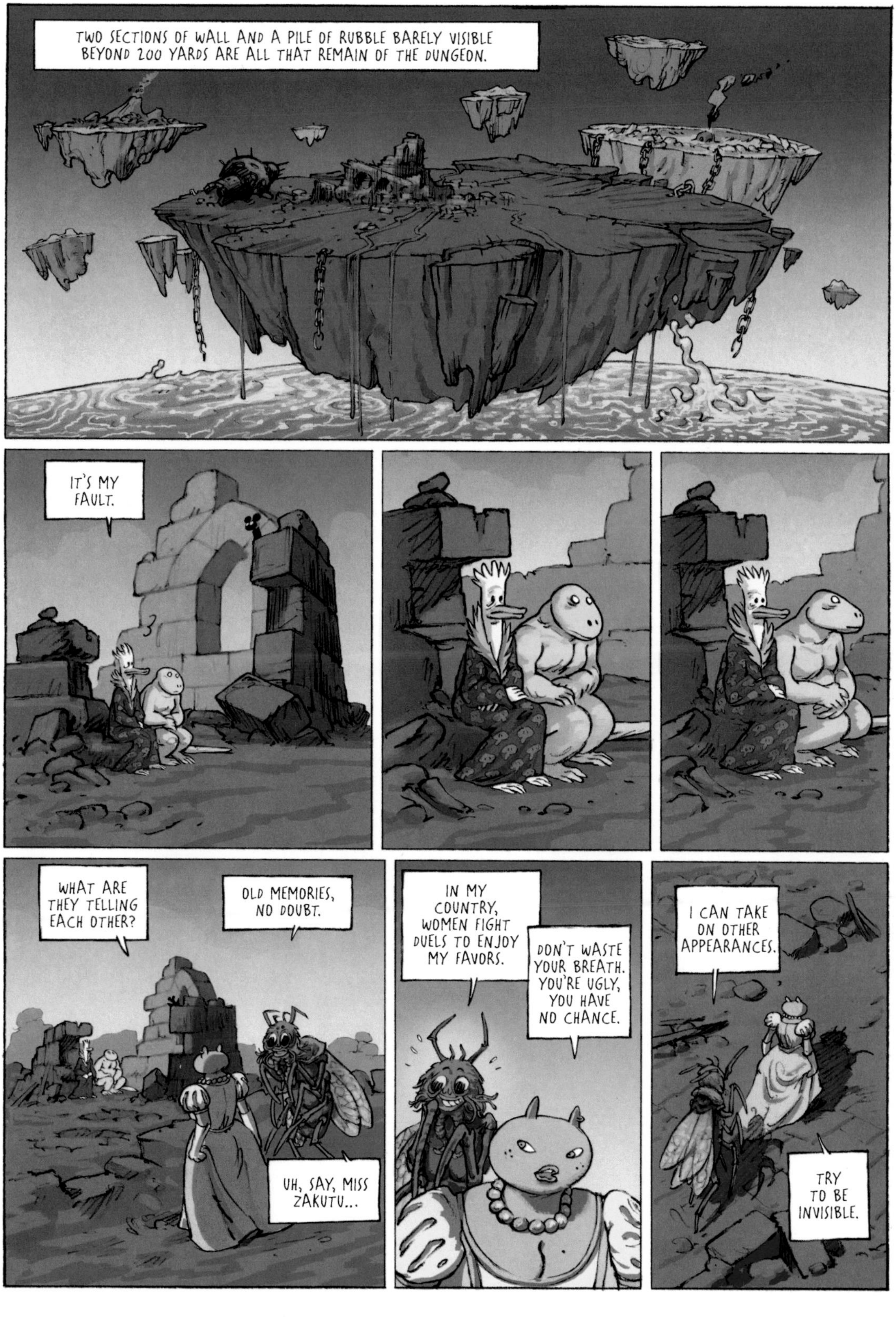
TWO SECTIONS OF WALL AND A PILE OF RUBBLE BARELY VISIBLE BEYOND 200 YARDS ARE ALL THAT REMAIN OF THE DUNGEON.
IT'S MY FAULT.
WHAT ARE THEY TELLING EACH OTHER?
OLD MEMORIES, NO DOUBT.
UH, SAY, MISS ZAKUTU...
IN MY COUNTRY, WOMEN FIGHT DUELS TO ENJOY MY FAVORS.
DON'T WASTE YOUR BREATH. YOU'RE UGLY, YOU HAVE NO CHANCE.
I CAN TAKE ON OTHER APPEARANCES.
TRY TO BE INVISIBLE.

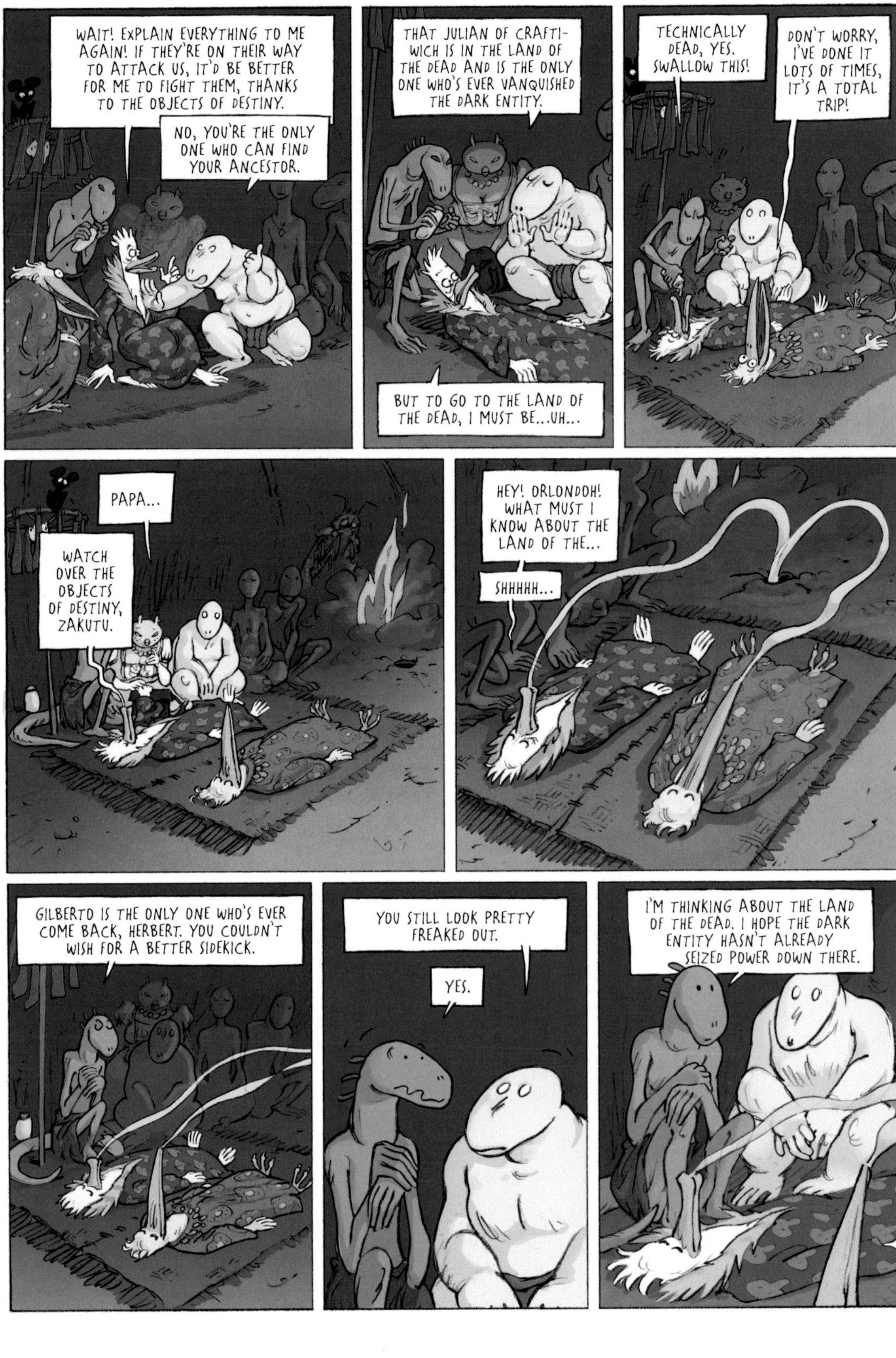
WAIT! EXPLAIN EVERYTHING TO ME AGAIN! IF THEY'RE ON THEIR WAY TO ATTACK US, IT'D BE BETTER FOR ME TO FIGHT THEM, THANKS TO THE OBJECTS OF DESTINY.
NO, YOU'RE THE ONLY ONE WHO CAN FIND YOUR ANCESTOR.
THAT JULIAN OF CRAFTI-WICH IS IN THE LAND OF THE DEAD AND IS THE ONLY ONE WHO'S EVER VANQUISHED THE DARK ENTITY.
BUT TO GO TO THE LAND OF THE DEAD, I MUST BE...UH...
TECHNICALLY DEAD, YES. SWALLOW THIS!
DON'T WORRY, I'VE DONE IT LOTS OF TIMES, IT'S A TOTAL TRIP!
PAPA...
WATCH OVER THE OBJECTS OF DESTINY, ZAKUTU.
HEY! ORLONDOH! WHAT MUST I KNOW ABOUT THE LAND OF THE...
SHHHHH...
GILBERTO IS THE ONLY ONE WHO'S EVER COME BACK, HERBERT. YOU COULDN'T WISH FOR A BETTER SIDEKICK.
YOU STILL LOOK PRETTY FREAKED OUT.
YES.
I'M THINKING ABOUT THE LAND OF THE DEAD. I HOPE THE DARK ENTITY HASN'T ALREADY SEIZED POWER DOWN THERE.

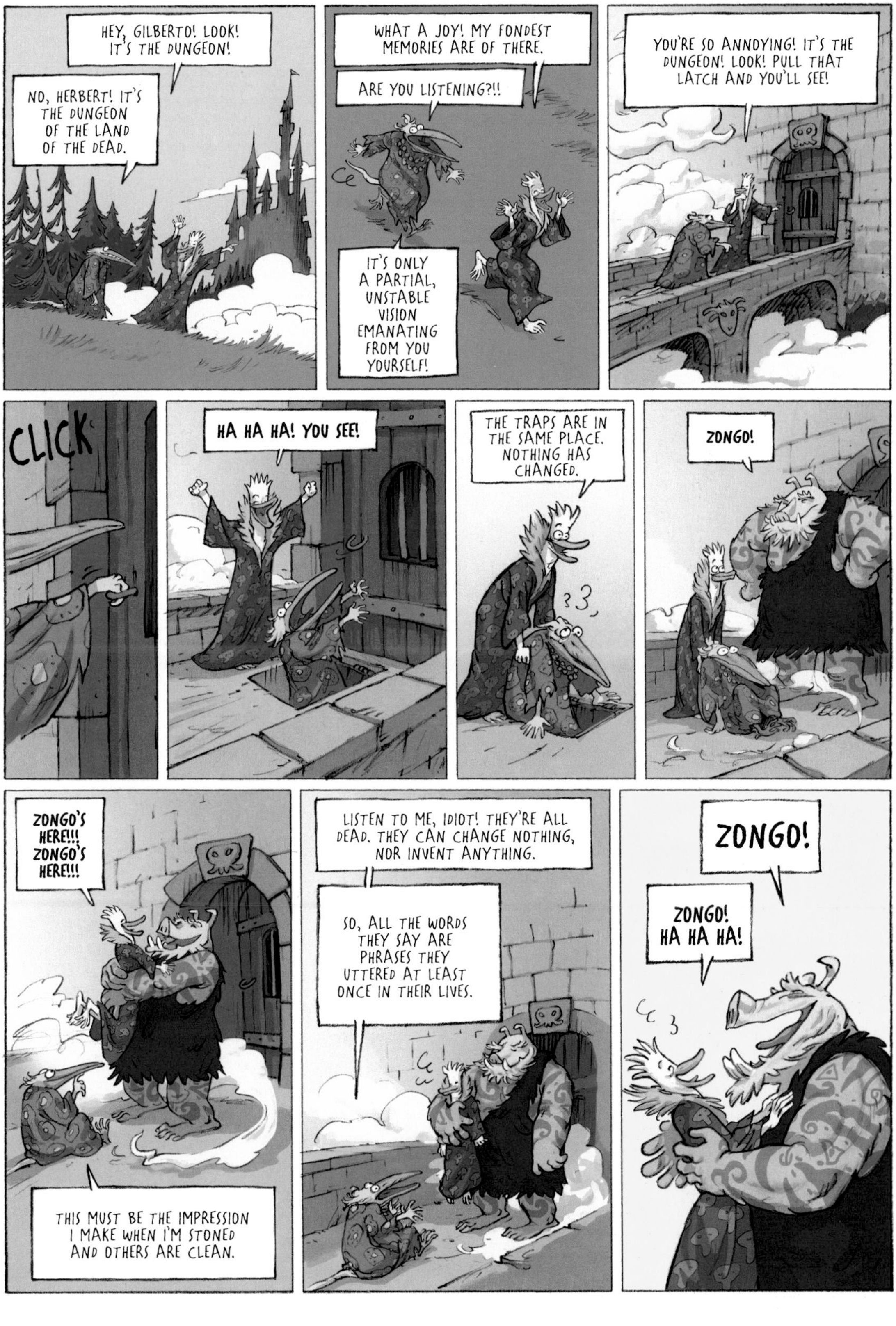
HEY, GILBERTO! LOOK! IT'S THE DUNGEON!
NO, HERBERT! IT'S THE DUNGEON OF THE LAND OF THE DEAD.
WHAT A JOY! MY FONDEST MEMORIES ARE OF THERE.
ARE YOU LISTENING?!!
IT'S ONLY A PARTIAL, UNSTABLE VISION EMANATING FROM YOU YOURSELF!
YOU'RE SO ANNOYING! IT'S THE DUNGEON! LOOK! PULL THAT LATCH AND YOU'LL SEE!
CLICK
HA HA HA! YOU SEE!
THE TRAPS ARE IN THE SAME PLACE. NOTHING HAS CHANGED.
ZONGO!
ZONGO'S HERE!!! ZONGO'S HERE!!!
THIS MUST BE THE IMPRESSION I MAKE WHEN I'M STONED AND OTHERS ARE CLEAN.
LISTEN TO ME, IDIOT! THEY'RE ALL DEAD. THEY CAN CHANGE NOTHING, NOR INVENT ANYTHING.
SO, ALL THE WORDS THEY SAY ARE PHRASES THEY UTTERED AT LEAST ONCE IN THEIR LIVES.
ZONGO!
ZONGO! HA HA HA!

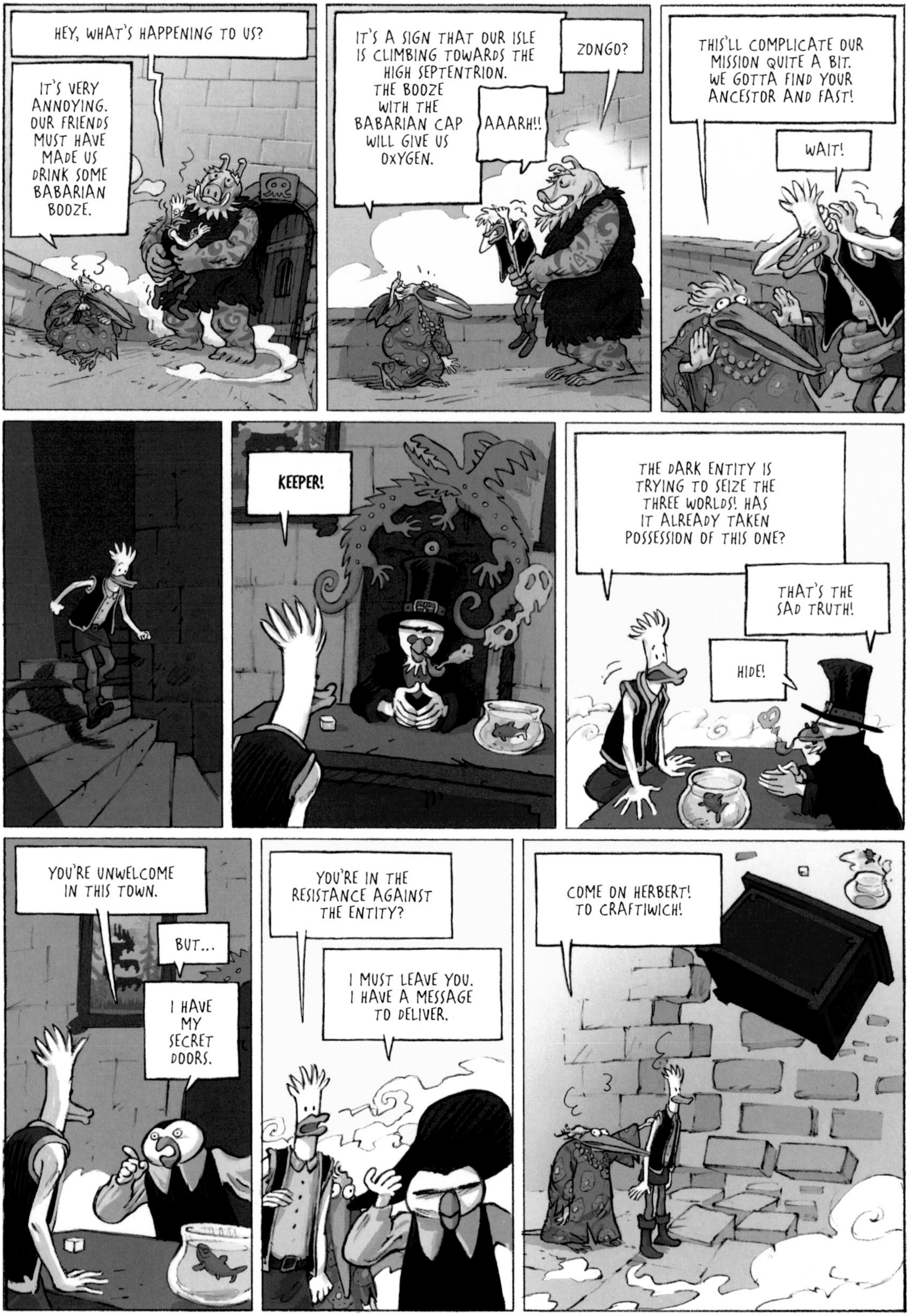
HEY, WHAT'S HAPPENING TO US?
IT'S VERY ANNOYING. OUR FRIENDS MUST HAVE MADE US DRINK SOME BABARIAN BOOZE.
IT'S A SIGN THAT OUR ISLE IS CLIMBING TOWARDS THE HIGH SEPTENTRION.
THE BOOZE WITH THE BABARIAN CAP WILL GIVE US OXYGEN.
ZONGO?
AAARH!!
THIS'LL COMPLICATE OUR MISSION QUITE A BIT. WE GOTTA FIND YOUR ANCESTOR AND FAST!
WAIT!
KEEPER!
THE DARK ENTITY IS TRYING TO SEIZE THE THREE WORLDS! HAS IT ALREADY TAKEN POSSESSION OF THIS ONE?
THAT'S THE SAD TRUTH!
HIDE!
YOU'RE UNWELCOME IN THIS TOWN.
BUT...
I HAVE MY SECRET DOORS.
YOU'RE IN THE RESISTANCE AGAINST THE ENTITY?
I MUST LEAVE YOU. I HAVE A MESSAGE TO DELIVER.
COME ON HERBERT! TO CRAFTIWICH!

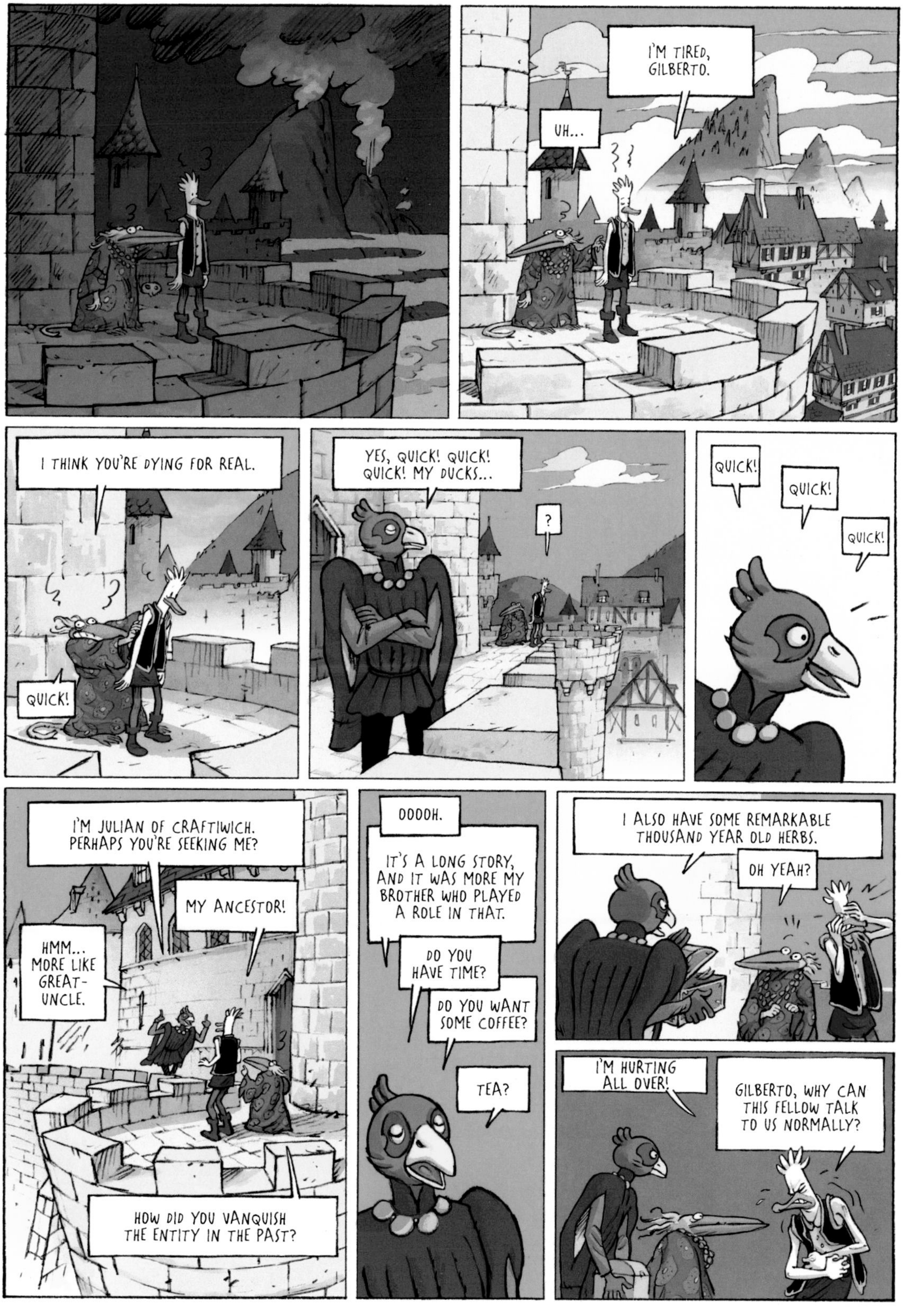
I'M TIRED, GILBERTO.
UH...
I THINK YOU'RE DYING FOR REAL.
QUICK!
YES, QUICK! QUICK! QUICK! MY DUCKS...
?
QUICK!
QUICK!
QUICK!
I'M JULIAN OF CRAFTIWICH. PERHAPS YOU'RE SEEKING ME?
MY ANCESTOR!
HMM... MORE LIKE GREAT-UNCLE.
HOW DID YOU VANQUISH THE ENTITY IN THE PAST?
OOOOH.
IT'S A LONG STORY, AND IT WAS MORE MY BROTHER WHO PLAYED A ROLE IN THAT.
DO YOU HAVE TIME?
DO YOU WANT SOME COFFEE?
TEA?
I ALSO HAVE SOME REMARKABLE THOUSAND YEAR OLD HERBS.
OH YEAH?
I'M HURTING ALL OVER!
GILBERTO, WHY CAN THIS FELLOW TALK TO US NORMALLY?

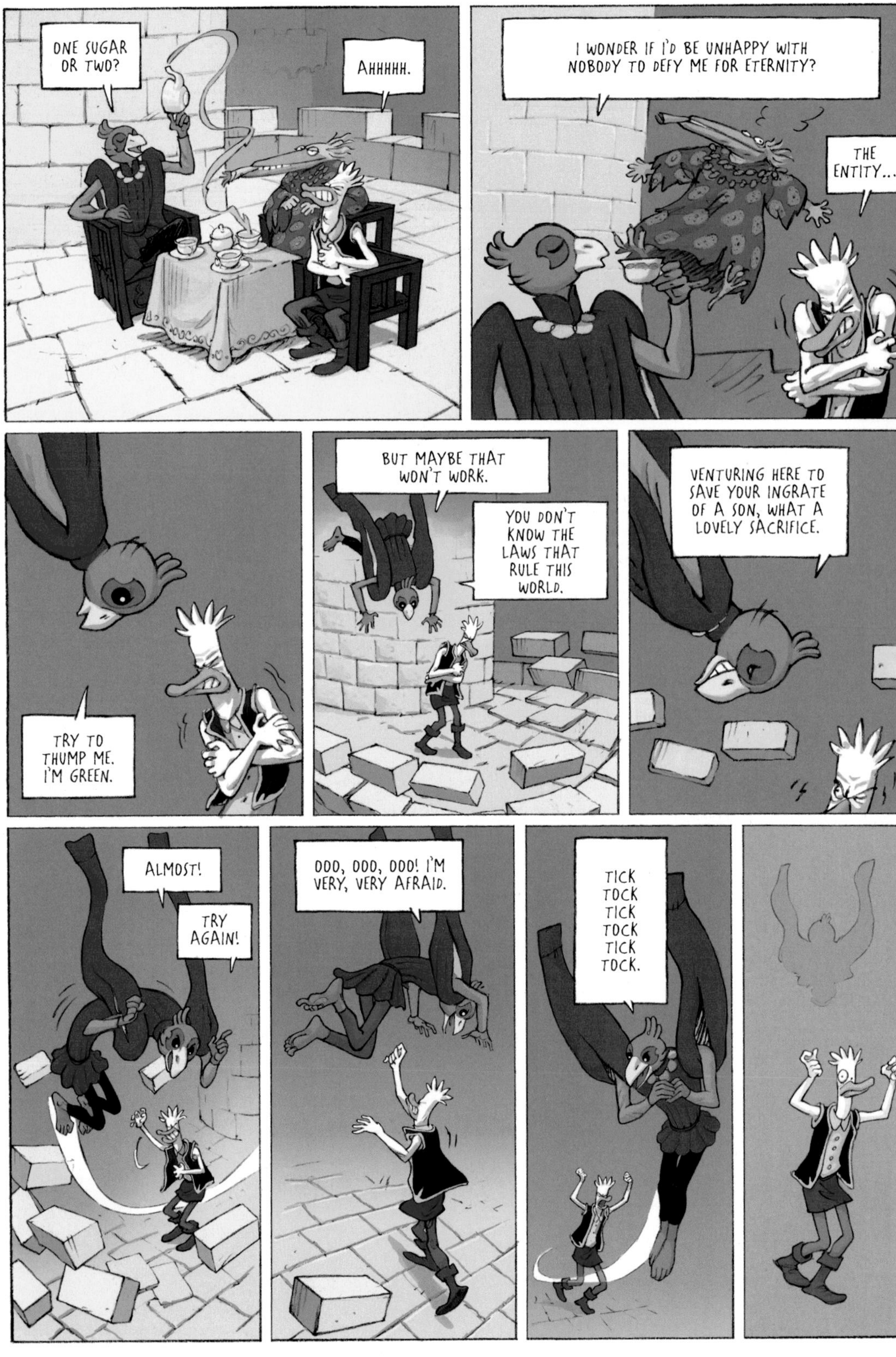
ONE SUGAR OR TWO?
AHHHHH.
I WONDER IF I'D BE UNHAPPY WITH NOBODY TO DEFY ME FOR ETERNITY?
THE ENTITY...
TRY TO THUMP ME. I'M GREEN.
BUT MAYBE THAT WON'T WORK.
YOU DON'T KNOW THE LAWS THAT RULE THIS WORLD.
VENTURING HERE TO SAVE YOUR INGRATE OF A SON, WHAT A LOVELY SACRIFICE.
ALMOST!
TRY AGAIN!
OOO, OOO, OOO! I'M VERY, VERY AFRAID.
TICK TOCK TICK TOCK TICK TOCK.

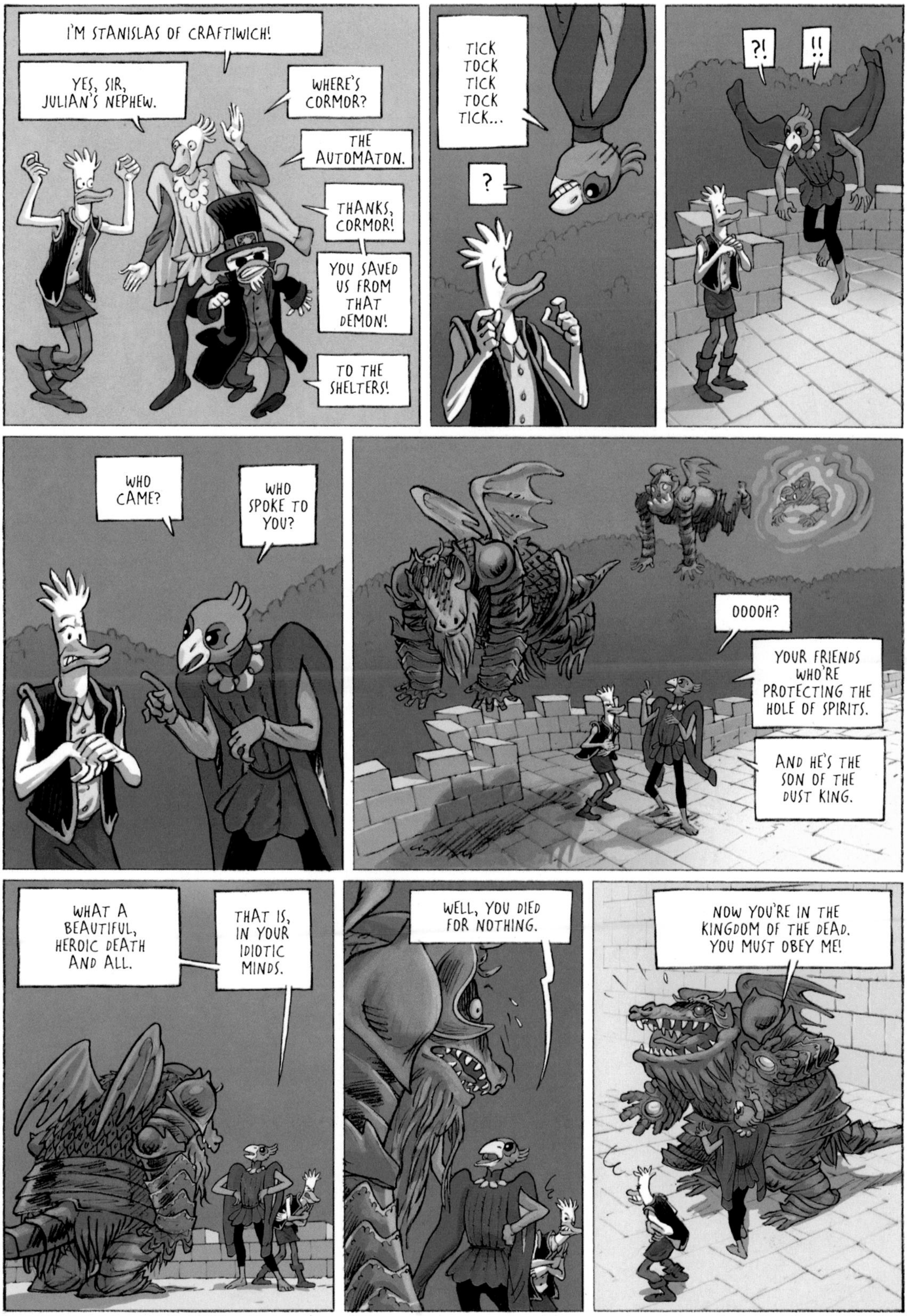
I'M STANISLAS OF CRAFTIWICH!
YES, SIR, JULIAN'S NEPHEW.
WHERE'S CORMOR?
THE AUTOMATON.
THANKS, CORMOR!
YOU SAVED US FROM THAT DEMON!
TO THE SHELTERS!
TICK TOCK TICK TOCK TICK...
?
?!
!!
WHO CAME?
WHO SPOKE TO YOU?
OOOOH?
YOUR FRIENDS WHO'RE PROTECTING THE HOLE OF SPIRITS.
AND HE'S THE SON OF THE DUST KING.
WHAT A BEAUTIFUL, HEROIC DEATH AND ALL.
THAT IS, IN YOUR IDIOTIC MINDS.
WELL, YOU DIED FOR NOTHING.
NOW YOU'RE IN THE KINGDOM OF THE DEAD. YOU MUST OBEY ME!

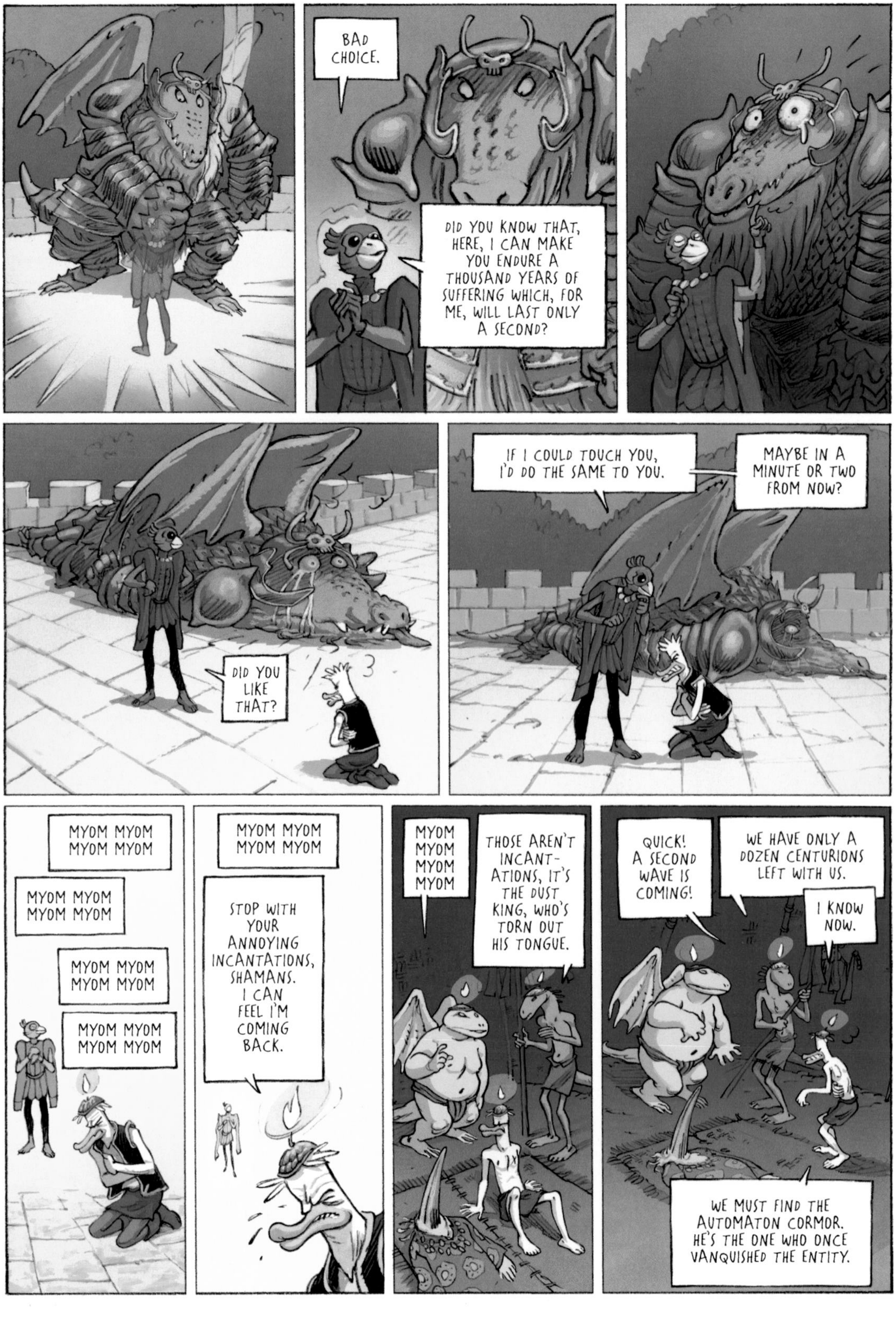

BAD CHOICE.
DID YOU KNOW THAT, HERE, I CAN MAKE YOU ENDURE A THOUSAND YEARS OF SUFFERING WHICH, FOR ME, WILL LAST ONLY A SECOND?
DID YOU LIKE THAT?
IF I COULD TOUCH YOU, I'D DO THE SAME TO YOU.
MAYBE IN A MINUTE OR TWO FROM NOW?
MYOM MYOM MYOM MYOM
MYOM MYOM MYOM MYOM
MYOM MYOM MYOM MYOM
MYOM MYOM MYOM MYOM
MYOM MYOM MYOM MYOM
STOP WITH YOUR ANNOYING INCANTATIONS, SHAMANS. I CAN FEEL I'M COMING BACK.
MYOM MYOM MYOM MYOM
THOSE AREN'T INCANT-ATIONS, IT'S THE DUST KING, WHO'S TORN OUT HIS TONGUE.
QUICK! A SECOND WAVE IS COMING!
WE HAVE ONLY A DOZEN CENTURIONS LEFT WITH US.
I KNOW NOW.
WE MUST FIND THE AUTOMATON CORMOR. HE'S THE ONE WHO ONCE VANQUISHED THE ENTITY.

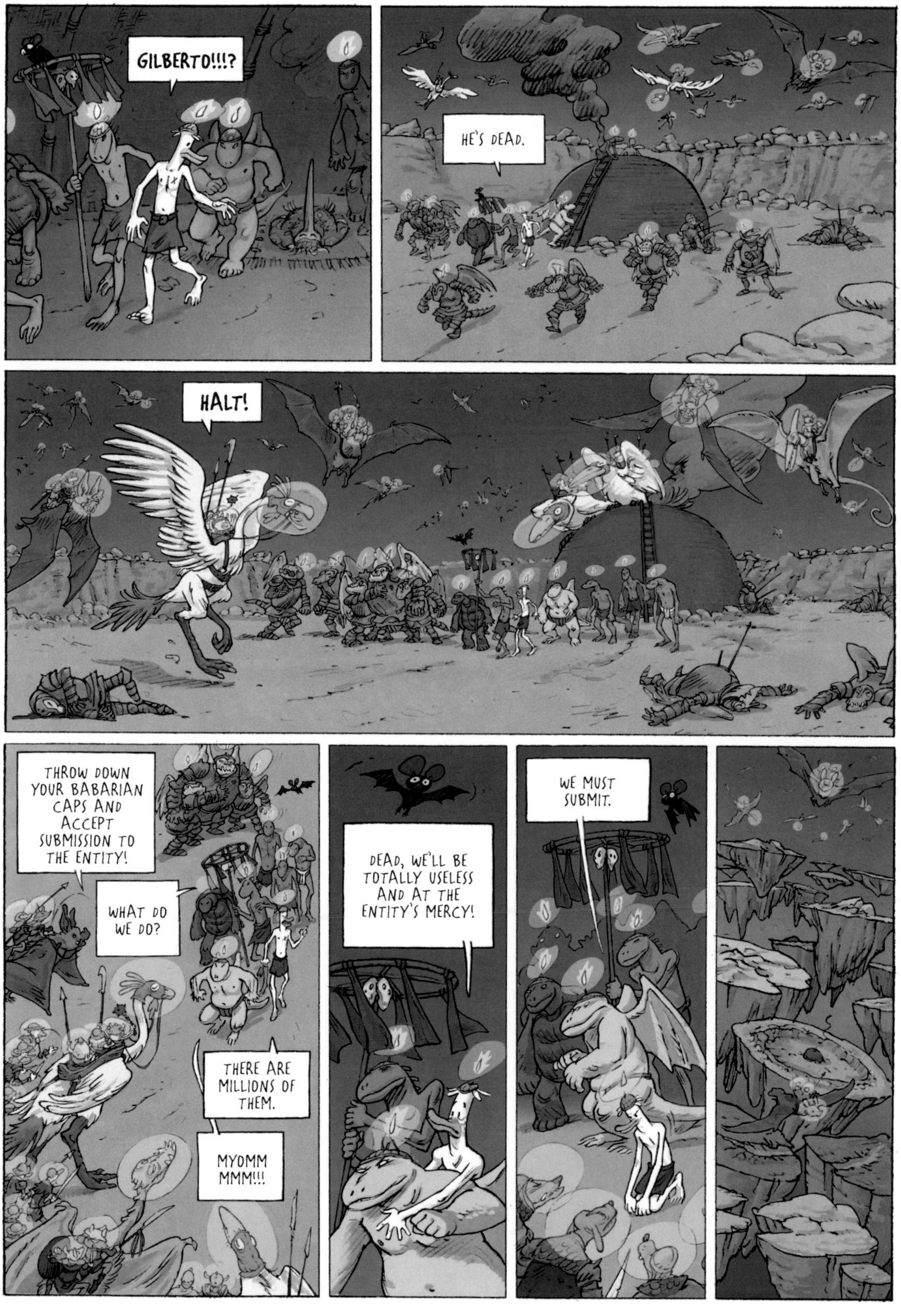
GILBERTO!!!?
HE'S DEAD.
HALT!
THROW DOWN YOUR BABARIAN CAPS AND ACCEPT SUBMISSION TO THE ENTITY!
WHAT DO WE DO?
THERE ARE MILLIONS OF THEM.
MYOMM MMM!!!
DEAD, WE'LL BE TOTALLY USELESS AND AT THE ENTITY'S MERCY!
WE MUST SUBMIT.

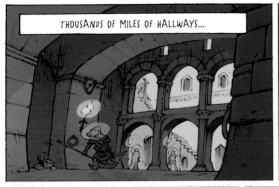

THOUSANDS OF MILES OF HALLWAYS...

OF CELLS WITH UNBREAKABLE BARS AND IMPREGNABLE DOORS...

IT'S THE DUNGEON OF CRAFTIWICH.

THAT'S WHERE THE ENTITY'S NEW SUBJECTS ARE IMPRISONED, THE TIME IT TAKES THEM TO UNDERSTAND THAT NO REBELLION IS POSSIBLE.

HAVE YOU UNDERSTOOD?

IF ONE OF YOU GETS CAUGHT DOING ANYTHING WHATSOEVER AGAINST THE MASTER OF THE THREE WORLDS, HE'LL NO LONGER HAVE HIS OXYGEN BUBBLE.

HIS BUBBLE WILL DISAPPEAR IN THE BLINK OF AN EYE.

LIKE THAT!

?!

HMMM, YOU TWO, THERE! I HAVE TO TALK TO YOU!

YOU'RE ENTITLED TO SPECIAL TREATMENT!

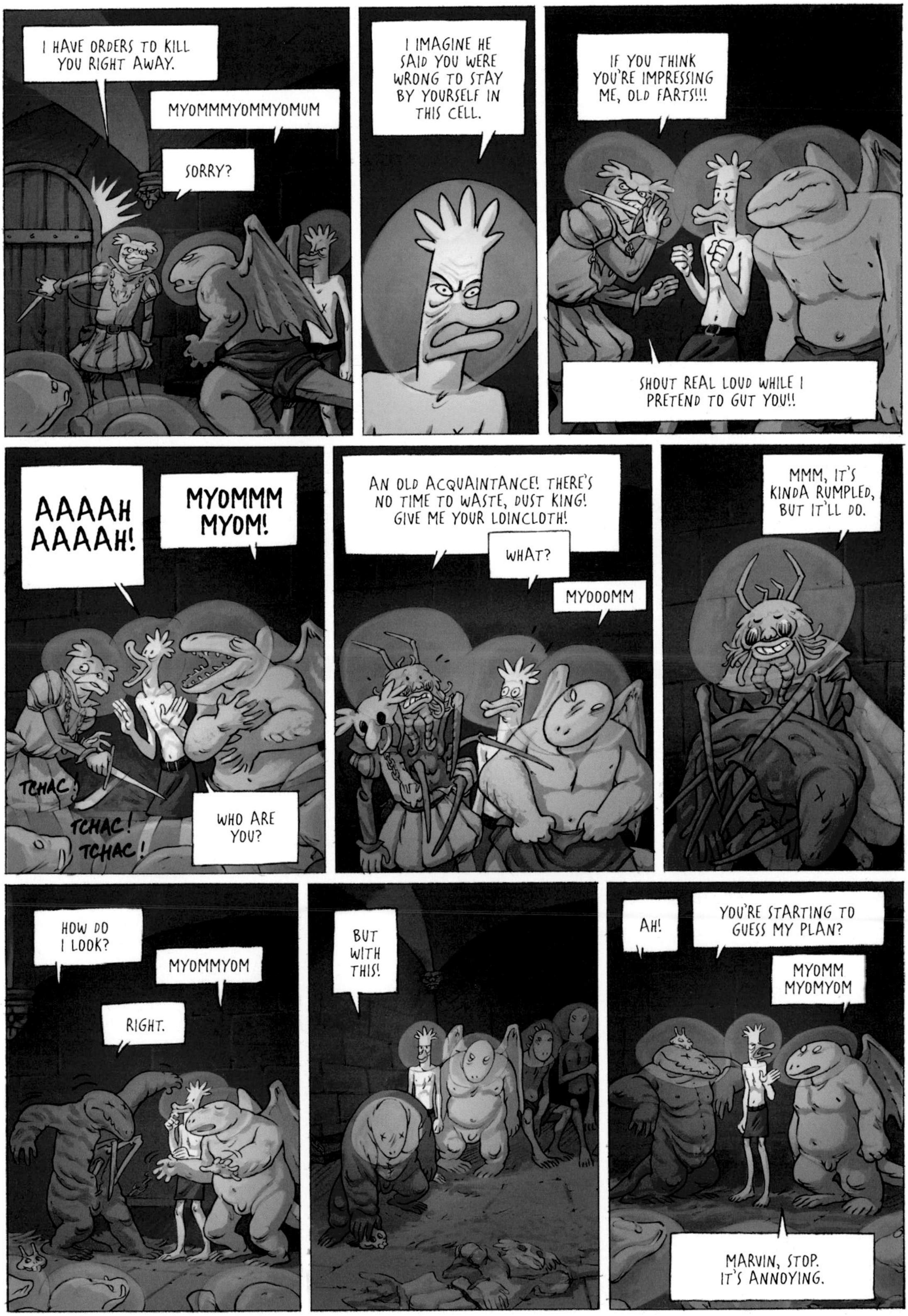

I HAVE ORDERS TO KILL YOU RIGHT AWAY.
MYOMMMYOMMYOMUM
SORRY?
I IMAGINE HE SAID YOU WERE WRONG TO STAY BY YOURSELF IN THIS CELL.
IF YOU THINK YOU'RE IMPRESSING ME, OLD FARTS!!!
SHOUT REAL LOUD WHILE I PRETEND TO GUT YOU!!
AAAAH AAAAH!
MYOMMM MYOM!
TCHAC!
TCHAC!
TCHAC!
WHO ARE YOU?
AN OLD ACQUAINTANCE! THERE'S NO TIME TO WASTE, DUST KING! GIVE ME YOUR LOINCLOTH!
WHAT?
MYOOOMM
MMM, IT'S KINDA RUMPLED, BUT IT'LL DO.
HOW DO I LOOK?
MYOMMYOM
RIGHT.
BUT WITH THIS!
AH!
YOU'RE STARTING TO GUESS MY PLAN?
MYOMM MYOMYOM
MARVIN, STOP. IT'S ANNOYING.

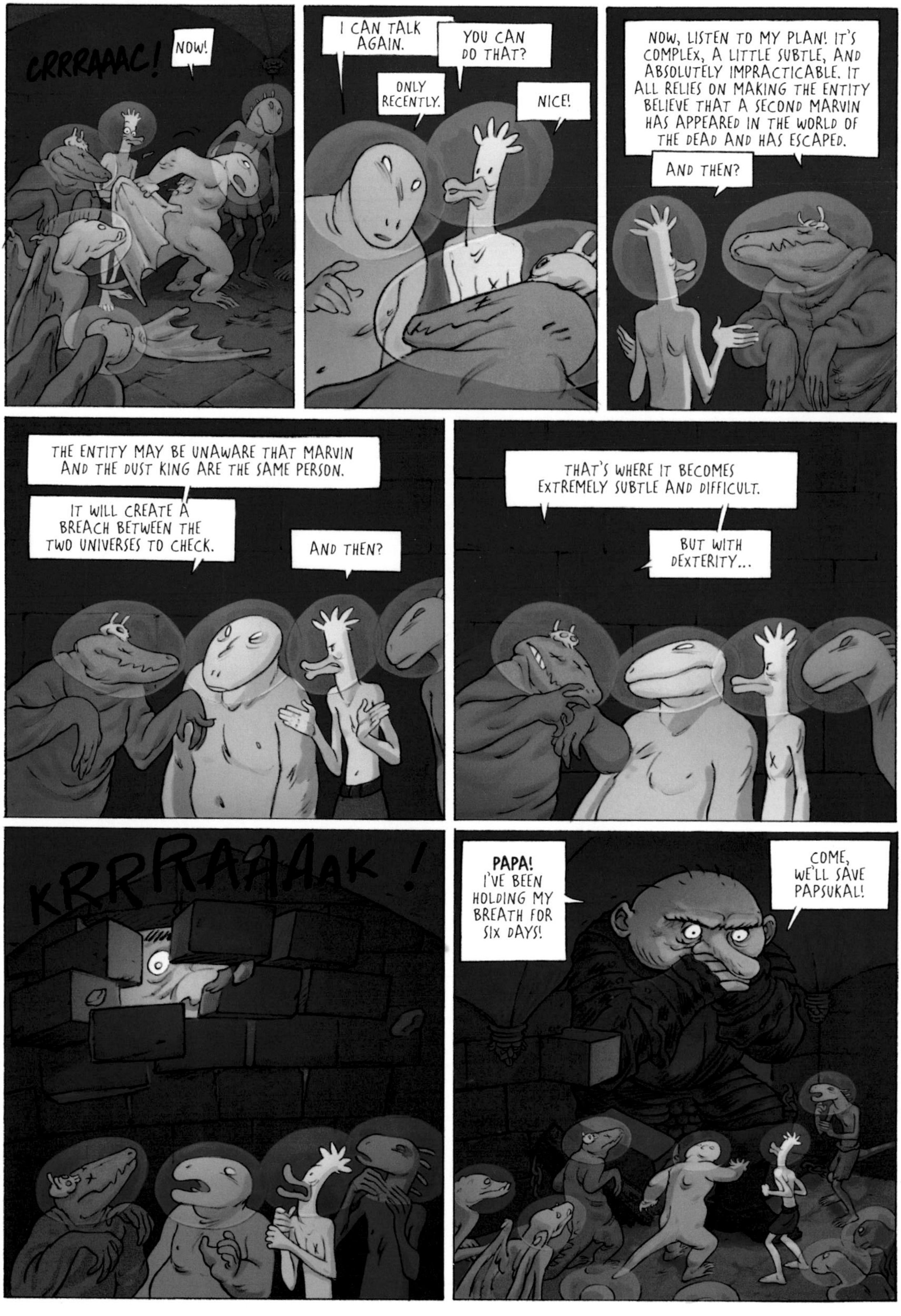

CRRRAAAC!
NOW!
I CAN TALK AGAIN.
YOU CAN DO THAT?
ONLY RECENTLY.
NICE!
NOW, LISTEN TO MY PLAN! IT'S COMPLEX, A LITTLE SUBTLE, AND ABSOLUTELY IMPRACTICABLE. IT ALL RELIES ON MAKING THE ENTITY BELIEVE THAT A SECOND MARVIN HAS APPEARED IN THE WORLD OF THE DEAD AND HAS ESCAPED.
AND THEN?
THE ENTITY MAY BE UNAWARE THAT MARVIN AND THE DUST KING ARE THE SAME PERSON.
IT WILL CREATE A BREACH BETWEEN THE TWO UNIVERSES TO CHECK.
AND THEN?
THAT'S WHERE IT BECOMES EXTREMELY SUBTLE AND DIFFICULT.
BUT WITH DEXTERITY...
KRRRAAAAK!
PAPA! I'VE BEEN HOLDING MY BREATH FOR SIX DAYS!
COME, WE'LL SAVE PAPSUKAL!

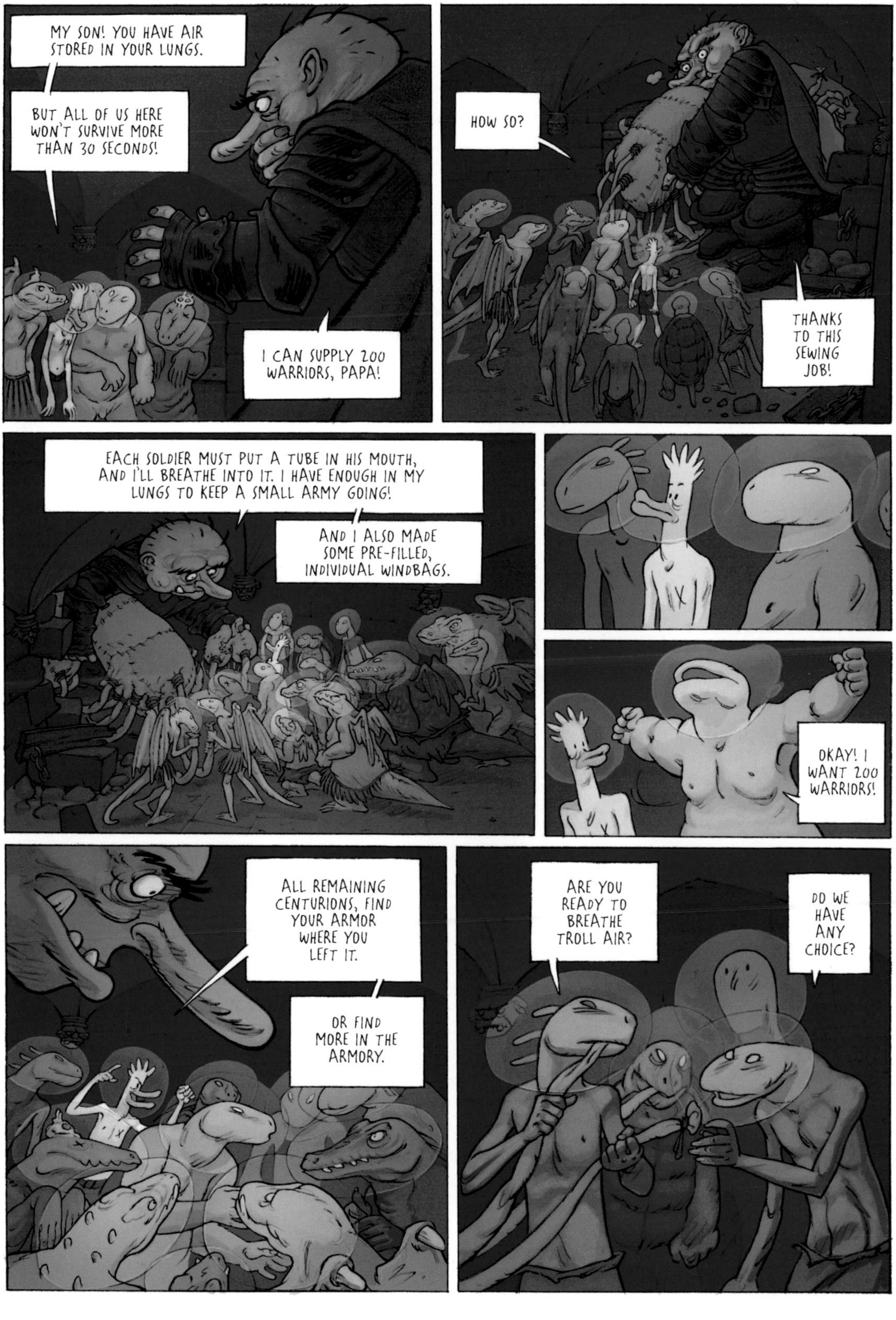
MY SON! YOU HAVE AIR STORED IN YOUR LUNGS.
BUT ALL OF US HERE WON'T SURVIVE MORE THAN 30 SECONDS!
I CAN SUPPLY 200 WARRIORS, PAPA!
HOW SO?
THANKS TO THIS SEWING JOB!
EACH SOLDIER MUST PUT A TUBE IN HIS MOUTH, AND I'LL BREATHE INTO IT. I HAVE ENOUGH IN MY LUNGS TO KEEP A SMALL ARMY GOING!
AND I ALSO MADE SOME PRE-FILLED, INDIVIDUAL WINDBAGS.
OKAY! I WANT 200 WARRIORS!
ALL REMAINING CENTURIONS, FIND YOUR ARMOR WHERE YOU LEFT IT.
OR FIND MORE IN THE ARMORY.
ARE YOU READY TO BREATHE TROLL AIR?
DO WE HAVE ANY CHOICE?

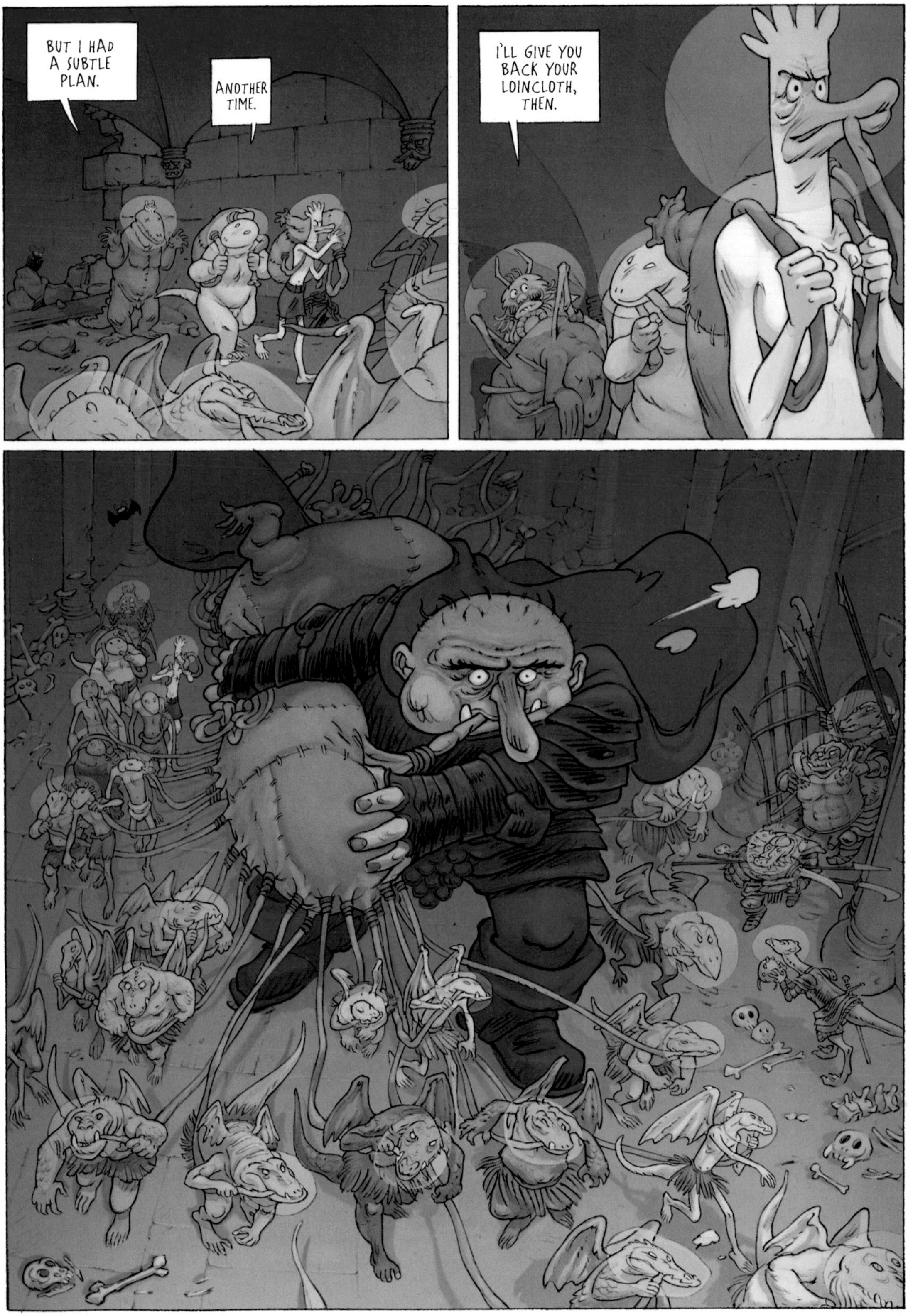
BUT I HAD A SUBTLE PLAN.
ANOTHER TIME.
I'LL GIVE YOU BACK YOUR LOINCLOTH, THEN.

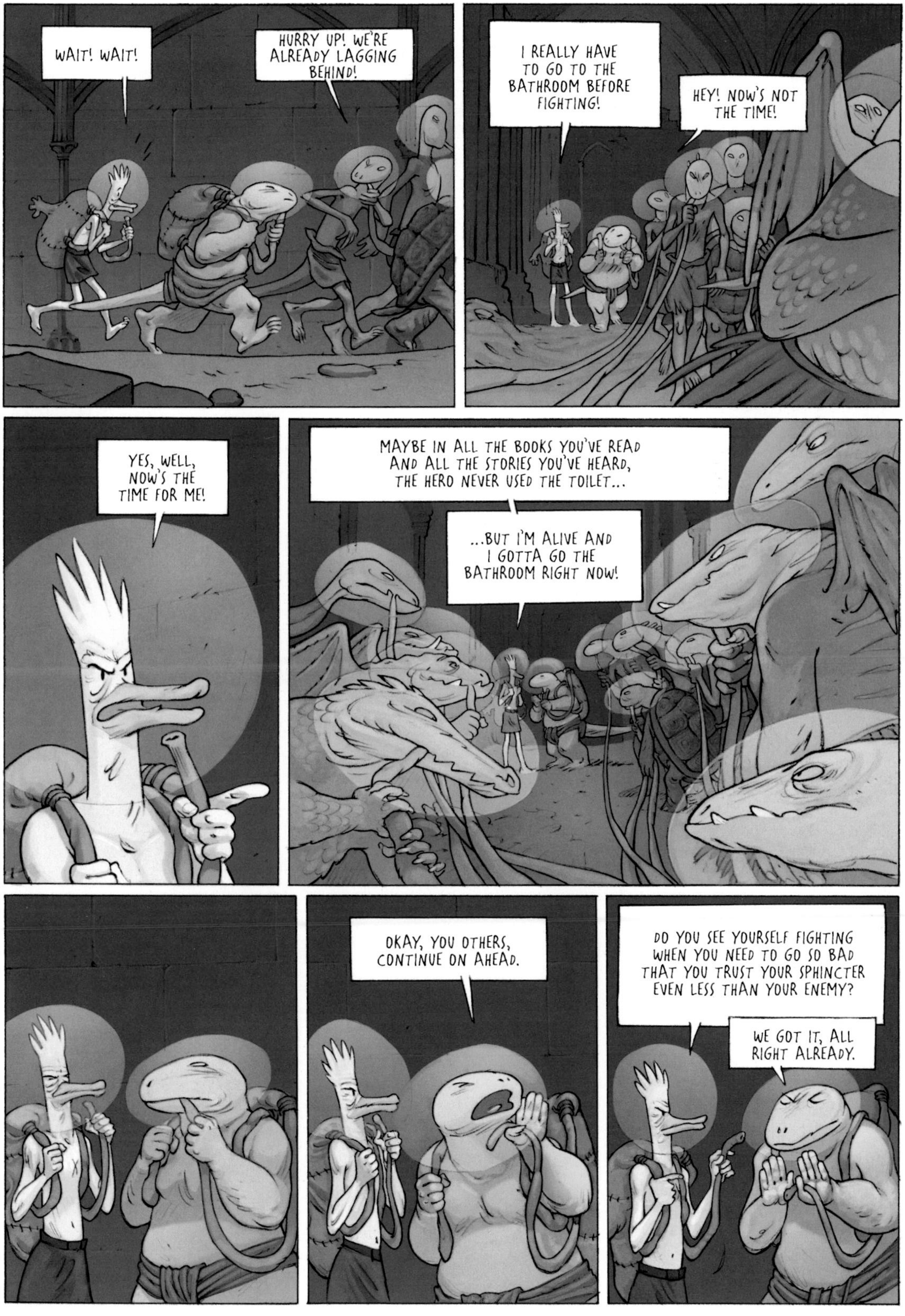
WAIT! WAIT!
HURRY UP! WE'RE ALREADY LAGGING BEHIND!
I REALLY HAVE TO GO TO THE BATHROOM BEFORE FIGHTING!
HEY! NOW'S NOT THE TIME!
YES, WELL, NOW'S THE TIME FOR ME!
MAYBE IN ALL THE BOOKS YOU'VE READ AND ALL THE STORIES YOU'VE HEARD, THE HERO NEVER USED THE TOILET...
...BUT I'M ALIVE AND I GOTTA GO THE BATHROOM RIGHT NOW!
OKAY, YOU OTHERS, CONTINUE ON AHEAD.
DO YOU SEE YOURSELF FIGHTING WHEN YOU NEED TO GO SO BAD THAT YOU TRUST YOUR SPHINCTER EVEN LESS THAN YOUR ENEMY?
WE GOT IT, ALL RIGHT ALREADY.

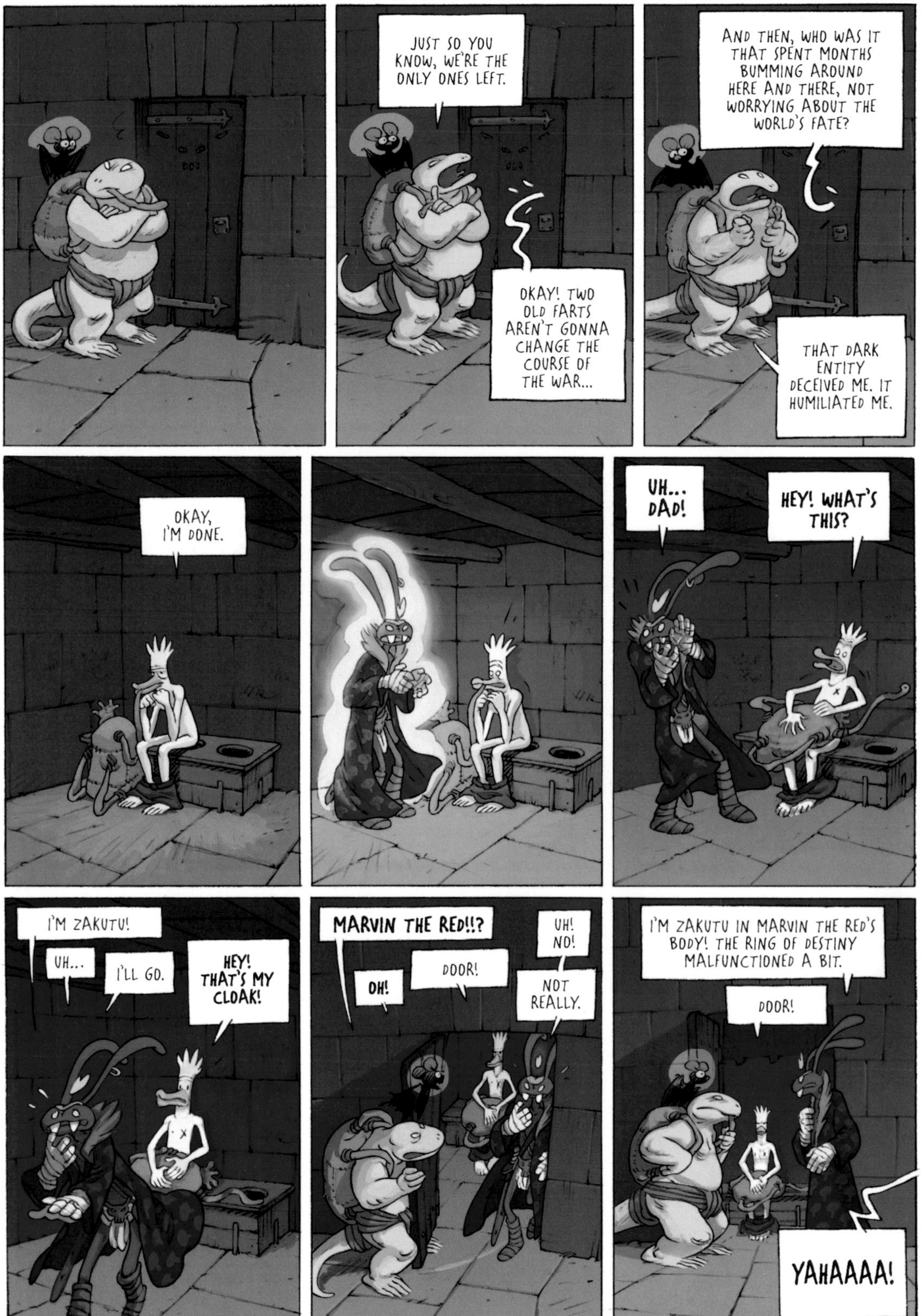
JUST SO YOU KNOW, WE'RE THE ONLY ONES LEFT.
OKAY! TWO OLD FARTS AREN'T GONNA CHANGE THE COURSE OF THE WAR...
AND THEN, WHO WAS IT THAT SPENT MONTHS BUMMING AROUND HERE AND THERE, NOT WORRYING ABOUT THE WORLD'S FATE?
THAT DARK ENTITY DECEIVED ME. IT HUMILIATED ME.
OKAY, I'M DONE.
UH... DAD!
HEY! WHAT'S THIS?
I'M ZAKUTU!
UH...
I'LL GO.
HEY! THAT'S MY CLOAK!
MARVIN THE RED!!?
OH!
DOOR!
UH! NO!
NOT REALLY.
I'M ZAKUTU IN MARVIN THE RED'S BODY! THE RING OF DESTINY MALFUNCTIONED A BIT.
DOOR!
YAHAAAA!

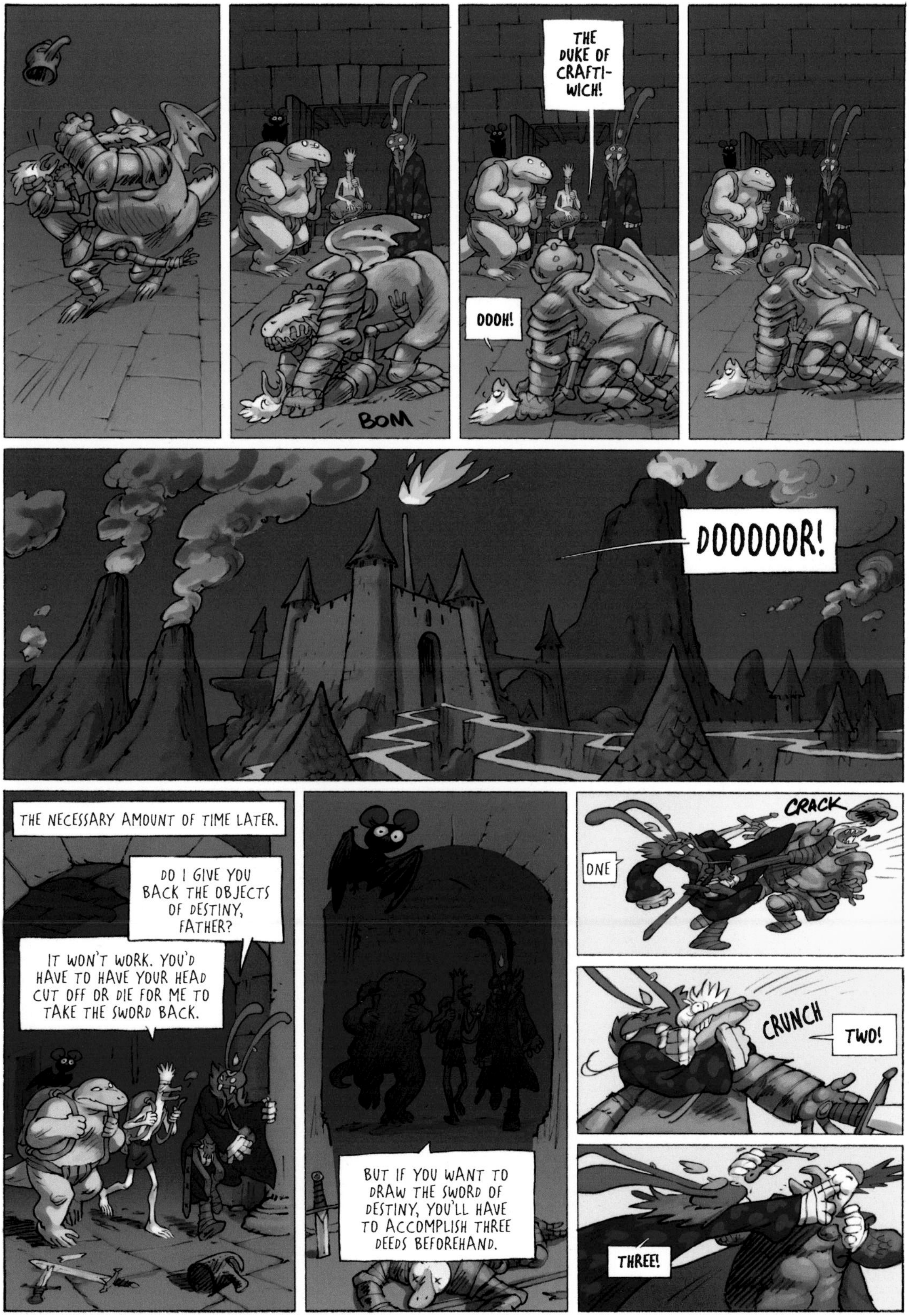

BOM
THE DUKE OF CRAFTI-WICH!
OOOH!
DOOOOOR!
THE NECESSARY AMOUNT OF TIME LATER.
DO I GIVE YOU BACK THE OBJECTS OF DESTINY, FATHER?
IT WON'T WORK. YOU'D HAVE TO HAVE YOUR HEAD CUT OFF OR DIE FOR ME TO TAKE THE SWORD BACK.
BUT IF YOU WANT TO DRAW THE SWORD OF DESTINY, YOU'LL HAVE TO ACCOMPLISH THREE DEEDS BEFOREHAND.
CRACK
ONE
CRUNCH
TWO!
THREE!

GOOD? CAN I DRAW THE SWORD?

UH...ONE SECOND, I'M THINKING.

I DON'T KNOW WHETHER THAT COUNTS AS THREE FEATS ACCOMPLISHED ON THE SAME DAY OR ONE SINGLE FEAT ACCOMPLISHED AS A BLOCK.

HEY!

DOES THIS MAKE YOU THINK ANY FASTER?

IT ANNOYS ME TO ADMIT THAT HAVING A LIGHT BODY ISN'T TOO BAD AT ALL!

OK?

CAN WE GO NOW?

YAAAH!

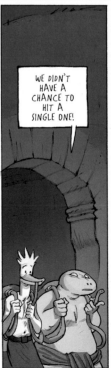

WE DIDN'T HAVE A CHANCE TO HIT A SINGLE ONE!

THAT'S MY GIRL!

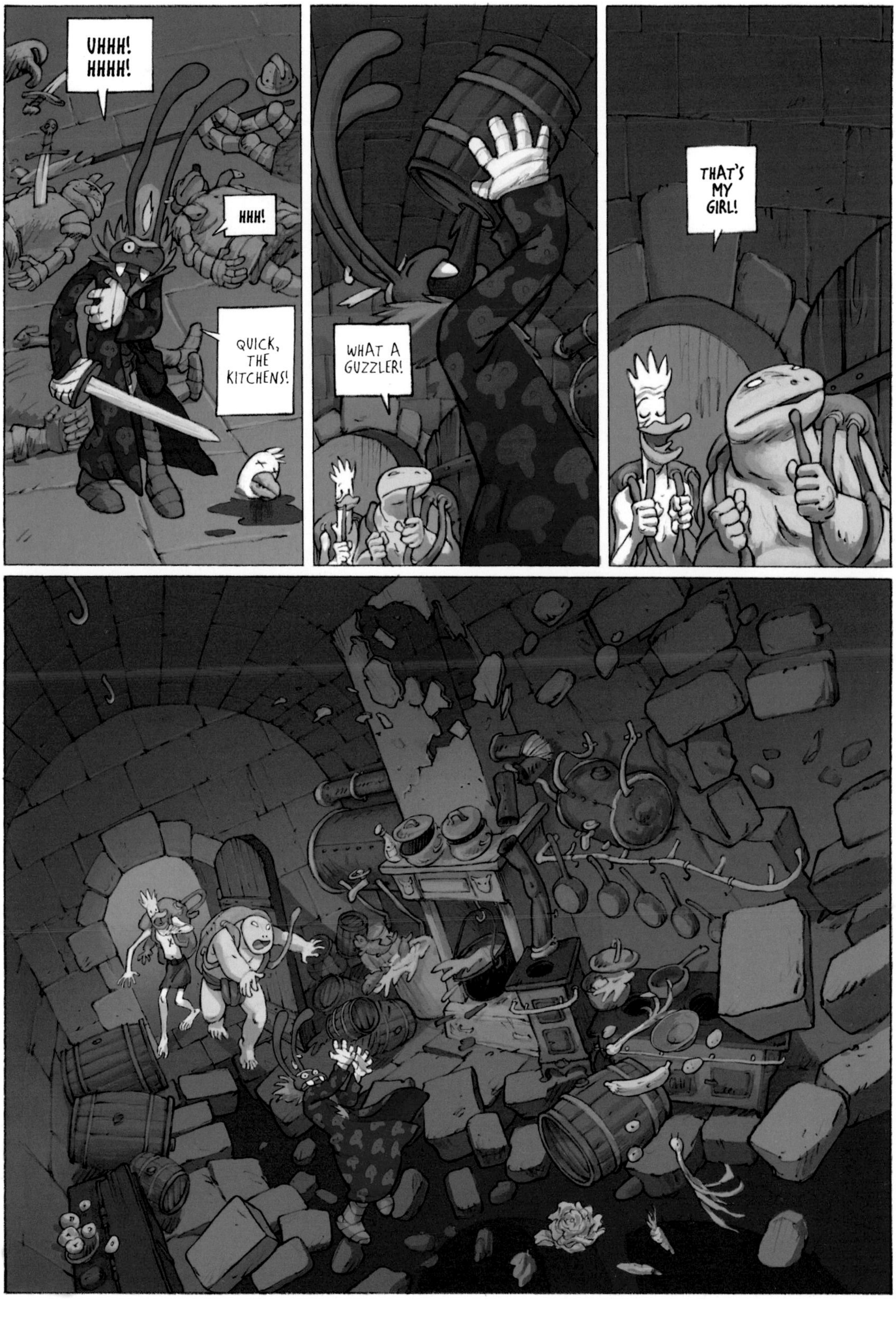
UHHH! HHHH!
HHH!
QUICK, THE KITCHENS!
WHAT A GUZZLER!
THAT'S MY GIRL!

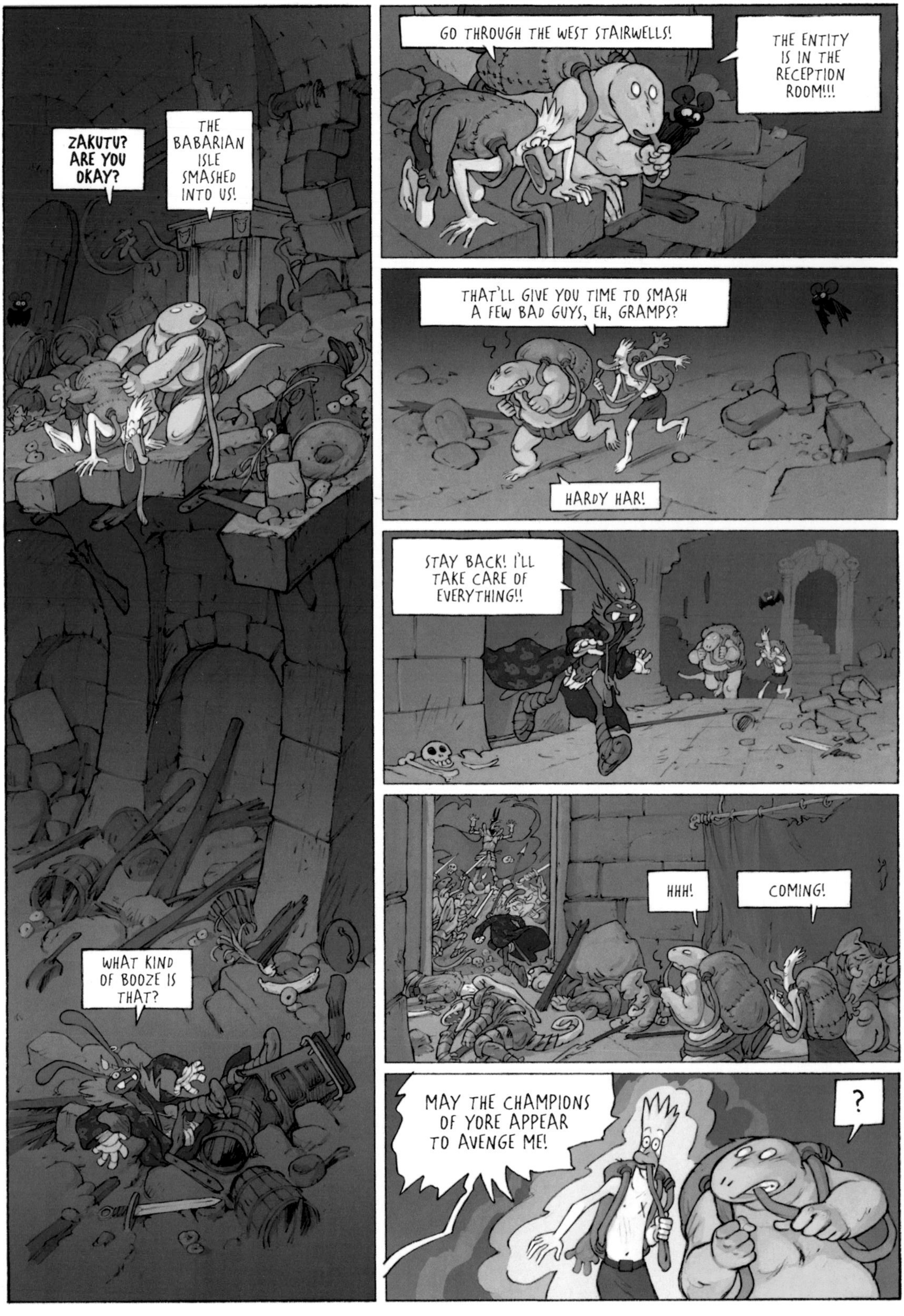
ZAKUTU? ARE YOU OKAY?
THE BABARIAN ISLE SMASHED INTO US!
WHAT KIND OF BOOZE IS THAT?
GO THROUGH THE WEST STAIRWELLS!
THE ENTITY IS IN THE RECEPTION ROOM!!!
THAT'LL GIVE YOU TIME TO SMASH A FEW BAD GUYS, EH, GRAMPS?
HARDY HAR!
STAY BACK! I'LL TAKE CARE OF EVERYTHING!!
HHH!
COMING!
MAY THE CHAMPIONS OF YORE APPEAR TO AVENGE ME!
?

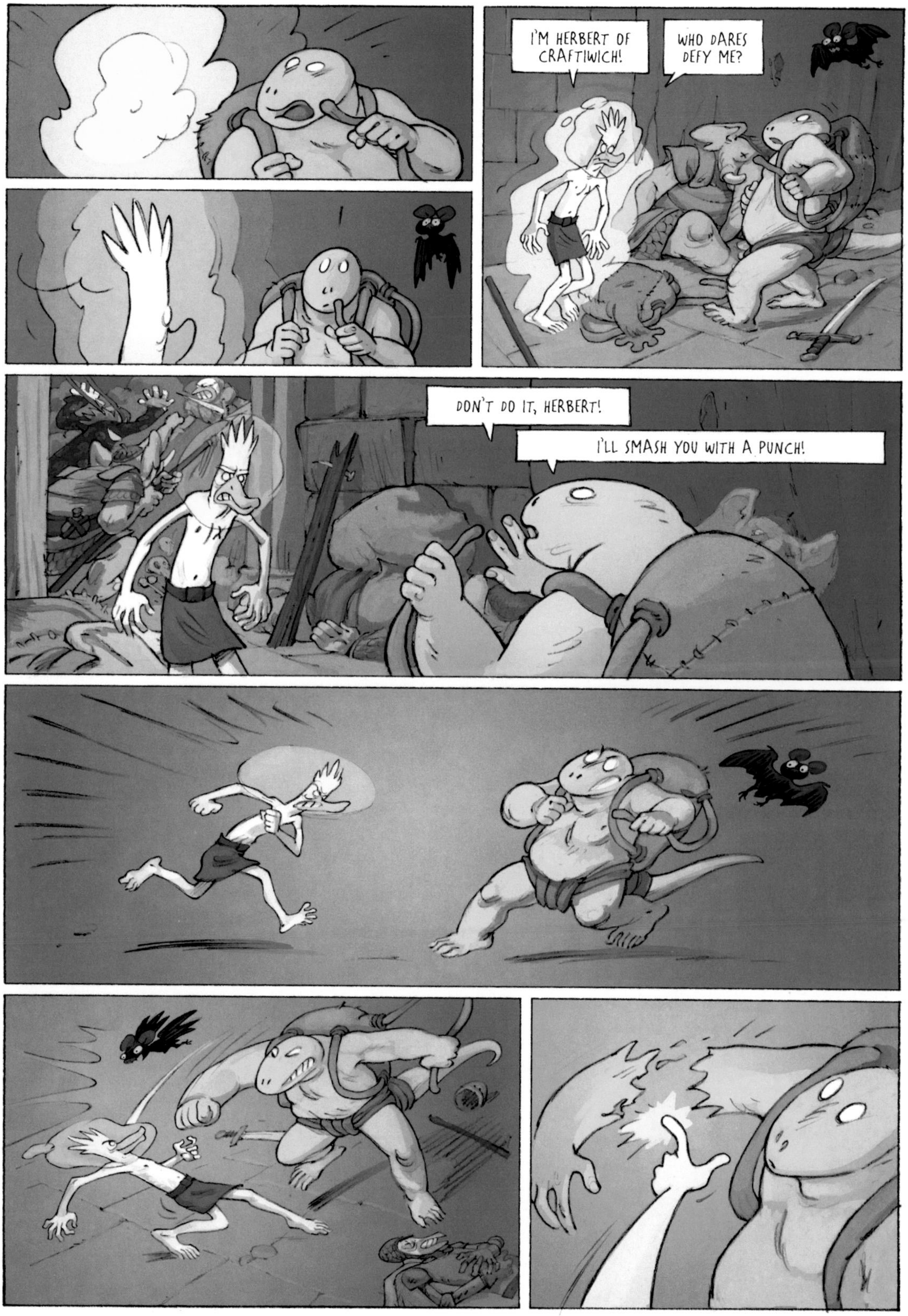
I'M HERBERT OF CRAFTIWICH!
WHO DARES DEFY ME?
DON'T DO IT, HERBERT!
I'LL SMASH YOU WITH A PUNCH!

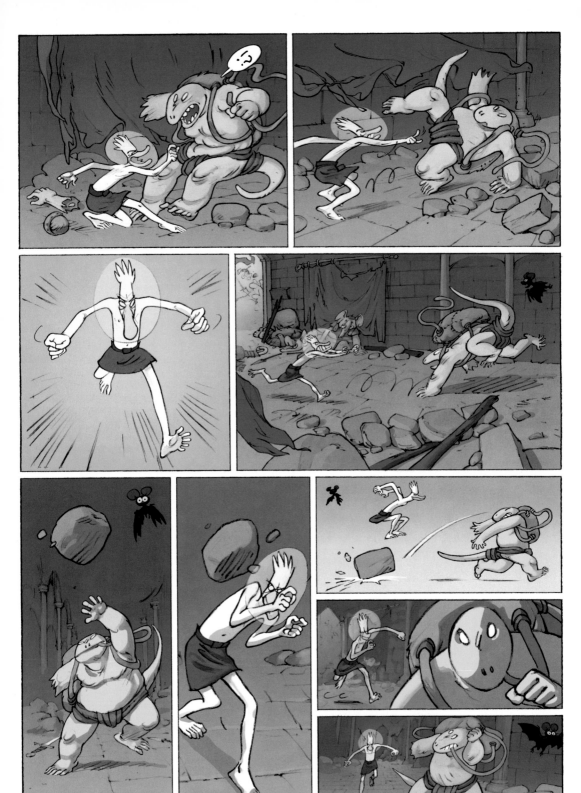

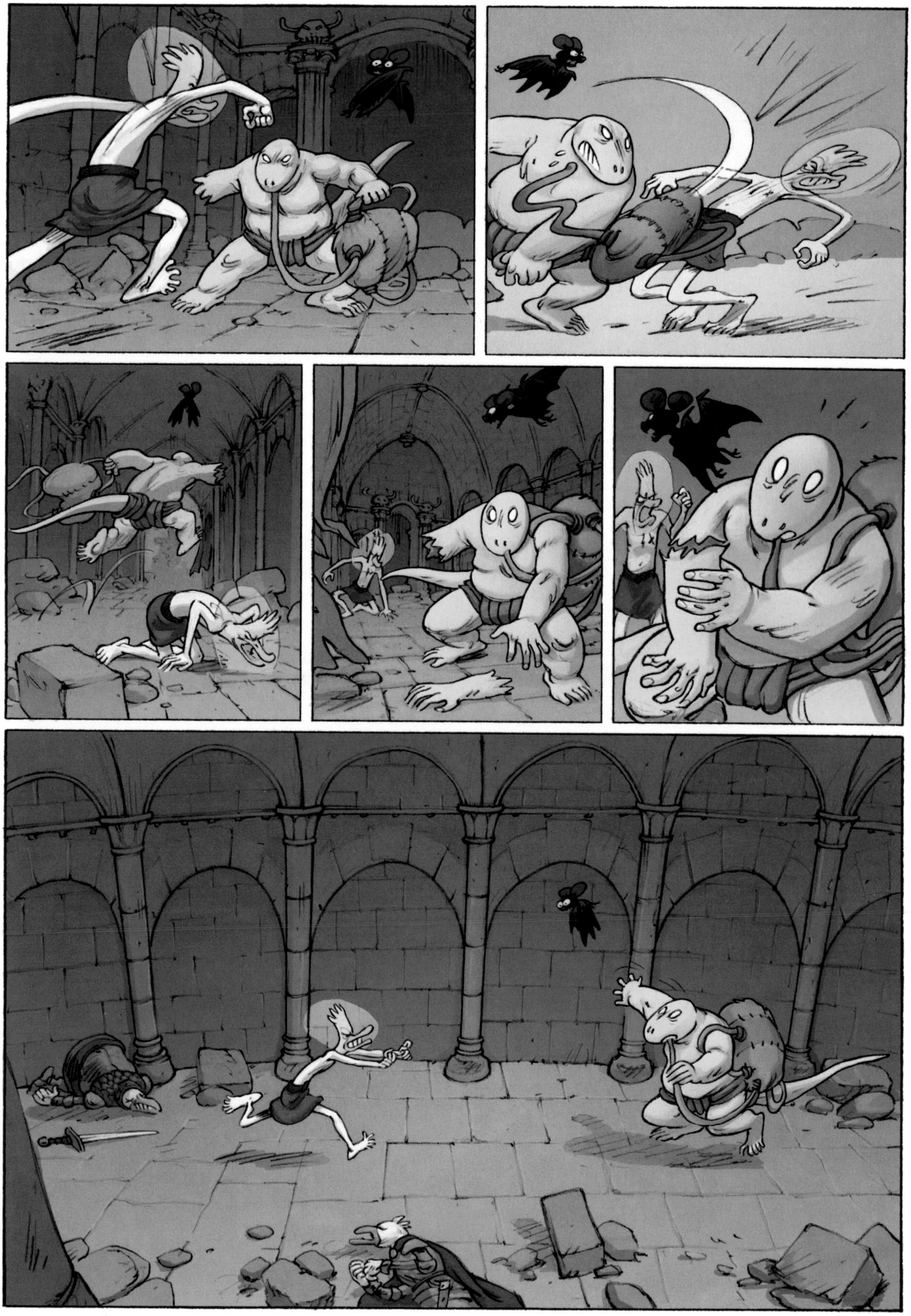

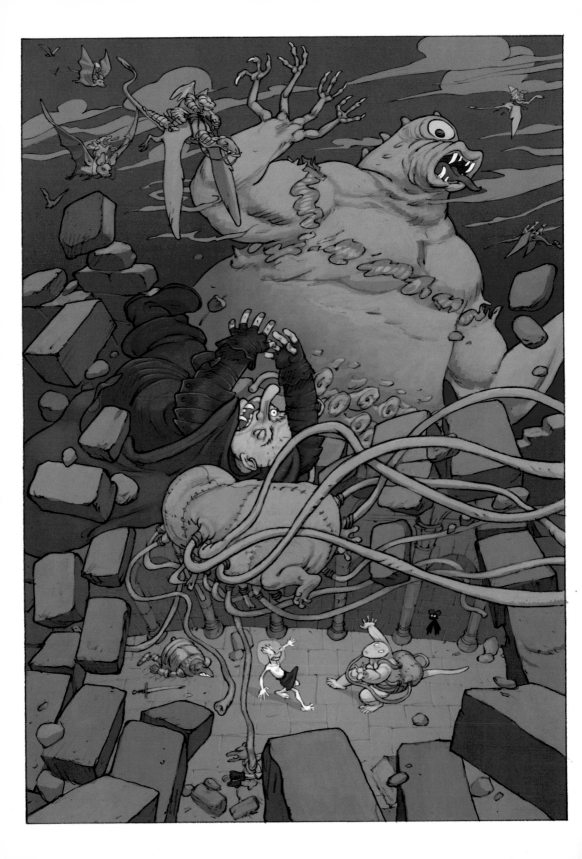

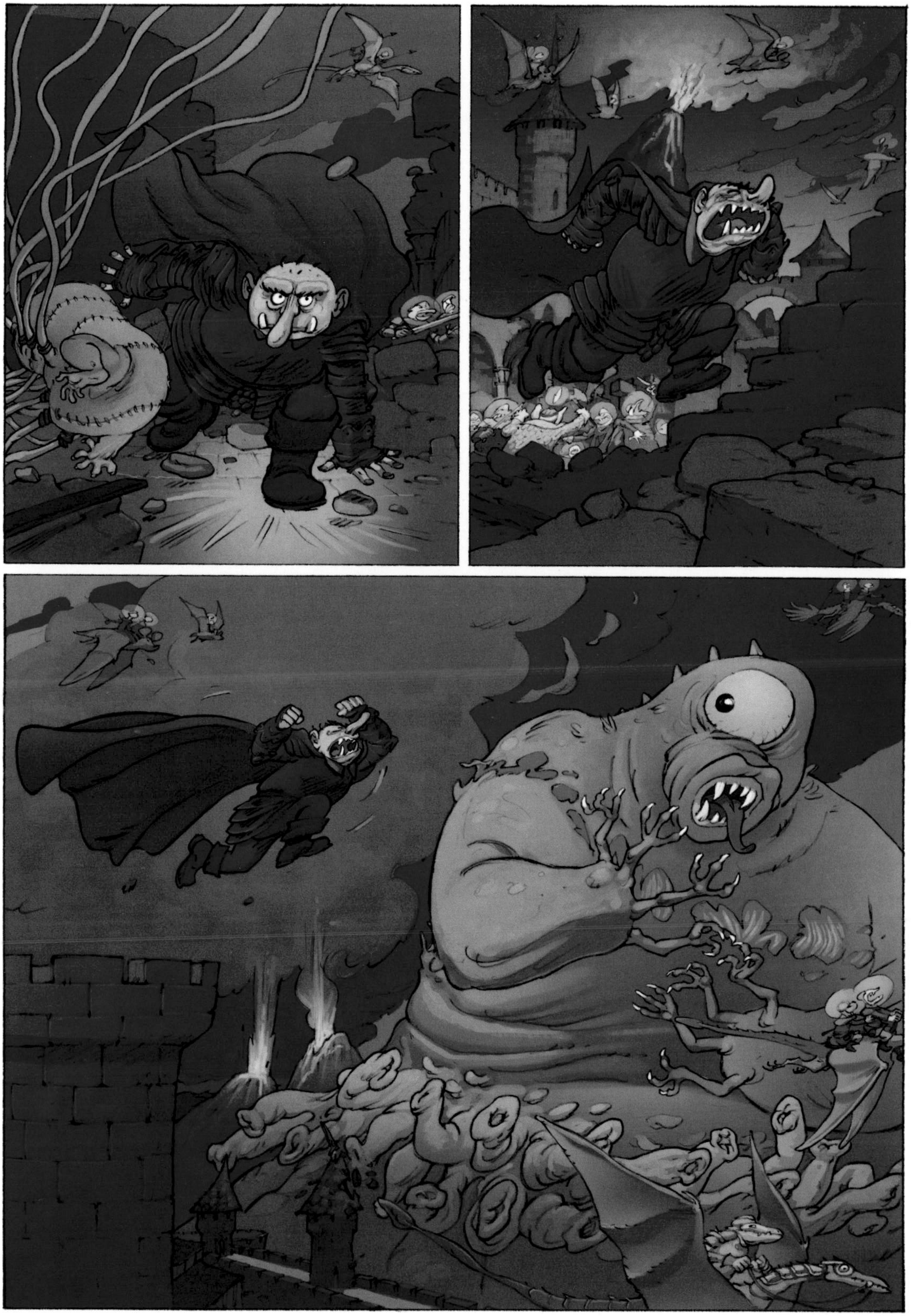

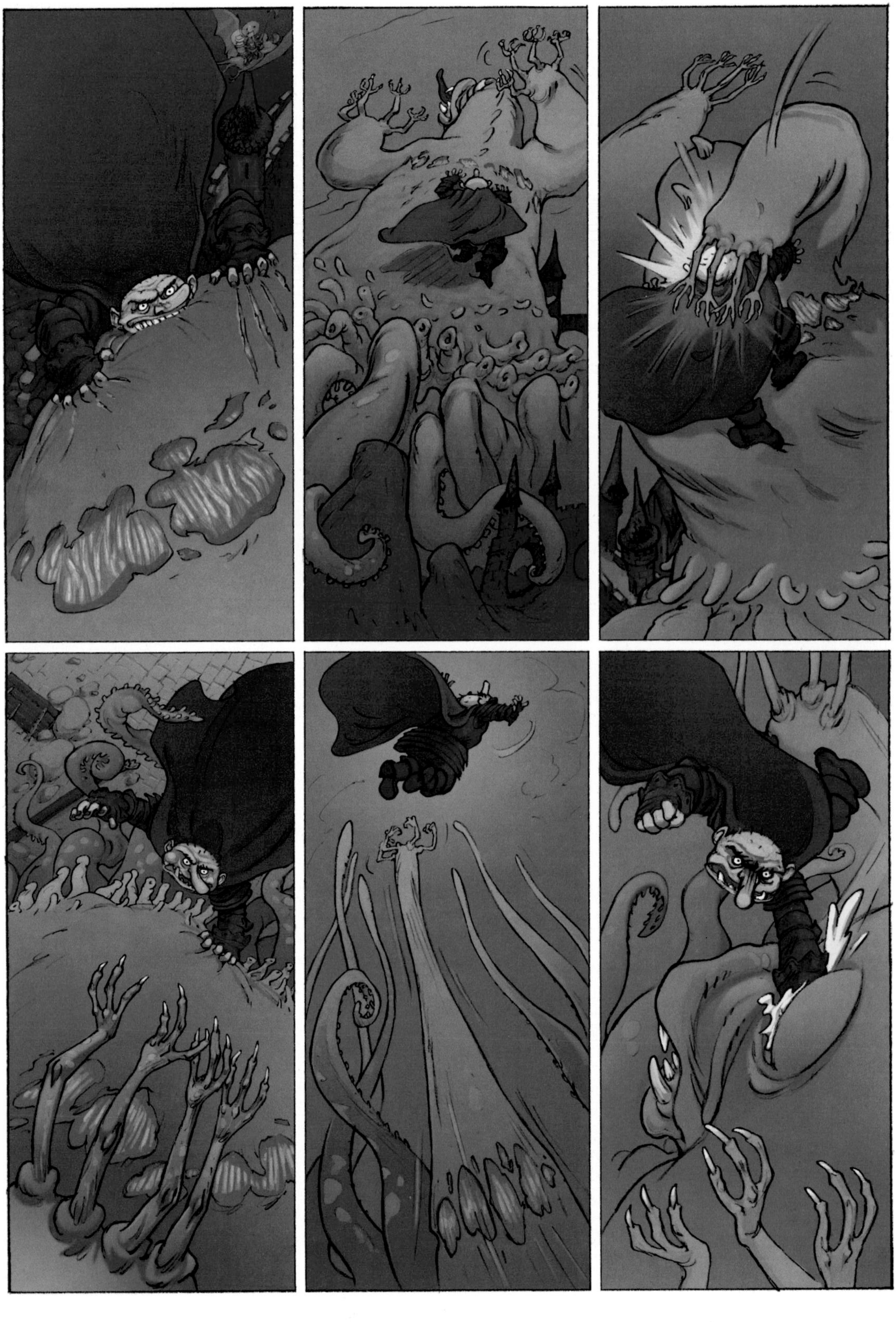

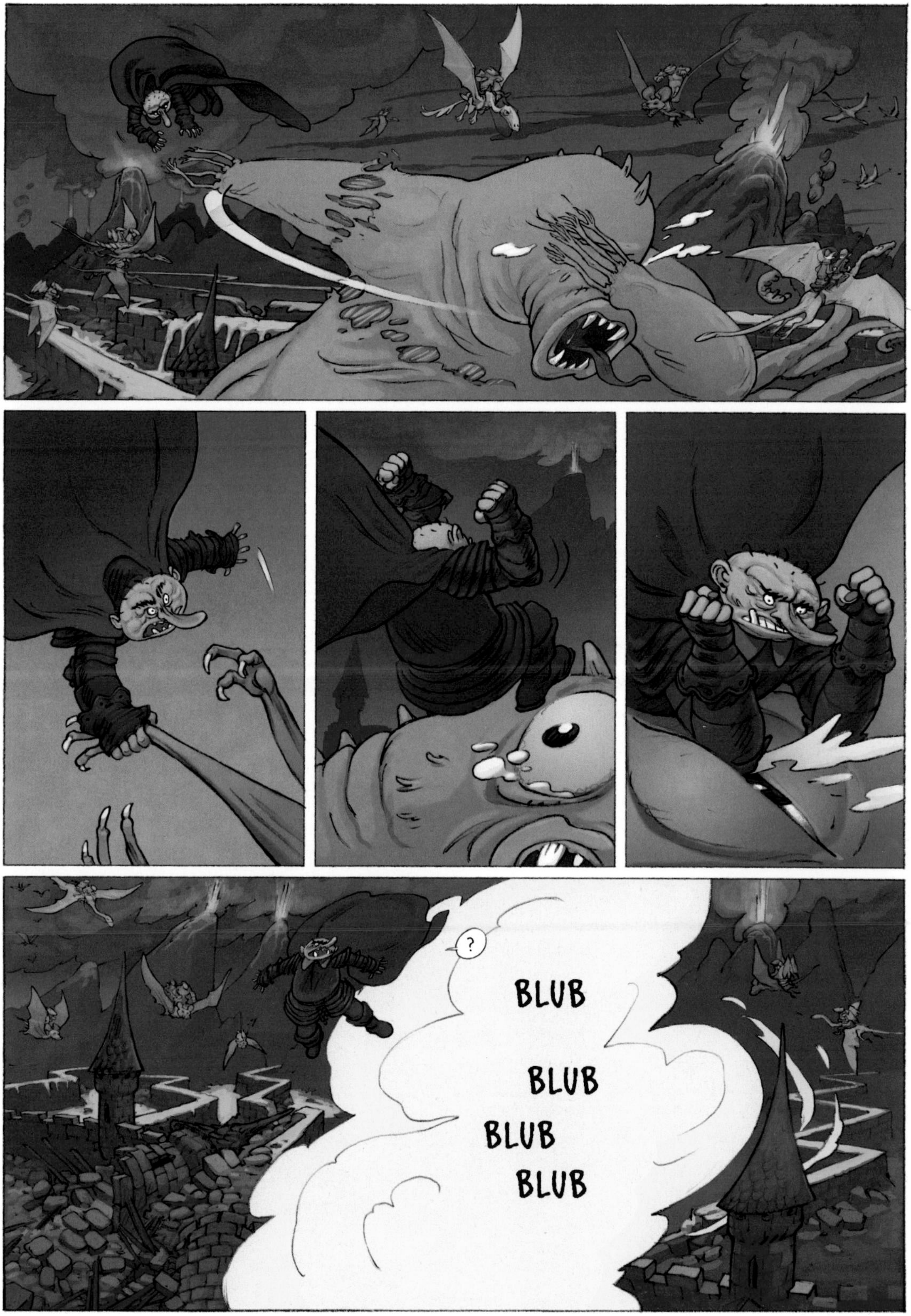
?
BLUB
BLUB
BLUB
BLUB

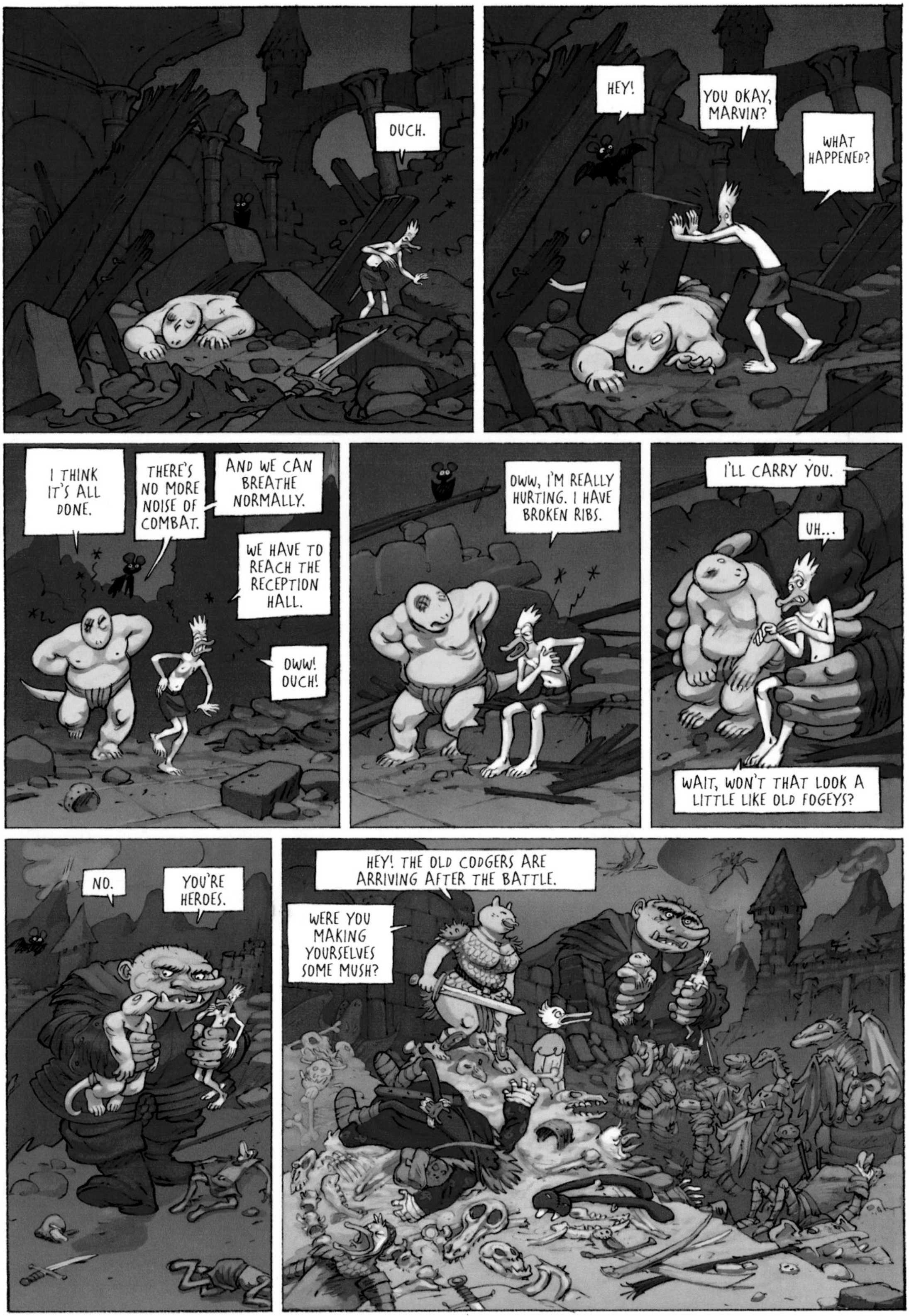

OUCH.
HEY!
YOU OKAY, MARVIN?
WHAT HAPPENED?
I THINK IT'S ALL DONE.
THERE'S NO MORE NOISE OF COMBAT.
AND WE CAN BREATHE NORMALLY.
WE HAVE TO REACH THE RECEPTION HALL.
OWW! OUCH!
OWW, I'M REALLY HURTING. I HAVE BROKEN RIBS.
I'LL CARRY YOU.
UH...
WAIT, WON'T THAT LOOK A LITTLE LIKE OLD FOGEYS?
NO.
YOU'RE HEROES.
HEY! THE OLD CODGERS ARE ARRIVING AFTER THE BATTLE.
WERE YOU MAKING YOURSELVES SOME MUSH?

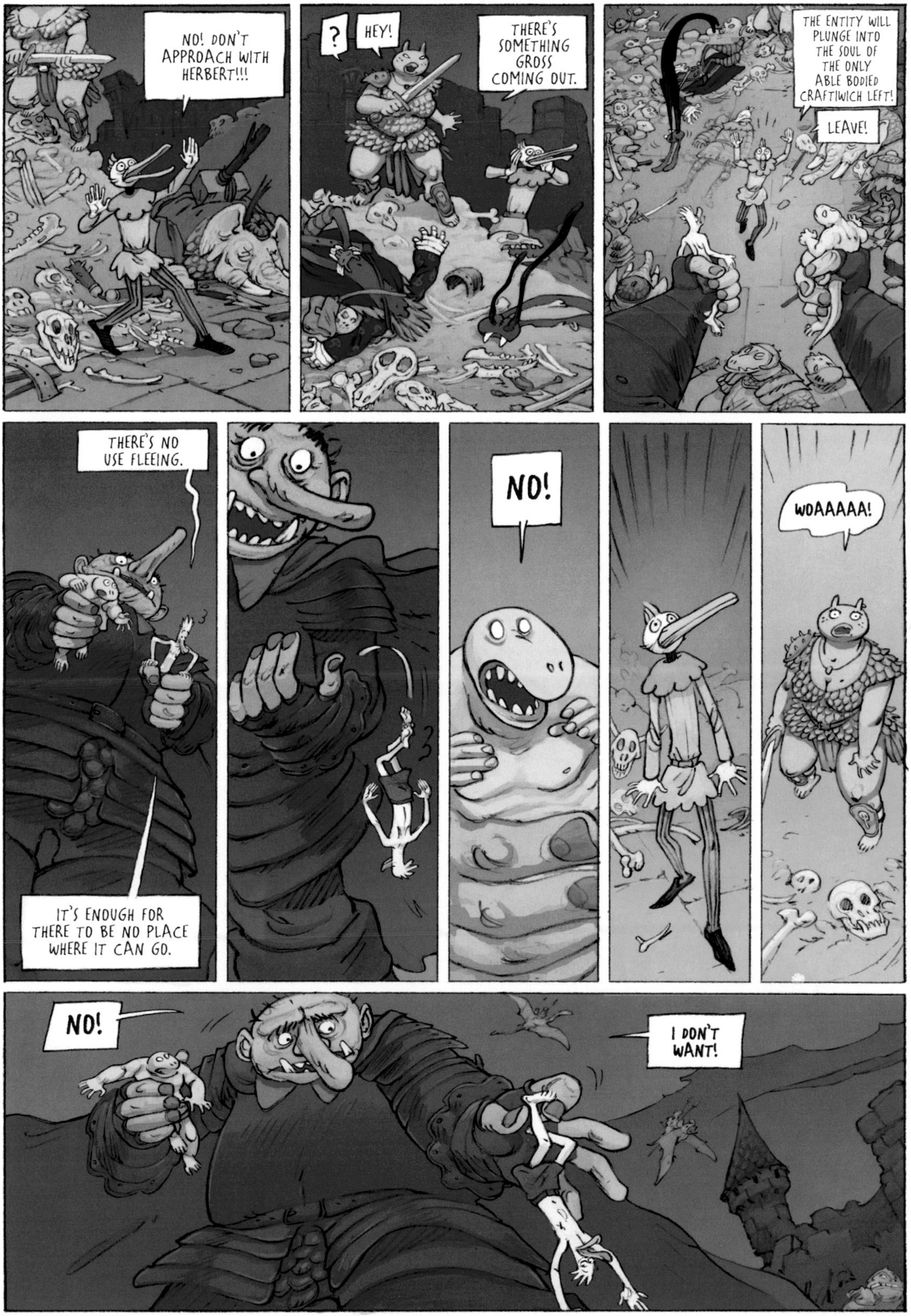
NO! DON'T APPROACH WITH HERBERT!!!
?
HEY!
THERE'S SOMETHING GROSS COMING OUT.
THE ENTITY WILL PLUNGE INTO THE SOUL OF THE ONLY ABLE BODIED CRAFTIWICH LEFT!
LEAVE!
THERE'S NO USE FLEEING.
IT'S ENOUGH FOR THERE TO BE NO PLACE WHERE IT CAN GO.
NO!
WOAAAAA!
NO!
I DON'T WANT!

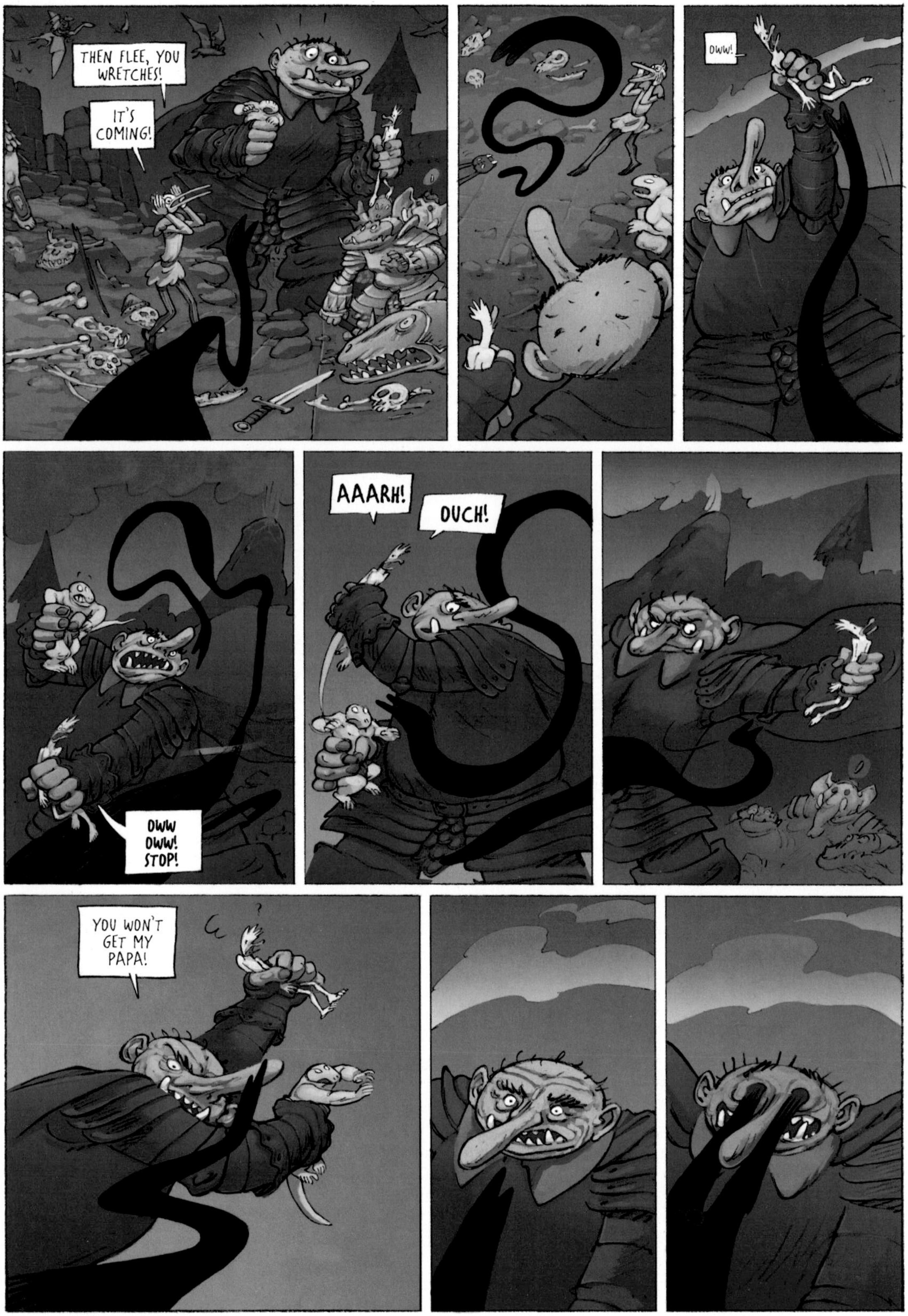
THEN FLEE, YOU WRETCHES!
IT'S COMING!
OWW!
AAARH!
OUCH!
OWW OWW! STOP!
YOU WON'T GET MY PAPA!

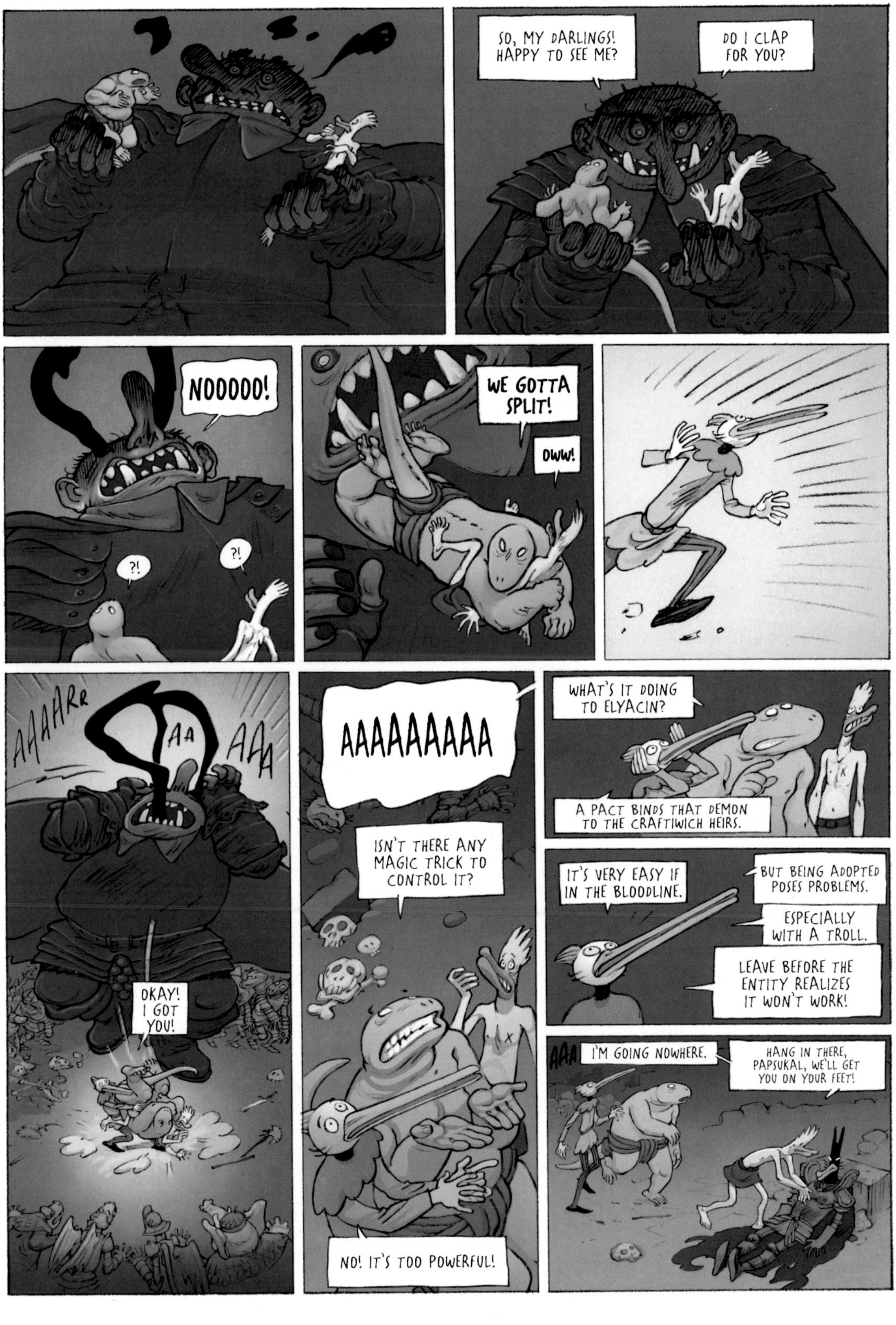
SO, MY DARLINGS! HAPPY TO SEE ME?
DO I CLAP FOR YOU?
NOOOOO!
?!
?!
WE GOTTA SPLIT!
OWW!
AAAARR
AA
AAAA
OKAY! I GOT YOU!
AAAAAAAAA
ISN'T THERE ANY MAGIC TRICK TO CONTROL IT?
NO! IT'S TOO POWERFUL!
WHAT'S IT DOING TO ELYACIN?
A PACT BINDS THAT DEMON TO THE CRAFTIWICH HEIRS.
IT'S VERY EASY IF IN THE BLOODLINE.
BUT BEING ADOPTED POSES PROBLEMS.
ESPECIALLY WITH A TROLL.
LEAVE BEFORE THE ENTITY REALIZES IT WON'T WORK!
AAA
I'M GOING NOWHERE.
HANG IN THERE, PAPSUKAL, WE'LL GET YOU ON YOUR FEET!

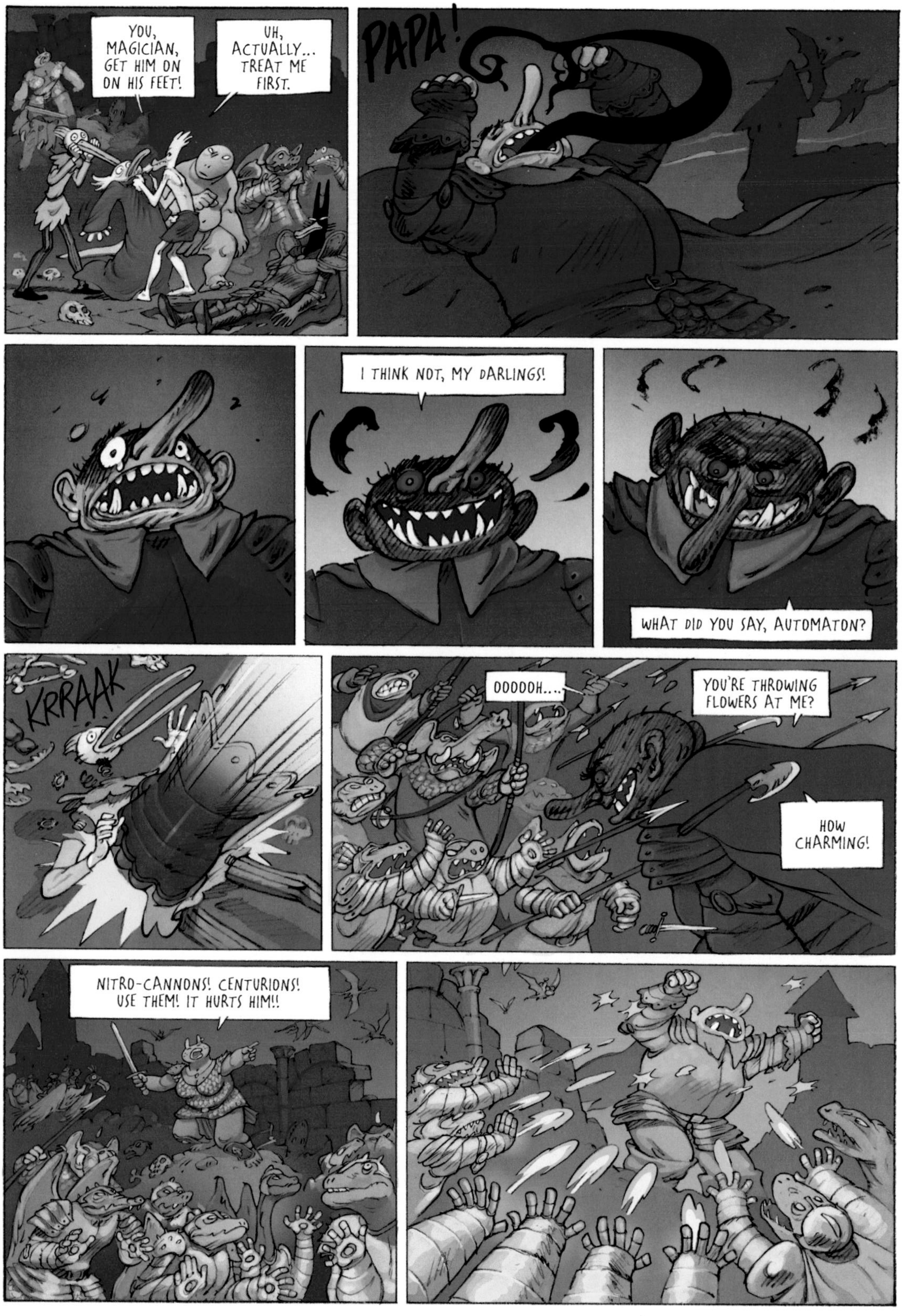
YOU, MAGICIAN, GET HIM ON ON HIS FEET!
UH, ACTUALLY... TREAT ME FIRST.
PAPA!
I THINK NOT, MY DARLINGS!
WHAT DID YOU SAY, AUTOMATON?
KRRAAK
OOOOOH....
YOU'RE THROWING FLOWERS AT ME?
HOW CHARMING!
NITRO-CANNONS! CENTURIONS! USE THEM! IT HURTS HIM!!

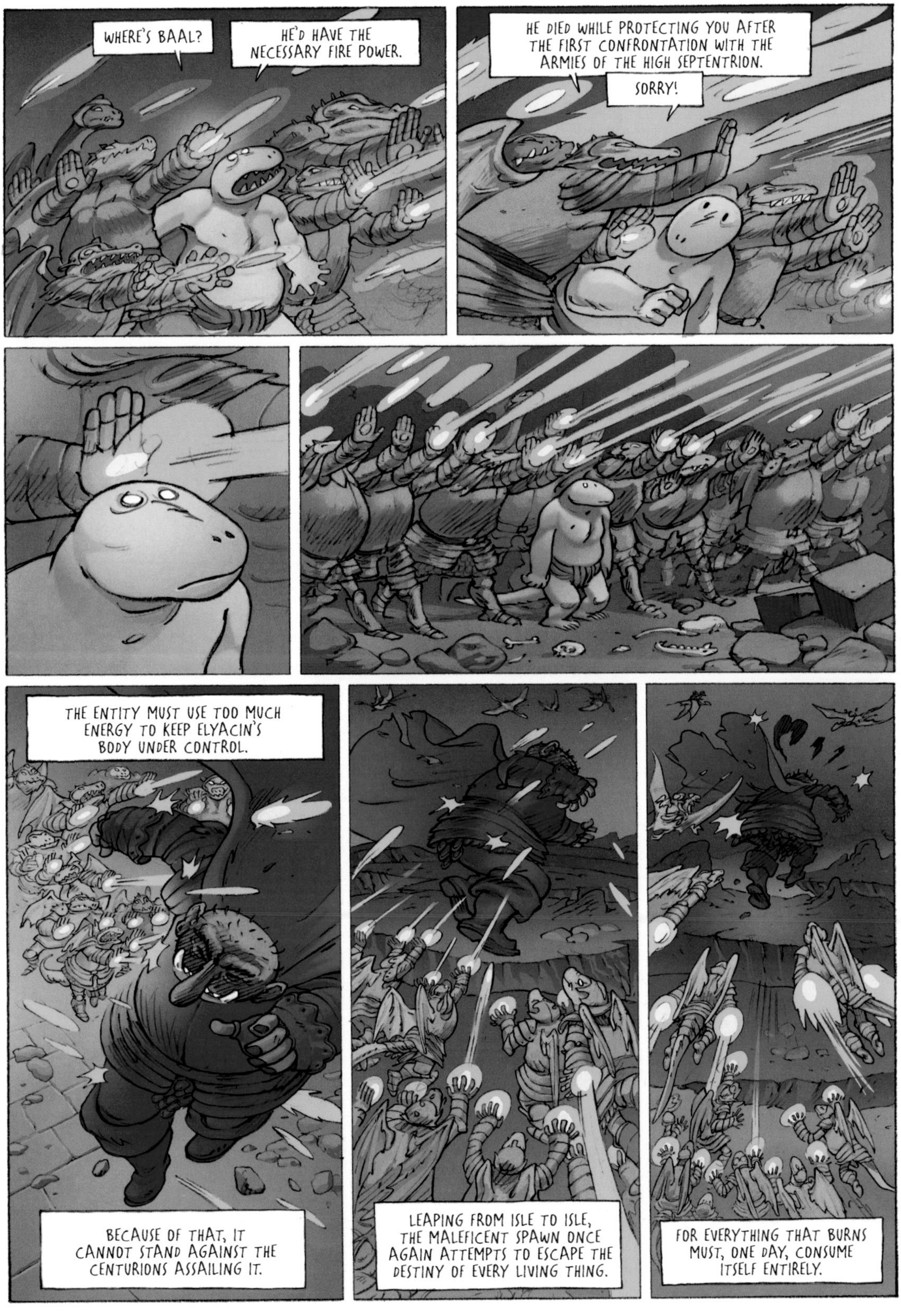
WHERE'S BAAL?
HE'D HAVE THE NECESSARY FIRE POWER.
HE DIED WHILE PROTECTING YOU AFTER THE FIRST CONFRONTATION WITH THE ARMIES OF THE HIGH SEPTENTRION.
SORRY!
THE ENTITY MUST USE TOO MUCH ENERGY TO KEEP ELYACIN'S BODY UNDER CONTROL.
BECAUSE OF THAT, IT CANNOT STAND AGAINST THE CENTURIONS ASSAILING IT.
LEAPING FROM ISLE TO ISLE, THE MALEFICENT SPAWN ONCE AGAIN ATTEMPTS TO ESCAPE THE DESTINY OF EVERY LIVING THING.
FOR EVERYTHING THAT BURNS MUST, ONE DAY, CONSUME ITSELF ENTIRELY.

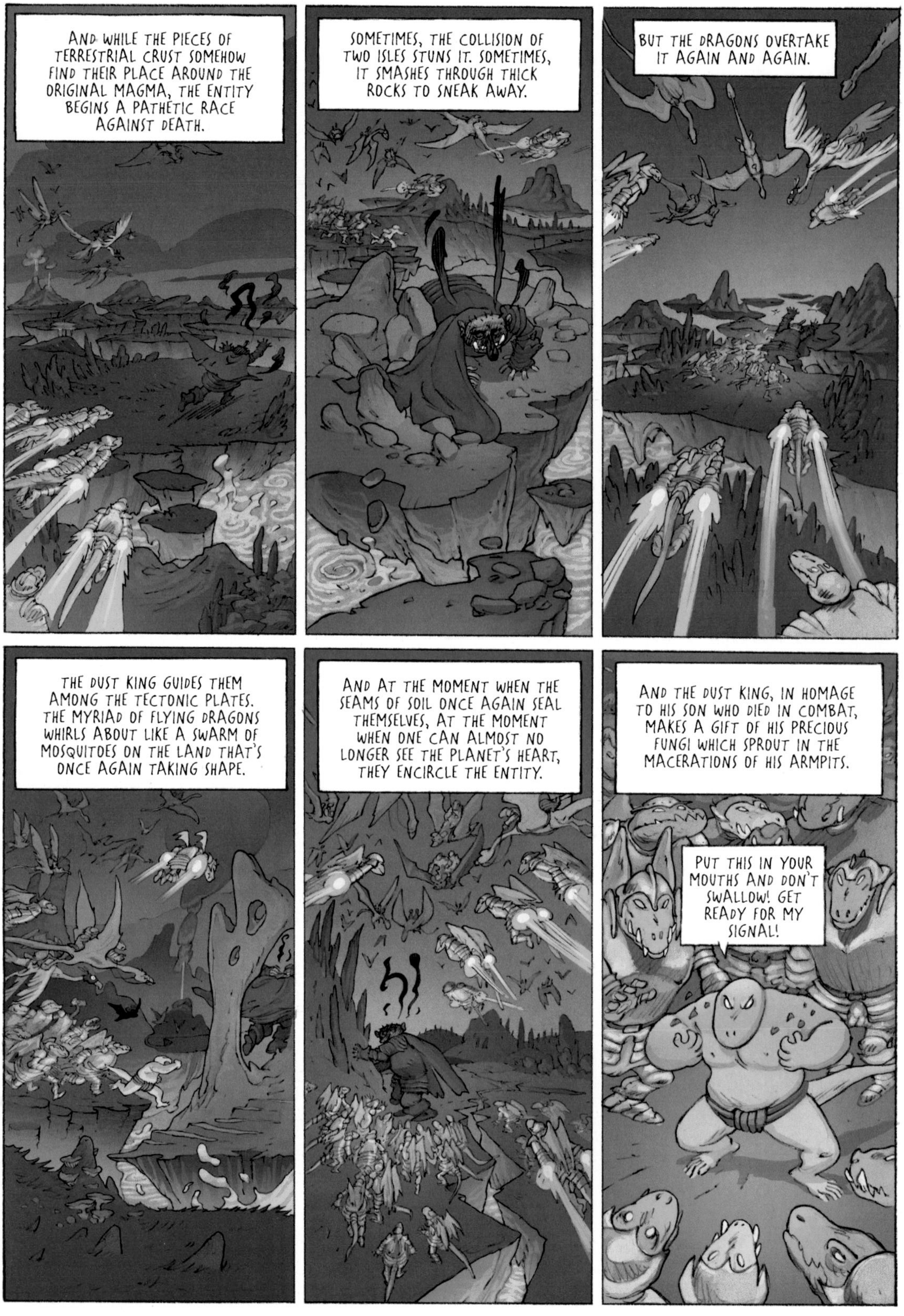
AND WHILE THE PIECES OF TERRESTRIAL CRUST SOMEHOW FIND THEIR PLACE AROUND THE ORIGINAL MAGMA, THE ENTITY BEGINS A PATHETIC RACE AGAINST DEATH.
SOMETIMES, THE COLLISION OF TWO ISLES STUNS IT. SOMETIMES, IT SMASHES THROUGH THICK ROCKS TO SNEAK AWAY.
BUT THE DRAGONS OVERTAKE IT AGAIN AND AGAIN.
THE DUST KING GUIDES THEM AMONG THE TECTONIC PLATES. THE MYRIAD OF FLYING DRAGONS WHIRLS ABOUT LIKE A SWARM OF MOSQUITOES ON THE LAND THAT'S ONCE AGAIN TAKING SHAPE.
AND AT THE MOMENT WHEN THE SEAMS OF SOIL ONCE AGAIN SEAL THEMSELVES, AT THE MOMENT WHEN ONE CAN ALMOST NO LONGER SEE THE PLANET'S HEART, THEY ENCIRCLE THE ENTITY.
AND THE DUST KING, IN HOMAGE TO HIS SON WHO DIED IN COMBAT, MAKES A GIFT OF HIS PRECIOUS FUNGI WHICH SPROUT IN THE MACERATIONS OF HIS ARMPITS.
PUT THIS IN YOUR MOUTHS AND DON'T SWALLOW! GET READY FOR MY SIGNAL!

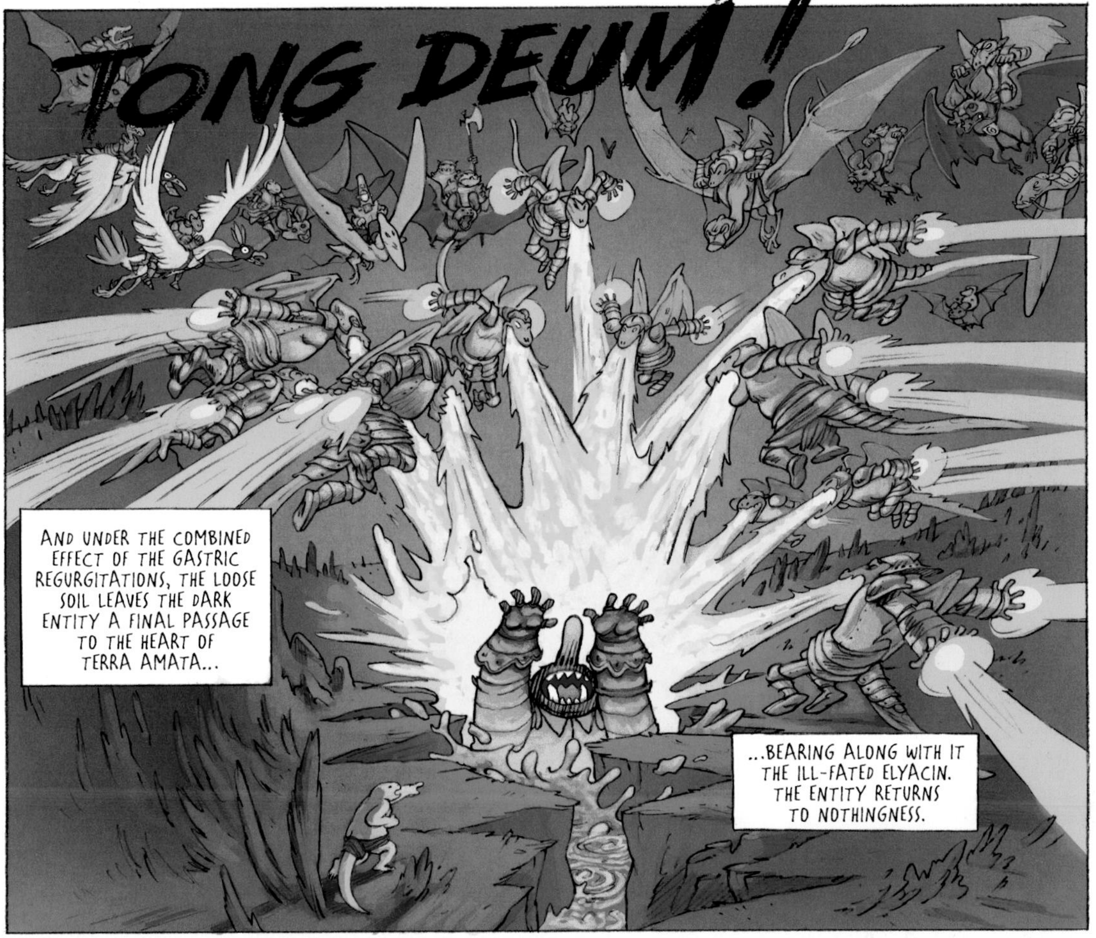
TONG DEUM!
AND UNDER THE COMBINED EFFECT OF THE GASTRIC REGURGITATIONS, THE LOOSE SOIL LEAVES THE DARK ENTITY A FINAL PASSAGE TO THE HEART OF TERRA AMATA...
...BEARING ALONG WITH IT THE ILL-FATED ELYACIN. THE ENTITY RETURNS TO NOTHINGNESS.

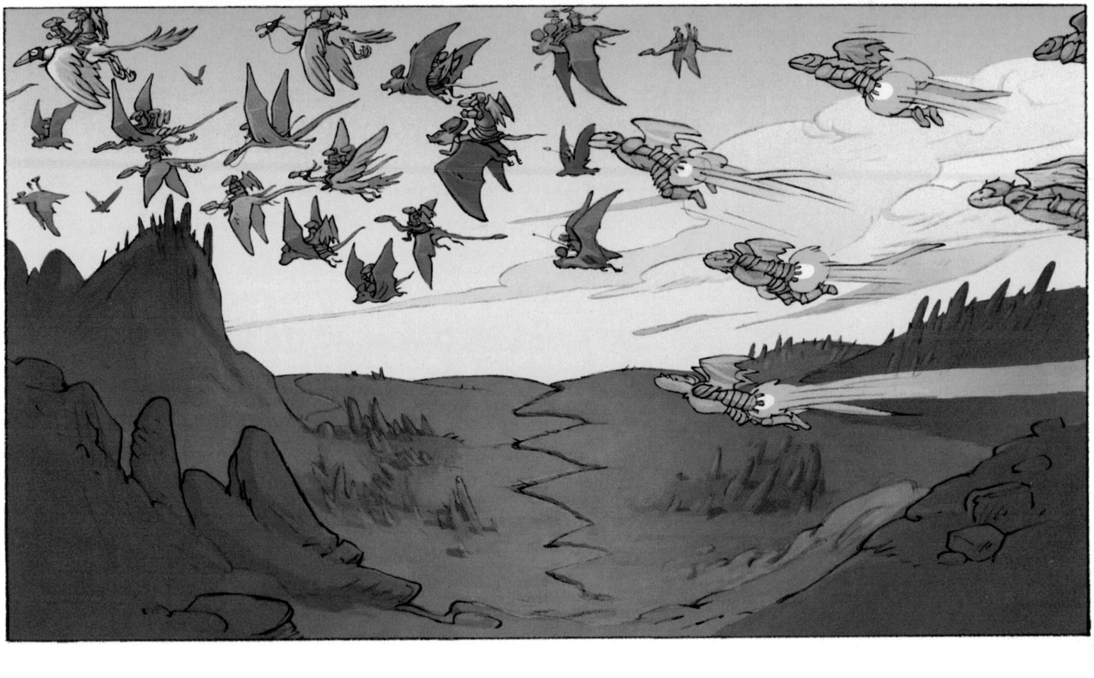

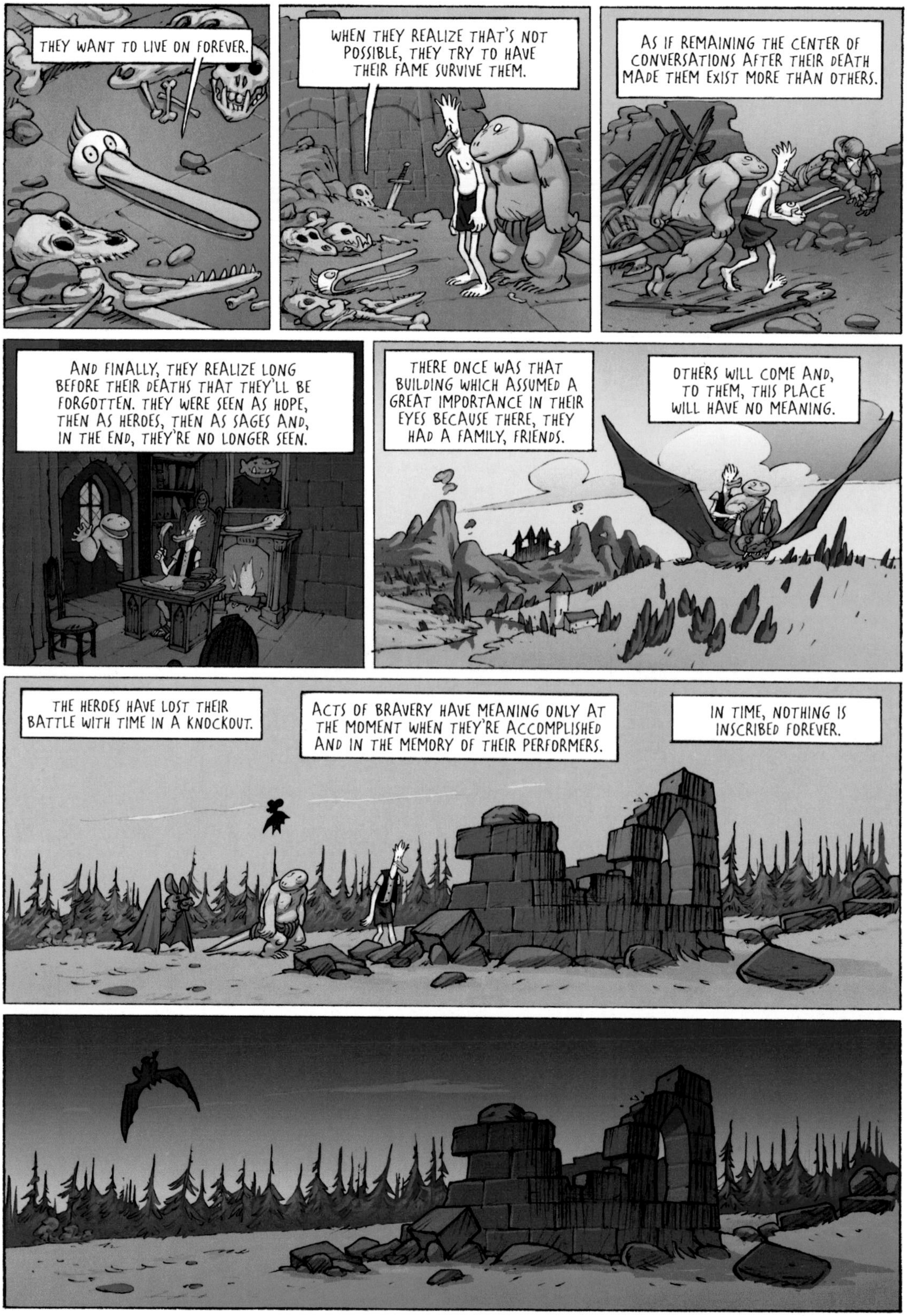

THEY WANT TO LIVE ON FOREVER.
WHEN THEY REALIZE THAT'S NOT POSSIBLE, THEY TRY TO HAVE THEIR FAME SURVIVE THEM.
AS IF REMAINING THE CENTER OF CONVERSATIONS AFTER THEIR DEATH MADE THEM EXIST MORE THAN OTHERS.
AND FINALLY, THEY REALIZE LONG BEFORE THEIR DEATHS THAT THEY'LL BE FORGOTTEN. THEY WERE SEEN AS HOPE, THEN AS HEROES, THEN AS SAGES AND, IN THE END, THEY'RE NO LONGER SEEN.
THERE ONCE WAS THAT BUILDING WHICH ASSUMED A GREAT IMPORTANCE IN THEIR EYES BECAUSE THERE, THEY HAD A FAMILY, FRIENDS.
OTHERS WILL COME AND, TO THEM, THIS PLACE WILL HAVE NO MEANING.
THE HEROES HAVE LOST THEIR BATTLE WITH TIME IN A KNOCKOUT.
ACTS OF BRAVERY HAVE MEANING ONLY AT THE MOMENT WHEN THEY'RE ACCOMPLISHED AND IN THE MEMORY OF THEIR PERFORMERS.
IN TIME, NOTHING IS INSCRIBED FOREVER.

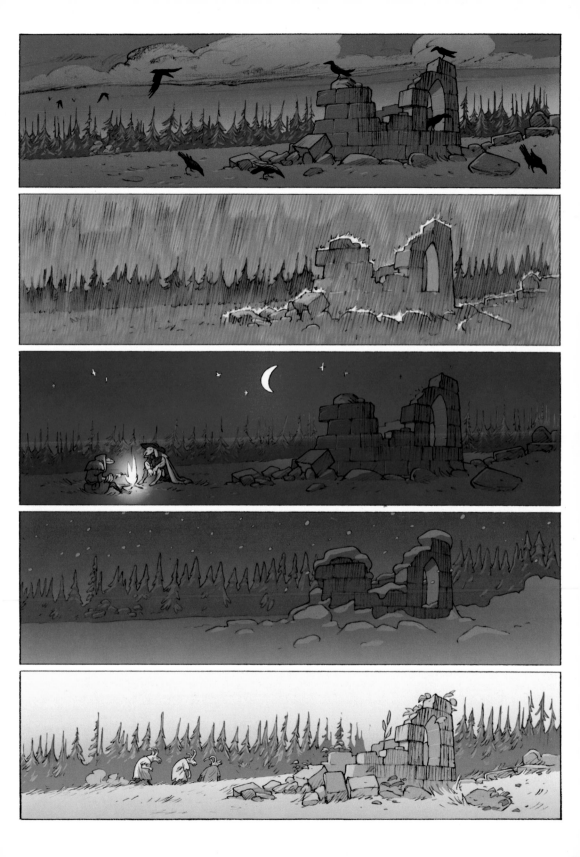

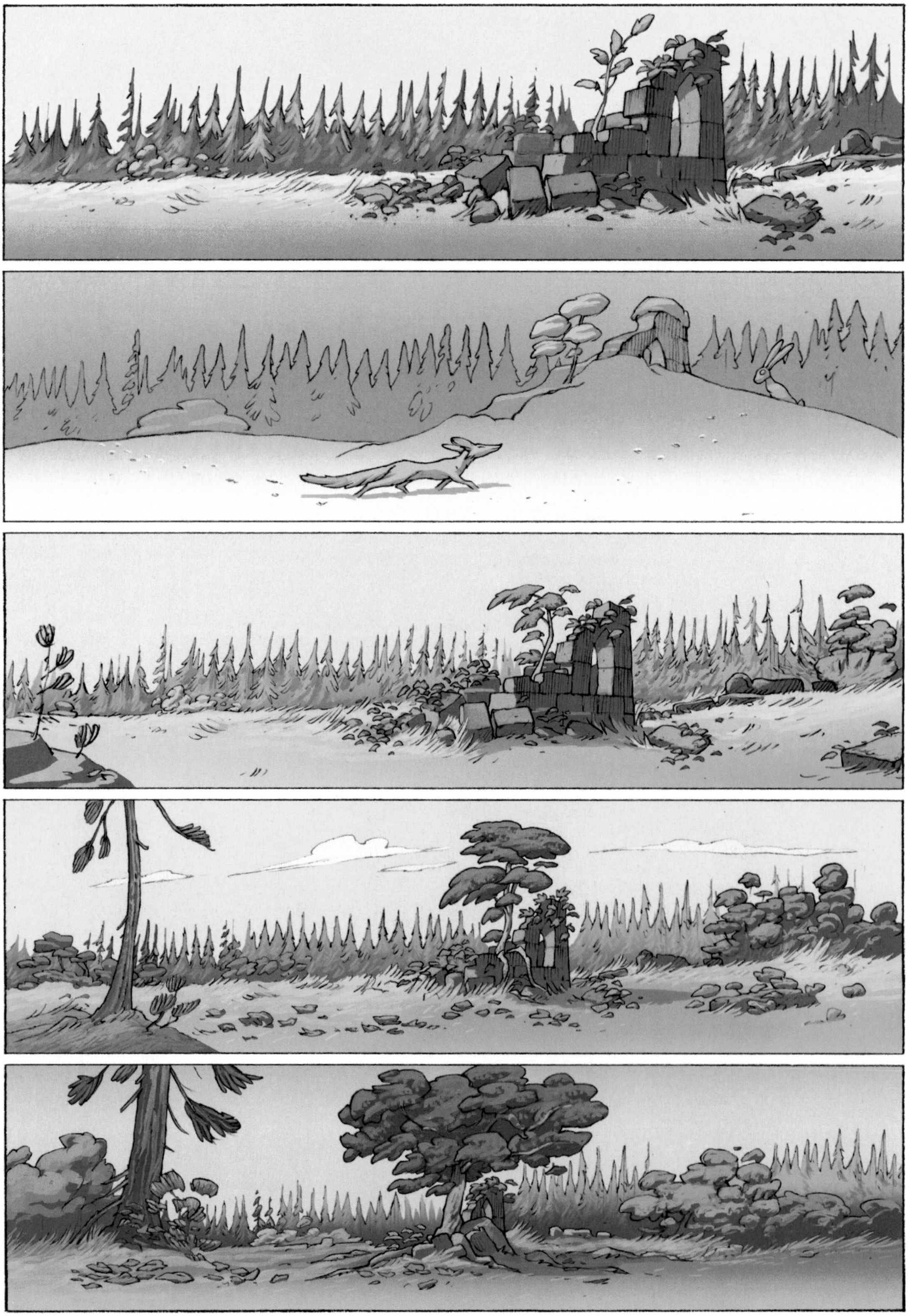

mazan Joann Sfar